# BEN FRANKLIN

# BEN FRANKLIN

An Affectionate Portrait

*by Nelson Beecher Keyes*

HANOVER HOUSE

GARDEN CITY, NEW YORK

TO

CHARLOTTE ISABEL BURNES KEYES

whose wifely portrait I have
carried in my heart these
many years — most
affectionately.

# Contents

# "Dear Friend"

CHILDREN adored him, and he, in turn, adored them. Having been the fifteenth among a family of seventeen, Franklin had been able to appreciate from his early years the child's restricted position in an adult world. And since friendliness was a lifelong and continuing vocation with him, he readily learned how to reach through to them and so captivate them that he built up firm friendships as well in the two generations younger than his own.

Even in the final, bedridden year of his life, prim little nine-year-old Deborah Bache presented herself daily at his bedside, her spelling book in hand, firm in the conviction that only her beloved grandfather could suitably hear her lesson. She and her six brothers and sisters romped in and out of his sickroom, amusing and delighting the old man up until almost the very hour of his death. This, too, despite the fact that his sufferings were such that he often had to seek relief from pain through sizable doses of laudanum.

Such harmonious relations were, however, by no means limited to his own children or grandchildren. As further evidence of his partiality for youngsters, consider how few sixty-five-year-old men there are who would graciously consent to an eleven-year-old daughter of friends as sole companion on a two-day chaise trip over England's abominable roads in the year 1771. Yet little Kitty Shipley, daughter of his recent host, together with this best-known private citizen in all the world, found plenty of topics to prattle about all the way from Twyford to London.

Then again, some seven years later, another eleven-year-old, but of the other gender, added his testimony to the fact that world-renowned Dr. Franklin was deserving of affectionate regard rather than stuffy formality. John Adams, much concerned with his son's schooling and upbringing, had taken young John

Quincy to Europe with him on his first mission abroad during the Revolution. A part of the year 1779 they had spent at Passy in France. En route home, there had been a long pause at Brest while waiting for ships to sail, and the future sixth president of the United States had improved his time by dashing off a brace of notes to young friends he had acquired at the little Paris suburb. These he had enclosed in a letter to the American envoy, with whom he had spent so many exciting and stimulating hours, despite a difference of better than sixty years in their ages.

This, it should be recalled, was an era of highly formal salutations. Most letters began with the blunt, "Sir," or "Madam." Even an adult beginning a letter to an own parent customarily wrote "Honored Madam," or "Honored Sir." But in the opinion of Master Adams any such ceremonious address would have been in the nature of an insult where this entrancing man was concerned. So he opened his letter to Benjamin Franklin quite spontaneously as, "Dear Friend." What could have been more appropriate?

Children and fools have a way of speaking the truth, and here was a person that was not only a friend of all mankind, but the "dear friend" of a host of men and women on two continents who knew him well and valued him highly. Any person who is innately gentle, kindly, companionable, sympathetic, and generous, and who is as interesting within himself as he is interested in others, has faculties that endear him not only to children, but to his peers as well.

Had he no enemies? Ah yes! No man spends the greater portion of his mature years in politics without breeding antipathy. Yet throughout his life he was very much a bungling amateur in the business of making adversaries, and their number was never legion. There were occasions when his mobile mind and quick reasoning caused his words or acts to be construed as craftiness. But there were few indeed who misjudged his integrity, benevolence, and abundant good humor, so that his warm, vital, humane nature attracted hundreds for every one it repelled.

He abhorred cruelty, injustice, rapacity, and arbitrary conduct. Crass and unreasonable actions could, and occasionally did, arouse his indignation. While he was ever slow to anger, he flared up at times, and could be direct and devastating. Yet it was seldom that he lost his composure, and those who attempted to make an enemy of him found the going difficult when they sought to paint him as a monster or ogre.

This South Boston boy developed into quite an imposing man. He was just a shade under six feet, stocky, broad of beam, and powerfully built. His head was of a size to give concern to the French wigmakers, and his large hands were strong, dextrous, and capable, and by means of them he expressed his well-defined mechanical bent. In his younger manhood he swam with the ease and grace of a dolphin.

To the end of his active life he thought of himself first as a "printer." Still, he had retired from that activity a wealthy man by the time he was forty-two, and certain of his other activities and accomplishments add up to a more lasting heritage. By the outbreak of the War for Independence probably more people had some conception of his personal appearance than any man who had lived up to that time. Not long after he went to live in France he wrote to his daughter that his face was virtually as well known there as that of the moon. He was definitely the leading private citizen of his time, and probably the finest exponent of the American way of life, to the patterning of which he had contributed so abundantly.

While there is no record of stars falling on New England at the time of his nativity, yet there was an incident on the very day of his birth that helps to illumine the spirit of the time and place, as well as the nature of his immediate forebear. So, it is on that wintry day at the start of the year 1706 when our story should logically begin.

# BEN FRANKLIN

# 1. A New England Boyhood

## 1706–1723

*I shall conclude this with my own character, which (one would think) I should be best able to give. Know then, that I am the enemy of vice, and a friend to virtue. I am one of an extensive charity, and a great forgiver of private injuries: A hearty lover of the clergy and all good men, and a mortal enemy of arbitrary government and unlimited power. I am naturally very jealous for the rights and liberties of my country: And the least appearance of an encroachment on these invaluable privileges, is apt to make my blood boil exceedingly. I have like-wise a natural inclination to observe and reprove the faults in others, at which I have an excellent faculty. I speak of this by way of warning to all such whose offenses shall come under my cognizance, for I never intend to wrap my talent in a napkin.—Sixteen-year-old Ben Franklin writing under the pen name of "Silence Dogood" in the New England Courant.*

BOSTON can be bitter indeed when the early January wind backs into the east, and then races in beneath leaden skies from off a wintry ocean freighted with tiny, biting snowflakes. And tradition stoutly maintains that the first Sunday of the year 1706 was just such a day. By the "old style" reckoning then employed in Britain and its possessions, the date would have been the sixth. Thus the year was young, yet well supplied with snow and ice, a heritage from the December terminated but a week before. But despite the cold and the bad going under foot, the customary goodly number had picked their way to the meetinghouse on Milk Street, wearing the paths to a high burnish that made them especially treacherous.

Directly opposite this Presbyterian house of worship was a smallish, clapboarded home. There had been dim candlelight in some of its rooms during much of the previous night, and more than the customary stir about it this Sabbath morning. Some of the children of the family living there had been readied and sent over to the meetinghouse in charge of one of the eldest of them. At home were two more toddlers and the mother and father, much concerned over the lusty crying of a baby boy only a matter of a few hours old.

There seemed to be but one way to quiet the clamor, so the mother laid aside her own heavy shawl, unswathed the child from several layers of woolen wrappings, opened the front of her waist, and set him to nursing. The father divested himself of his great-coat, peeled the outer clothing from the two small children, pokered up the fire, and drew a chair before it for his wife.

She was indeed pale and wan, yet fully resolute, after her very recent eighth bout with childbirth, finding it considerably more exacting at thirty-nine than formerly. But Abiah Franklin was from sturdy stock, the seafaring Folgers of Nantucket Island, and she had the bearing of two more children and forty-six years of life still before her. With all the host of family and household matters with which she was faced, her chief concern at that moment was the very same as her husband's, to get this latest of their offspring over the way to the church so that he might receive baptism. A human soul was at stake.

They would be late for service, that was certain. But it was hoped they might not be late enough for the sermon to have started. That would run for an hour to an hour and a half, and it would never do for this woman in her weakened condition, or her less-than-day-old son, to stay longer than need be in the unheated, barny structure on so bleak a day. So the feeding was terminated as promptly as possible, the contingent again arrayed in their heavy outer garments, and another start made. The objective is known today as the Old South Church.

There on the very day of his birth, so the written record claims, Josiah Franklin's tenth son underwent the sacrament of the cleansing from sin, and was carried to the kirk, so legend says, by none other than his mother. Perhaps she made an especial effort in his case, for he was a *tenth* son, and thus one to be "tithed" and set aside for God's purposes, a point which held great significance for this pious man and wife.

Even to have a child baptized in a church of which you were a *member* was also significant. Josiah had attended faithfully for nine long years before he had been accorded a place on the rolls. This gave him considerable distinction, for, quite contrary to the general impression, hardly twenty per cent of the inhabitants of Puritan Boston achieved church membership at the turn into the eighteenth century.

Little Ben's father was descended from an old Northampton-shire family. Actually the name Franklin had once been a Middle English noun meaning a *freeholder*, and had come to denote the class of freeborn landholders ranking next below the gentry. For many generations they had been yeomen blacksmiths and armorers in the East of England. And then the blacksmithing trade had come to be the "mystery," or craft of the first-born only. Thus this most recent Ben Franklin had little chance of working at the anvil, for he proved to be the youngest son of the youngest son back for five generations.

Josiah, his immediate forebear, had been trained to the dyer's trade, and had acquired a wife and three children before leaving Banbury in Oxfordshire in the year 1683, heading to America with other Dissenters seeking religious freedom. On this side of the ocean this first wife had presented him with four more chil-dren, or seven in all, before her demise in 1689 when the seventh was born. This child had expired in but a few days, and another, too, had died before being weaned. But the five children remain-ing could not be taken lightly, and the benighted father and husband began an immediate search for another helpmeet.

Since there had not been sufficient work here in the dyer's line to furnish a livelihood, he had shifted to tallow chandlery and soap boiling. It was a "smelly" occupation, but within six months Josiah had found a woman that would not only tolerate the reek of simmering fat, but the demands of five children not her own, and a husband nine years her senior.

Soon she was adding a brood of her own: two boys, a girl, another boy and girl, then three boys including Ben, and after him two more girls, or ten in all. Her fourth son, Ebenezer, came to a distressing end by drowning at the age of sixteen months in one of the tubs of sudzy fluid that cluttered his father's little shop. All the remainder of Abiah's children, however, lived to maturity, and Jane, the youngest, outlived her brother Benjamin.

The difference in age between members of these two broods was considerable, and most of the elder children had left the parental roof before the last of Abiah's off-spring appeared. Yet Franklin claims to have recalled at least one occasion on which no less than thirteen sat down to a meal together in their parents' home.

This may well have been in the larger, corner house that Josiah purchased at Union and Hanover Streets when Ben was but six. It would be in this home, most likely, that the boy remembered his father singing psalm tunes in the evening, accompanying himself on the violin. And it was here, too, that an outsider would occasionally sup with the family, and the conversation be turned to topics the discussion of which might benefit the children, and aid their understanding of the world in which they lived.

America, only about a century old with regard to the English colonies along the Atlantic seaboard, was developing rather rapidly now. Three quarters of a million souls were scattered from Maine to Carolina, yet only three of the towns in this huge area would have qualified as "large." They were Boston, New York, and Philadelphia, in that order, and even staid little Boston of Ben's boyhood was hardly citified. It is more than probable that one of the small boy's daily chores was to escort the family cow to and from pasture on the Common.

He tells in his *Autobiography* of swimming in its ponds, and there are stories of other childish play at the edges of the compact little town, somewhat cramped for space on a spit of land virtually an island. But in an age when children were frequently "bound out" and thus were self-sustaining at seven, playtime would have been curtailed by the number of tasks in candle making and soap boiling that were within the competence of small hands.

With the majority of his children married or in trades, Josiah's finances were improving, and he began to realize that if his younger son was to be tithed to the Lord the time to do something about the matter was at hand. And so it was that at eight Ben was entered in the grammar school to begin the classical training that would ultimately prepare him for the ministry. Within the year he had pushed up to the head of his class, and then on into the next class above. But the father began to have a change of heart. The costs of the necessary schooling would come high, and, at the moment, the opportunities in the pulpit did not seem especially promising.

So at the end of his first year he was shifted to a private school kept by one George Brownell, there to specialize in writing and arithmetic. While he did quite acceptably in the former, he failed abjectly in the latter, and by the end of this second year his formal "schooling" was over, although his education had in reality just begun. He would be an avid student for the balance of his life, even begging the boys at noisy play outside his windows in the last years of his life to be quieter so he might better concentrate on his reading. And limited though his intake had been, he would still recall it most favorably more than seventy years later and will a hundred pounds to the Boston public school system, the proceeds to be used to provide silver medals as scholarly incentives through generations to come.

Josiah put the boy to work learning his own business, cutting wicks, dipping candles, and stirring boiling soap. These were not new labors, neither were they one whit more congenial now that they were full-time stints. Already fair-sized and stocky for his age, young Ben occasionally let drop some remark that left the impression he might, in the back of his mind, be considering stealing away to sea. These indications of his thinking gave the father real concern, and he perhaps piled jobs on the boy with the intention of keeping his mind employed and away from nonsensical ideas.

But it would take far more than the affairs of a tallow chandlery to keep Ben's keen and active mind occupied. It is said he had learned to read at five, and to write at seven, and there is every indication he practiced both accomplishments upon every possible occasion. The home atmosphere was not only heavy with soap fat, but also with a Calvinism that has grown less formidable in more recent years. Churchgoing then was something of a feat of endurance with two extensive services on the Sabbath, and a lengthy lecture on Thursday evening, in an age when five A.M. was the approved hour for arising. There was a small armful of books such as so pious a Dissenter as his father would have chosen. But apart from a copy of Plutarch's *Lives* the remainder were mostly polemics, and too much reading of the latter seems to have given young Ben mental indigestion rather than either comfort or clarity. Throughout his long life he maintained a distinct preference for sound morals over speculative theology, particularly when it seemed to be a theology of terror such as fed the "hell fire" preaching of colonial times. Slowly he would evolve a religion of his own—a Religion of Love—love of his fellowman, which he sedulously practiced.

There has been some conjecture as to what the result might have been if this eager-minded boy had had a somewhat more sympathetic guide than his father, or his equally devout and prejudiced Uncle Benjamin. The air he breathed during his formative years was rather prim and stuffy, and urged him toward escape, and encouraged the original and provocative cast of mind he did acquire. Still, the Puritan weighed values, and he might have been far less of a moral and ethical personality had he not undergone the associations of his early childhood.

Piracy was just then parting with its aura of semi-respectibility, privateering was still in good repute, and there was something romantic and appealing about the ships that tied up at the wharves little more than a long stone's throw from the Franklin home. Also the boy's mother was from a seafaring background. The ocean's open spaces had intoxicated the next to the eldest half-brother, Josiah, who had in a measure disgraced the family by running off to sea. And now Ben, at least of cabin-boy size, seemed to have a hankering for "life on the ocean wave." The situation had the parents thoroughly perplexed.

Whenever there was a moment that could be spared from the business, Josiah took his youngest son in hand and marched him about the town so he might see artisans and craftsmen at their work. It was hoped that he might give some inkling of where his natural preferences lay. But none seemed to make a strong appeal. Josiah had a cousin, Samuel, who had come recently from England and was seeking to establish himself as a cutler, or maker of knives and cutting instruments. So Ben went to him on approval, but, since a fee was expected if he was apprenticed, he was brought home again. It was touch and go for a time.

Then James, his full brother, about ten years Ben's senior, arrived home from having served his apprenticeship to the printer's trade in London and perhaps saved the day. With him he had brought type and a press preparatory to opening up for himself. There were in 1718 two other printers already established in the city, Thomas Fleet of Pudding Lane, and Samuel Kneeland in Prison Lane. Between them they seemed to furnish capacity equal to local printing needs. But the young man just back from the British capital was quite optimistic, and took space in a house on Court Street at the corner of what later came to be called Franklin Avenue.

And no sooner was he ready to function than Josiah apprenticed "bookish Ben" to the older James.

Thus at twelve he left the soap kettle for the type case, and his father's home as well. But he was saved from the sea, which he later came to realize would have been a most distasteful means of livelihood. He would look to and accept advice from his father on occasion, but for better than four years Brother James would attempt to be his "master," while from age seventeen on Benjamin Franklin would be very much his *own* master.

Being bound out generally proved to be little better than a legalized and accepted type of slavery. Ben's indentured term of training was to have been nine years, or until he was twenty-one. During the last year he would receive journeyman's wages. He began learning his trade no doubt by washing used type, distributing it in the cases, running errands, and making himself generally useful. Surely he soon had a stick in his hand and was trying his competence at setting type. One gets the impression that James was not deluged with business, and there were probably odd moments for a variety of employments.

Ben used some of them by scribbling a little "poetry." Word had seeped up the coast from the South of how plucky Vir-

ginians had pounced on Teach, or Black-beard, in his hideaway
in Carolina waters, and then sailed home after the set-to with
the pirate's ornate head lashed to the sprit of one of their sloops.
Sensing that this news might have quite an emotional impact in
this seaport town, the youngster began a recital of the incident
as follows:

> Will you hear of a bloody Battle
> Lately fought upon the seas,
> It will make your ears to rattle
> And your admiration cease.
> Have you heard of Teach, the Rover,
> And his knavery on the Main;
> How of Gold he was a lover,
> How he loved all ill-got gain?

This small serving will be adequate as a sample of what the
balance was like. But such doggerel sold, and he was soon on the
streets with a supply of penny sheets under his arm, hawking his
poetic wares. With James' encouragement there were a number
of other similar compositions before the boy's father indicated
to him the true value of such efforts, and assured him that
rhymsters, as a rule, died of starvation.

Being a printer's apprentice he was naturally thrown in contact with the apprentices of some of the local booksellers. With
one or more of the latter the artful youngster made a highly
advantageous deal. He arranged to borrow books, sitting up
much of the night to read them through, so they might be
returned the following morning before they were missed or
wanted. With an appetite whetted by a much broader reading
diet, he quite naturally began to wish to have books he could call
his very own. Suddenly his reading indicated a possible means to
such an end.

One author had strongly advocated the benefits of a meatless
regimen, making it evident as well what a saving it would accomplish. Unmarried James was forced to board out his apprentices and workmen, and his smart younger brother soon made
him a proposition—he would feed himself if James would agree
to pay him one half his present board bill. This proposition was
accepted promptly, and Ben was gratified to find he could satisfy

both hunger and health and still have one half the cash advanced to him left over. Out of such funds he began to acquire a library.

To catalog fully his reading during this period is perhaps not justified. Still, the fact deserves to be emphasized that it was well-chosen, substantial fare. He would be heavily indebted for the remainder of his life for the philosophic approach he early acquired from John Locke, particularly his *Essay Concerning Human Understanding*. There was a similar obligation to Sir Isaac Newton for his *Principia*, and a lesser one to Francis Bacon. It was perhaps at this time that he read Sir William Petty's *Treatise on Taxation and Contributions*, for in years ahead he seems to have leaned heavily upon his economic theories. Also chancing upon a copy of Cocker's text on numbers, he now filled the void of his school days by teaching himself arithmetic and lower mathematics, along with geometry and navigation. His time was well employed.

Two other works made a mighty impact upon his impressionable mind. One was steadfast old Cotton Mather's *Essays to Do Good*, which made a lifelong "do-gooder" of the finest type of Franklin; the other was Daniel Defoe's *Essay on Projects*. This latter impressed upon his plastic mind the need for municipal improvements crying to be made in every hamlet, town, and city of that age, and helped to develop him as one of the most civic-minded men of the eighteenth century.

While his reading helped, perhaps the most immediately beneficial activity at that time was his use of Joseph Addison's writings in the *Spectator* as a textbook in composition. By diligent application he taught himself to write with one of the most direct and cogent styles of the age in which he would play so conspicuous a role. And by the fall of the year when he was fifteen he found an opportunity to put his newly achieved writing ability to effective use.

James had both ambition and plant capacity, and in August of 1721 began the publication of the *New England Courant*, fourth paper in the Colonies, and the third in Boston. While it was printed two sides of a half sheet of crown paper, and consequently had a trim size of but 6 1/8 by 10 inches, even this minute tabloid had to be filled with copy, and news alone was often insufficient

to that purpose. Also it was its proprietor's feeling that a newspaper should be entertaining and opinion-forming, rather than
dully matter-of-fact. He soon gathered about him a group of
cronies willing to write short bits for publication, and not above
taking occasional potshots at local stuffed shirts both in the
church and the government. It was to prove a precarious past-
time but still at times an amusing one.

Young Ben, about ready to turn sixteen, must have watched
this gentle sport of ragging local worthies such as Increase and
Cotton Mather with much interest. Despite his youth, he began
to want a place in the fray. So he chose himself a fictitious
character to hide behind, penned a letter as though written to the
paper by this remarkable female, a minister's widow named
Silence Dogood, and tucked his first literary effort, other than
the doggerel poetry, beneath the print-shop door during the
hours of darkness.

Found the next morning, it caused much amusement, was
judged good enough to print, so good in fact that the clique of
close companions spent much time trying to guess who had the
ability to turn it out. Published in the issue of April 2, 1722, other
bits from Mistress Dogood's facile pen arrived mysteriously each
two weeks from then on. Finally, after several had appeared and
made something of a stir, their author felt the time had come to
acknowledge his offspring. While this knowledge advanced the
boy somewhat in the estimation of the literary aspirants that made
the plant a rendezvous, it irked the rather testy James. The too-
pert-at-times younger brother felt that his "master" beat him too
frequently without justification, a breech threatened, and old
Josiah had to step in and adjust the matter.

There is the old contention that the artist unconsciously
sketches his own likeness, and something of this nature seems to
have occurred in the word picture the young printer's devil
drew of the feminine creature he chose to hide behind. In reading
the quote from his first installment which appears at the beginning
of this chapter, it would be well to bear in mind certain of the
characteristics he lists. In virtually every respect they are the very
characteristics he himself developed as he grew to manhood.

There were fourteen communications in all bearing the pseudonym "Silence Dogood" during the summer and fall of 1722, and by the time he had composed that many the apprentice had mined this vein of all its recoverable gold, and the lady lapsed into the limbo. But this had been the first positive step down the road to a journalistic career, the profession to which Benjamin Franklin was destined to give the greater share of his efforts in the years ahead.

But James and his literary bully boys began to inflate their confidence and sharpen their darts aimed at both clergy and magistrates. Finally someone so far overstepped the bounds of current propriety that James was in sore trouble. In fact he was briefly in jail, and the local government served notice on him to cease and desist from the publication of his news sheet. For a time it looked as though that edict might terminate the *Courant*. But a way out of the impasse suggested itself to the apologetic but still determined publisher. It would be issued in the name of the young brother, Benjamin Franklin.

To give greater credence to such a move, the indenture binding Ben to him as an apprentice was hauled out and rather publicly destroyed. That James drew another secret contract, which he forced his brother to sign, indicated his real intent. And so, with the issue of February 11, 1723, the seventeen-year-old Franklin became to all appearances a newspaper publisher. In fact his name would continue to be used in that manner for more than three years, until the *Courant's* termination. By that time Ben would be long gone from Boston, and even from America.

It could be that it was on the very day that James tore up the first indenture that his brother "grew up." From then on their relations, always strained, soon became insufferable. Finally Ben screwed up his courage and told James the apprenticeship was fully completed as far as he was concerned. The older brother promptly notified other printers in the neighborhood, asked them to refuse employment, and felt he had stopped this insurrection before it was well under way. This action did bring the younger man face to face with the circumstances, for at that time there were but four other printers in all the remaining colonies, one in

New London in Connecticut, another in New York, and two in Philadelphia. But Ben's courage still held, and he was determined to see what his fortune might be in New York.

Selling some of his books to obtain passage money, he schemed through a friend to be put secretly aboard a sloop heading down the coast, and when it sailed on a late September day in 1723, he hurriedly left family and friends behind him. Three days later he landed in the town on the tip of the island at the mouth of the Hudson, and made his way to the shop of William Bradford, "at the sign of the Bible," on Hanover Square. This elder of the Bradford clan had come to Philadelphia with the Quakers early in the 1680s, but had left in 1693 to become public printer of the New York colony. Having no work for this likely-looking youngster in his own plant, he recommended that the "journey-man" go on to Philadelphia, where he was convinced his son would make a place for him in his printery in the Quaker City.

There were three routes between New York and Philadelphia in those days. One led across the Hudson and then over a trail through the Jersey woods to Camden opposite Philadelphia. The second was by boat down the Lower Bay, about Staten Island to Amboy, then overland to Burlington, and the last eighteen miles again by boat down the Delaware River. The third was to await the rather infrequent sloops that coasted along the Jersey shoreline, and then up the Delaware Bay and River. Forced to stretch his fast-diminishing capital to the utmost, he chose the second route, taking a boat for a stormy passage to Amboy.

It was fall, there was a drenching rain and chilling wind, and Ben sensed he was running a temperature as he went ashore. Already his lifelong interest in medicine and health was developing, and years later he recalled that, "I found myself very fever-ish, and went in to bed; but having read somewhere that cold water drunk plentifully was good for fever, I followed the prescription, sweat plentifully most of the night, my fever left me, and in the morning, crossing the ferry, I proceeded on my journey on foot." He would ever be ready to pioneer new cures that seemed to him to have merit, and was more than a century ahead of his time with regard to frequent bathing and plenty of fresh air.

Making his way to Burlington, his prudence and level-headedness kept him from unfortunate escapades, and thus probably from the hands of the authorities as a suspected servant. There he was forced to await a boat, and when one unexpectedly offered close to dark on a Saturday evening, he went aboard. The night was cold, and he, together with some of the other passengers, took a turn at the oars. Finally they took shelter in the mouth of a creek, made a fire of old fence rails, and remained until daylight.

At last, about eight o'clock of a bright October Sunday morning, they tied up at the wharf in Philadelphia at the foot of the street leading up to the market. Stepping ashore from that small craft on a Sabbath morning had in it something of the entering of the promised land. It would indeed hold much of promise for this New England lad attempting to escape from a Puritanic background and the conventional restrictions of the age. He was in the process, too, of taking the plunge from boyhood into manhood, which is not always accomplished with facility. Such rewards as came to him in this adopted home he won through his own ability; and while the Lord surely had his hand upon the young man's shoulder, Ben Franklin always subscribed to the belief that "God helps them that help themselves."

## II. Philadelphia and London

### 1723–1726

*He that drinks fast pays slow.*

*Men and melons are hard to know.*

*Where there is marriage without love there will be love without marriage.*

*He that would have a short Lent, let him borrow money to be repaid at Easter.*

—*Sayings of* Poor Richard.

PENN'S "greene country towne," founded on the west bank of the Delaware some forty years before, was by the time of Franklin's arrival in the fall of 1723 very definitely astir. While its Quaker settlers fought shy of formal creeds, believing them to be from the head rather than the heart, their innate humility bred a very tolerant attitude toward the religious beliefs of others. Such genuine sufferance had already attracted a very large influx of Germans, and now the Scotch-Irish were beginning to enter Philadelphia by the shipload. While much of this immigration flowed on through the port into the back country, some remained to swell the local population. But in either event the traffic was profitable, and the town was growing in numbers, in wealth, and in opportunities. While it still inclined to the drab and the prudential, its vitality and substance were quite as apparent.

Its twenty-five hundred houses and structures were closely huddled within a triangular space whose principal side ran for about a mile along the river's high western bank. Its apex was a bare four blocks from the river on the central east-west thorough-fare, High Street, even that early being referred to as the "market street," which name it bears today. In the center of this wide street stood the market house and accompanying stalls, and the jail. On one of its corners was the largest of the Friends' meeting-houses, while facing it from either side were the places of business of some of the local tradesmen, their living quarters being behind and above their stores, counting rooms, and shops, which were customarily in front at street level.

Soiled from his travels, and unkempt in his "second-best" garments, the young printer made anything but a prepossessing figure. But he was anxious to look the town over, and also nearly famished. Pushing up the steep pitch immediately behind the line of wharves, he was given directions to a bakeshop that was open. He entered, drew some copper coins from his pocket, and asked for the customary Boston threepenny loaf. Such was not baked in Philadelphia, and in its place he found himself with three huge, outsized rolls. Since his coat pockets were already stuffed with some of his belongings, he tucked one under each arm, and began munching on the other as he strode off up the High Street.

There were bills on some of the houses, announcing that they were to be let. These gave him a trace of momentary concern, lest they indicate slack times. Both the houses and the people with whom he passed the time of day were plain, yet somehow both were reassuring. And then he saw something else that heightened his interest in this Quaker city. He had crossed the third of the main north-and-south streets and come almost to the last of the houses on the High Street, when he spied a pleasingly well-filled-out young lady of near his own age standing in a doorway. The rather quizzical look she gave him was returned with one of frank admiration. Later on he was to learn her name was Deborah Read, and that she was unmarried.

Swinging south, he strolled a block or two along Chestnut Street in the direction of the river, moved on through to Walnut, and was soon on the riverbank, and back at the boat from which he had landed. In it a woman and child who had been passengers the night before still waited to travel further on downstream. They most willingly accepted the two untouched rolls; and, after a bit of conversation, he strolled back toward the growing activity on the town's streets. Most of the folk seemed headed in one direction, and following along, he quickly found himself in the large meetinghouse at the corner of Second and High Streets. Since a Quaker meeting is always quiet and relaxed, and

Ben was exhausted after a sleepless night, his chin was soon on his chest, and he slept soundly through the hour or hour-and-a-half session.

Gently awakened, he trudged out, learned that the Crooked Billet Inn on the wharf just above Chestnut Street was a fully reputable place, and there had his first real meal in many hours. There, too, he found a bed, slept through the rest of the day until awakened for supper, and then dropped back into bed and slept on through the night.

With his finances running perilously low, he was up early, made himself as presentable as possible, and, drawing on his reserve from the two full meals of the day before, went off break-fastless in search of Andrew Bradford's printing shop. He was the son to whom William Bradford in New York had recommended he pay a visit. The younger man had taken over from the father when the latter quitted the province, and since December of 1719 had been issuing the *Mercury*. This had secured his position in local affairs and won him the postmastership, highly essential to the publisher of a paper, since it provided carrier service.

Ben was somewhat surprised to find the elder Bradford on hand as well, the trip from New York having been made with greater dispatch on horseback. He was disappointed to learn that Andrew had already replaced a journeyman that had just died, but was pleased to join the two older men at breakfast. Seemingly he made a good impression, for he was offered lodging in return for an occasional odd job, an arrangement he had little choice but to accept. And beyond that it was suggested that the competing printer, Samuel Keimer, might well be in need of help, and that a call on him would not be amiss.

Wanting to run down this lead as soon as possible, Ben was about to start off when William Bradford agreed to go along, presumably to introduce him to Keimer. This seemed a little irregular when it was disclosed that these two printers had never met. But the young workman from Boston was introduced quite impressively, and Keimer, believing his sponsor to be some local person of consequence, was most affable. Ben quickly proved his ability; and then the "crafty old sophister," as he is called in the

*Autobiography*, gave evidence of why he had come along. By subtle questioning he led his son's competitor on and learned all his prospects and plans. Having finally plucked the goose clean, he left.

There was no work immediately available, but Keimer promised that he would surely take him on in just a few days. So Ben stayed for a while, did what he could to improve the workings of the decrepit press and to put the small shop into better order. Then he drifted back to Bradford's and such small jobs as might turn up there.

But Keimer kept his promise, sent for him within a short time, and put him at regular work. He, too, was single, and, like James, had to board out his hands, and the arrangements he made would strongly influence Ben's life. The Boston boy suddenly found himself a member of the Read household, and thus living in the same home with the first young woman in Philadelphia who had seriously attracted his attention. The winter just ahead promised to be a pleasant one.

And so it was. Keimer, rather a vapid eccentric, was more amusing than inspiring. However, the wages he paid proved a new and pleasing experience for the young man. Through Deborah Read, as well as by his own admirable aptitudes, he soon acquired a considerable circle of worthwhile friends. His being "from Boston" gave him preferred standing among young people of his own age, enough of whom were "lovers of reading" and other meritorious pursuits, so that he spent his unemployed time happily and profitably. There was the eternal tang of freedom in the air, too—freedom from restraints imposed by a zealous father and a slightly arrogant brother. Yet he had enough native prudence so that neither the few coins to spend in his pocket, nor the lack of a checkrein, was his undoing.

In some manner, word of his being in Philadelphia spread on down the river to New Castle, capital of the Delaware province. There it came to the attention of a brother-in-law, Robert Holmes, husband of one of Ben's older sisters, whose trading vessel had put in at the downriver port. From there he wrote his young relative by marriage a letter, telling him of the family's concern for him, suggesting his return to Boston, and perhaps

offering free passage by way of inducement. Young Ben thanked
him by return post for his interest, but stated with great clarity
his reasons for staying on where he now was.

Once again, as will so frequently be apparent throughout
Franklin's long life, he was fortunate in being on hand and well
equipped to profit by circumstances. On this occasion it happened
that Captain Holmes was visiting with Sir William Keith, governor of Pennsylvania, on official business in New Castle, and
showed him the letter he had just received. Ben was discussed,
and Sir William evinced a lively interest in him, maintaining that
any young man who wrote so well should be encouraged. If he
would but set himself up in business, the official printing of both
Pennsylvania and Delaware would be his. The sequel Franklin
relates in his *Autobiography* as follows:

"One day Keimer and I being at work near the window, we
saw the governor and another gentleman (which proved to be
Colonel French, of New Castle), finely dressed, come directly
across the street to our house, and heard them at the door. Keimer
ran down immediately, thinking it a visit to him; but the governor inquired for me, came up, and with condescension and
politeness I had been quite unused to made me many compliments, desired to be acquainted with me, blamed me kindly for
not having made myself known to him when I first came to the
place, and would have me go away with him to the tavern, where
he was going with Colonel French to taste, as he said, some
excellent Madeira. I was not a little surprised, and Keimer stared
like a pig poisoned. . . . Over the Madeira he proposed my setting
up my business, laid before me the probabilities of success, and
both he and Colonel French assured me I should have their interest
and influence in procuring the public business of both govern-
ments. On my doubting whether my father would assist me in it,
Sir William said he would give me a letter to him, in which he
would state the advantages, and he did not doubt of prevailing
with him. So it was concluded I should return to Boston in the
first vessel, with the governor's letter recommending me to my
father."

Keimer's hired hand decided not to let his "master" in on his
secret, despite the fact he was invited to dine occasionally with

the governor, who soon polished his newly-made young friend to a fine luster with the potent wax of flattery. The days rolled along, and it was toward the end of April in 1724 when a vessel offered for Boston. Explaining hurriedly to Keimer that he felt he should make peace with his family, from whom he had so hastily departed, he picked up the promised letter from Keith, and was aboard when the craft sailed. It managed to strike a shoal while descending the river. This started a leak that necessitated almost continual pumping all the way to Boston, and at which the passenger was obliged to take his turn. Consequently he put in a rugged and most unpleasant fortnight, and was very likely glad he had not chosen a career at sea.

Dressed in brand-spanking new clothing from head to toe, sporting a watch, and with five pounds sterling in silver lining his pockets, this was in no sense a return of the prodigal son. After his absence of about seven months he managed to pleasantly surprise his family, and when he dropped in at his brother's plant he achieved quite a sensation. What a tingle of satisfaction he must have found in spreading his silver coins across one of the composing stones for the edification of men accustomed to the paper money seen almost exclusively in Boston. And the crowning act of this courtesy call came when, upon leaving, he plunked down a Spanish dollar for a round of drinks. Needless to say this visit did nothing to improve relations between the estranged brothers, James protesting volubly that he had been roundly insulted before his working people.

Also, the letter Ben delivered to his father left old Josiah speechless. At least for some days he made no reference to it to his son. Captain Holmes happened into port, so it was shown to him, and his opinion of Keith solicited. The elder Franklin was confident the governor must be daft when he suggested setting an eighteen-year-old boy up in business. Despite Holmes's staunch defense of the scheme, Ben's ultracautious parent turned it down cold.

He did thank Sir William, however, for his interest and patronage, and the governor's communication was by no means a total loss. It did elevate Ben somewhat in the father's opinion, although not enough to accomplish the son's purposes. The visit had amply indicated that James and Benjamin were not yet ready to be reconciled. Thus their father the more readily granted the younger son, still a minor, permission to return to Philadelphia where he seemed to be developing so promisingly on his own.

There being a vessel about ready to leave for New York, the visit was concluded, and Ben set off. While his father would live for another twenty years, to die at age eighty-seven, this tenth and youngest son was destined to see him but twice more. Since the ship made a stop at Newport there was an opportunity to visit an older brother, John, maker of the "Crown soap" which one day would, together with countless other items, be sold in Philadelphia by B. Franklin, Printer.

During this brief visit in Rhode Island he was introduced to a friend of the brother's, a Mr. Vernon. This gentleman was so impressed by the young man that he gave him an order on a debtor in the Philadelphia area to collect the then considerable sum of thirty-five pounds. He was to retain the money until advised as to the manner in which it was to be transferred. While it was in the nature of a compliment to be so trusted, this transaction would produce several years of heartache.

Continuing on to New York, he met there a boyhood friend, John Collins, who had come on ahead and proposed to accompany Ben to Philadelphia, hoping to find employment as a merchant's clerk. Formerly of excellent habits, he had, during Ben's absence, taken to "sotting with brandy." Unfortunately when his friend caught up with him young Collins was both drunk and broke.

Governor Burnet of the New York colony, having heard from the ship's captain that one of his passengers had a very considerable number of books with him, asked that the young man be brought to call upon his excellency. Ben would have willingly taken Collins, but this was out of the question. So he went alone, spent a pleasant hour or two looking over the governor's library and discussing books and authors with him. Naturally he was pleased that he had so conducted himself that he had been singled out for attention by the head of the second of the colonies. It was an unusual distinction.

As soon as his companion had sobered up sufficiently, they

started overland to Philadelphia. Mr. Vernon's thirty-five pounds were collected en route. This was fortunate in that otherwise they would have been destitute of funds, unfortunate in that it necessitated dipping into money belonging to another. Also with this sum on hand it seemed easier for Collins to borrow from Franklin than to sober up and do his best in finding work. He became so constant a financial drain that the funds collected for Mr. Vernon were at length exhausted, and with his tippling he was far less enjoyable as a companion. Finally he went off to Barbados to fill an opening for a tutor, full of promise of quickly restoring his borrowings, but was never heard from again. "The breaking into this money of Vernon's was one of the first great errata of my life," recalled Franklin forty-seven years later. Sober and temperate Ben, plagued and laid liable to confinement in a debtor's prison because of a sot and wastrel! Looking himself squarely in the face, he began to feel that perhaps his father had been right—he was as yet unequal to properly managing business affairs. Perhaps he was too well-read in books, and not discerning enough in human nature. Since he appeared to need it, he was due to have further harsh schooling along similar lines.

Back once again in Keimer's employ, he had also refitted himself into the circle of friends he had been acquiring. Student that he was and always would be, he still very much needed the stimulus of congenial companions of both sexes. On the male side his especial friends were Charles Osborne, Joseph Watson, and James Ralph, all eager readers, and all, too, aspiring writers of both prose and particularly of poetry. In the warmer months their meeting place was in any one of dozens of beautiful spots along the banks of the Schuylkill River, about two miles west of town. There they read and then tore apart each other's compositions, and eagerly picked each other's minds for every bit of interesting information.

Boarding again at Read's, Ben and Deborah began to take each other seriously, and active courtship was soon in progress, and marriage even talked about. But a new trend in affairs quickly moved any such prospects well into the future. Sir William's immediate reaction to Josiah Franklin's refusal to finance his son was that "he was too prudent." Well then, he would set Ben up himself, and he asked for an inventory of what would be necessary.

This offer made by the man chosen by the Penn family to guide the affairs of the province appeared to be completely reliable. Also it seemed but common sense and good business to hold the entire matter in strictest secrecy. As a consequence, the eighteen-year-old boy kept his own counsel, and perhaps missed an opportunity to be set right respecting Keithian promises.

The inventory, which ran to the substantial sum of about one hundred pounds, evidently was quite satisfactory to the governor. It was autumn again, and the annual ship, the only one regularly plying between London and Philadelphia, would be sailing shortly. Ben visualized the inventory stowed aboard it when it returned from England, and wondered if he could stretch out his patience until the press, type, and supplies arrived possibly a year hence.

Thus he was somewhat astounded to have Sir William suggest it might be a good move if he went to England and made the selection of the properties in person. It would also afford him a chance to meet London stationers and booksellers, with whom profitable connections might be made. The *London Hope*, Captain Annis in command, tied up at about this time at the local wharves, and Ben was told to get himself ready to leave shortly. His letters of credit and of introduction would be available by sailing time.

The next few days were busy ones. The break was made with Keimer, while that with Deborah Read, whose father had died suddenly in September, was softened with assurances he would be back as speedily as possible, and, once established as a tradesman, in real need of a wife. Somewhat to his astonishment though, the aspiring poet, James Ralph, suddenly determined to accompany him.

The man was married and had one child, but he explained to Ben that he was making the trip in search of goods he might handle on commission to his advantage. In the light of this plausible explanation his friend was quite delighted. A crossing took thirty days at the barest minimum, and could run to twice and even three times that long. Someone closer to his own age and tastes for a companion would make the journey, and the stay in London, much pleasanter.

Even at sailing time the letters promised by the governor had not been forthcoming, but Dr. Baird, his secretary, gave full assurance they would be turned over at New Castle, the last port of call. So Ben and Ralph went aboard, found their very limited quarters below decks, and the ship dropped downstream, and anchored at the Delaware capital.

The great cabin on the *London Hope* had been taken by the famous lawyer, Andrew Hamilton, and his son James, together with a Mr. Thomas Denham, a local merchant, and two owners of an ironworks in the Maryland colony. But almost at the time of sailing, Mr. Hamilton received by post "an uncommon call in the way of business from Philadelphia . . . a fee of three hundred pounds sterling to save a rich ship" in a case in the admiralty court. Hurrying back upriver with his son, he left his space in the great cabin vacant, and his food stores intact.

Just as the ship was about to shake out its sails Colonel French came aboard with the mailbag containing the governor's dispatches, and presumably the letters in which Ben was interested. He showed so much deference to the young printer, who had been considered quite an "ordinary" person up until then, that, as Franklin later recounted, "I was more taken notice of, and, with my friend Ralph, invited by the other gentlemen to come into the cabin, there being now room." He recalled too, with gratitude, the Hamilton supplies that had been "laid in plentifully."

It was a disagreeable crossing, yet it fortunately provided him the chance of establishing a firm friendship with the kindly Mr. Denham.

As they sailed through the Channel, Captain Annis opened the mailsack, as he had promised, allowed the governor's protégé to select the six or seven missives that seemed to be his. It was the day before Christmas when they tied up at the London wharves, and the ambitious young man lost no time in searching out a stationer to whom one of the letters was addressed, and presented it to the man in his shop.

Ben was rudely taken aback when the tradesman disclaimed

knowing any such person as Governor Keith. And he swallowed still harder when he found that it was not written by Sir William but by a knavish attorney named Riddlesden, whom the now angry stationer pronounced "a complete rascal," and stumped off to wait upon a customer. No communications such as the governor had agreed to had been put aboard the ship, and the young American was heartsick indeed when at last it was conclusive that Keith's high-sounding promises were totally worthless. The holiday season that year was a sober, barren period.

Seeking out Mr. Denham, he learned what he long since might better have found out, how utterly unreliable Keith's word could be. Just what his feelings were at that moment is not clear, but in all probability not too violent, for Franklin never seemed capable of intense and consuming hatred. Years later, when drafting his *Autobiography*, he even gives the impression of defending this little man, trying with empty promises to reinflate his ego. Very likely he even then looked upon this wild-goose chase as but another incident in his apprenticeship to life and living, and one that in the ultimate was fraught with good.

The Quaker merchant may have been seriously considering this young printer even then. But he advised Ben to seek immediately for employment in his own trade and further perfect his skill by learning the methods of the larger plants to be found in England. Also, since this chap Riddlesden, whose letter he had mistakenly delivered, appeared to be involved in some mischief with Keith, and "to the prejudice" of Lawyer Hamilton, he suggested the whole circumstances be committed to the latter when he arrived by the next ship. The information passed along to Hamilton months later proved a great favor to this influential man, and in return he did many kindnesses for Franklin in the years ahead.

When Ben and Ralph took stock of their finances, they were low enough to counsel extreme economy, so they found lodgings together in the rather humble section of the city known as Little Britain. The cost was roughly the equivalent of eighty-seven cents apiece per week. It was probably anything but consoling news to have Ralph announce that he was remaining in London, and abandoning his wife and child in the Colonies. The tight-woven moral fiber inherited from his Puritan forebears would have set Ben to searching his own words and acts for some trace of responsibility for or implication in this callous proceeding. It had seemed to him that he had helped to untether John Collins from family and friends in Boston, whereupon he spiraled off into drunkenness and duplicity. Had he not more recently in some manner been encouraging James Ralph to slip his moorings and run away from his obligations? His was a clearly exacting conscience.

These first days in the British capital were full of soul searching, and Ben attempted to get a firmer hold on himself and to put more real purpose and direction into his life. But he had been rather shamefully deceived and badly let down, and for a time there was a strong inclination to escape from the sobering experiences he was undergoing in the gaiety and excitement that London provided in such decided contrast to either Boston or Philadelphia. As an instance, the theater, banned in the Quaker City, was in full swing here. So they spent many evenings sampling its pleasures, to the rapid depletion of Ben's small reserve funds.

Applying at Palmer's, then a well-known printing establishment located in the Close adjoining the Church of St. Bartholomew, the oldest religious structure in the city, the young American readily obtained work. With Ralph becoming a decided drain, his new-found journeyman's wages were most welcome. However, any prospects of getting back to America soon seemed rather remote. In the face of this uncertainty, his first impulse was to do the right thing by Deborah Read and loosen any bonds there might be between them. So he addressed a letter to her, and had it readied in the post office for the first westbound packet in the spring, saying among other things that he "was not likely soon to return." That this was his sole communication with her later proved highly unfortunate, and forty odd years afterward he felt this niggardliness to have been another of the "great errata" of his life.

Ralph, with his head far up among the clouds, first sought a place on the stage, but to no avail. Certain he was bound to be one of the great writers of his time, he tried to find backing for a new magazine which he would both write and edit. One hope after another evaporated, and eventually he was down to the point of begging among the stationers and lawyers for such hack writing as they might toss in his direction. Obviously he had to eat and to find lodging, which he did at Ben's expense. The consequence was that this left little or no surplus out of which to accumulate passage money home.

There was a credit side to the ledger, however, and a few entries to be made in it. Next to the lodgings in Little Britain was a bookseller, one Wilcox, from whom arrangements were made to borrow secondhand volumes for a mere pittance. It was from this experience, at least in part, that six years later came the suggestion for fashioning the first circulating library in America.

Close to the Palmer plant was the type foundry of Thomas James. It is inconceivable that this youngster with such lively curiosity missed knowing every last detail of this companion business to the trade which would provide him both a living and a fortune. He was filling out Keimer's badly depleted fonts of type soon after his eventual return to America, and in 1744 he seems to have acquired a set of founder's tools through his London correspondent, William Strahan. Benjamin Franklin may well have been the first typecaster in his native land.

It was while at Palmer's that his work on Wollaston's *Religion of Nature* brought him into conflict with that author's reasoning. Fancying himself called upon to refute this Christian deist, he turned out a pamphlet titled *A Dissertation on Liberty and Necessity, Pleasure and Pain*. A small edition was struck off, which achieved a limited circulation. While Mr. Palmer applauded his workman's ingenuity, he considered his ethical reasoning "abominable." This enterprise later appeared to its immature author as another "erratum," and apparently committed him forever afterward to the practice of keeping his religious views out of print.

Nonetheless, his little polemic afforded him an entry to some of the clubs of "free-thinkers" that frequented certain coffee houses, and he met such celebrities as Dr. Bernard Mandeville, author of the *Fable of the Bees*. Another such acquaintance raised his hopes by offering to make him known to the then very aged Sir Isaac Newton, but such a meeting failed to transpire. He did, though, come to know Sir Hans Sloane through selling him a purse which he had brought from home made of rare asbestos. This item presumably found its way into the huge trove of curiosities Sir Hans gathered together, and which, following his death, became the nucleus of the British Museum.

Both Ralph's circumstances and moral attitude appear to have worsened. He became quite smitten with a young widow, a milliner, living in the same place with them. When she moved elsewhere, he followed, allowing her to support him. But her small child made three to be kept by her limited wages, and, they being quite inadequate, the ne'er-do-well at last was forced to take a teaching position in the country. Quite brazenly, too, he borrowed his companion's name, asking in a letter to be addressed in the reply as Mr. Franklin, schoolmaster.

Ralph was still determined to make a name for himself as a poet, and Ben endured the samples of his work poured upon him through the post largely because he still had hopes of collecting the considerable amount owed him. The young woman this scribbler had abandoned evidently had formed a strong attachment to him. She was personable, genteel, and interesting, and warm-blooded Benjamin Franklin soon sought to take Ralph's place in her affections. But she did not take his advances favorably at all, and communicated her indignation to Ralph, who employed the circumstances to break the friendship with Ben, maintaining that any and all obligations between them were now cancelled. Said an older and wiser Franklin years later, "I found myself relieved of a burden." At the moment it was still a most distasteful episode, and although he was learning, it continued to be in the hard way.

But the termination of the affair gave something of a new turn to Ben's circumstances. There had been a newness to London which, even in the face of depressing influences, had been stimulating. But its stimulation was wearing off, America seemed quite appealing, and the big objective quickly became sufficient passage money to get home again. This encouraged his shifting to Watt's, a larger printing house, near Lincoln's Inn Fields. Here he started in as pressman, feeling that he needed more exercise, and here he became something of a curiosity. The fifty other workmen, who drank little besides beer, and some as much as six pints between dawn and dark, looked rather contemptuously upon this "Water-American," as they dubbed him. Yet he regularly carried double the load of locked-up type they chose to attempt. Also he was soon running a very profitable loan business on the side, loaning back to his companions at high interest the money he saved by abstaining from their everlasting sotting.

But this virile young American with his breezy ways, and his strong inclination to and ability for building friendships, was soon well accepted among them, and "achieved considerable influence." He had been levied about five shillings, the equivalent of a day's wages, to buy drinks for his associates when he first entered the plant. When another similar contribution was demanded on his shift from the press to the composing room, he naturally rebelled. But he was subjected to so much mischief and anoyance that he at last was forced to comply. Still, his stay at Watt's seems to have been both pleasant and profitable.

He shifted into new lodgings closer to this second plant, and managed to cut his living expenses to two shillings, about fifty cents, a week. He discovered a few interesting companions, and in the warmer weather found much pleasure in bathing in the Thames and in teaching some of his friends to swim. For a time he even considered touring Europe and attempting to make a livelihood from exhibitions and the teaching of swimming.

It is very possible that he called on Mr. Denham to sound out that substantial businessman's reactions to such a plan, when the Quaker merchant proposed a scheme of his own. He was getting ready to return to America, and offered to take Ben along, make him his clerk, and, after a period of training, permit him to buy and sell on his own account to his very considerable advantage. While the fifty pounds a year he agreed to pay was not equal to what his compositor's wages in London were, Ben had become discerning enough to recognize the far larger prospects this proposal offered. Said he: "I now took leave of printing, as I thought, forever, and was daily employed in my new business, going about with Mr. Denham among tradesmen to purchase various articles, and seeing them packed up," and getting these goods aboard ship. There were a few days of leisure before sailing, and in them came another opportunity which might have warranted his staying in England, but his attachment to Mr. Denham, and to America, drew him home.

They sailed from Gravesend, twenty miles down the Thames, on July 23, 1726, but it would be October 11 before he was back in Philadelphia. There was an adventure or two, and some stimulating incidents, during these eleven weeks and more at sea, but by and large the passengers were pretty well bored by the time it was over. Much of his first two weeks Ben spent pumping his companions, by which time he had gained most of the information wanted. The last nine he gave to perfecting his *Journal* of the voyage, and also to a plan for "regulating my future conduct in life."

He also had ample time in which to reflect upon these last eighteen months of his life spent in England. He had worked hard, and spent but a minimum upon himself, some for seeing plays, but principally for books. His friend Ralph, whom he was forced to admit he continued to love for his many amiable qualities, had kept him poor. He stilled owed him some twenty-seven pounds, more than half the year's wages Mr. Denham now paid him, and almost three quarters of the money Ben still owed Mr. Vernon. In middle age he recalled that, "I had by no means improved my fortune; but I had picked up some very ingenious acquaintances, whose conversation was of great advantage to me; and I had read considerably."

It had been an education, and rather a liberal one, though expensive in time and effort.

## III. Apprenticeship to Life

### 1727–1730

*It is very common with Authors, in their first Performances, to talk to their readers thus; "If this meets with a SUITABLE Reception; Or, If this should meet with DUE Encouragement, I shall hereafter publish, &c." This only manifests the Value they put on their own Writings, since they think to frighten the Publick into their Applause, by threatening, that unless you approve what they have already wrote, they intend never to write again; when perhaps it mayn't be a Pin Matter whether they ever do or no. As I have not observed the Cricks to be more favourable on this Account, I shall always avoid saying any Thing of the Kind; and conclude with telling you, that, if you send me a Bottle of Ink and a Quire of Paper by the Bearer, you may depend on hearing further from, Sir, your most humble Servant.—Conclusion of* The Busy-Body.—No 1, *appearing in* Bradford's Mercury.

YOUNG Ben had left for London a year and a half before full of certainty he would bring back with him the facilities to set himself up as his own master. Instead he had returned virtually empty-handed. Yes, he had a job, but it was one in which he would be forced to start from scratch again. Still, he was a more matured person, and his unbounded ambition was intact. During the next twenty years he would apply himself with all his might to earning a living and to accumulating a competence. At the moment he seemed to have his feet firmly on the ground, a more certain course plotted, and to be unmistakably on his way. But what a jade Fortune could be!

Mr. Denham opened a store on Water (Front) Street, and Ben, with his customary alacrity, sought to learn accounting, selling, and his new craft of merchandising. He grew very fond of the good Quaker, with whom he boarded, and whom he accepted as a second father. It was sort of thrilling to be home again.

There had been changes, some of them quite apparent. Keith was no longer governor, and refused to speak to the young man he had so badly deceived when they passed on the street. Deborah Read had married a potter, named Rogers, but, so 'twas said, was most unhappy in these arrangements into which she had been hurried. It pricked his conscience more than a little to realize that he had contributed to her present dilemma. Keimer evidently was busy. At least he had five hands in the plant. There was also Ben's coterie of friends anxious to hear his astute impressions of London, the recital of which filled many a most pleasant evening. He prized these evening sessions, and his active mind began to wrestle with means of making them even more fruitful. And then misfortune struck again.

Shortly after he turned twenty-one, both he and Mr. Denham were stricken with grave illnesses. What the latter's ailment was is not known, but Ben had contracted a violent case of pleurisy that all but carried him off. Slowly he regained his strength, while his great and good friend and patron finally succumbed. Previous to his death he had left oral instructions that Ben was to be relieved from indebtedness for his passage money and some small advances beyond his salary—but—Ben was now out of employment.

Ben's ill luck, however, proved to be Keimer's good fortune. He quickly "tempted" the now highly skilled printer "with an offer of large wages by the year, to come and take the management of his printing-house." There being no openings for a merchant's clerk, he went back to work at a craft the mere manual practice of which evidently gave him but very indifferent satisfaction. Also he was to be associated, for a time at least, with a man whom he found it hard to tolerate.

The workmen Keimer had attached to himself with extravagant promises and stinting wages were rather a motley crew. The most promising among them was a countryman some nine years Ben's senior, who was at least honest and willing, although not too apt mechanically and inclined to be an over-zealous

drinker. His name was Hugh Meredith. Another, a wild Irishman
known only as John, decamped suddenly for parts unknown,
leaving but four to be managed and instructed by the new foreman.

Keimer kept to his stationery store and left the print shop in
far abler hands, and for a time Ben was very busy. The men had
to be taught typesetting, press work, or even bookbinding, while
he himself had to cast fill-ins for type characters in short supply,
mix ink, repair equipment, and bring order out of near chaos. He
was very much of a factotum, yet to it all there was one most
acceptable feature. They "never worked on Saturday, that being
Keimer's Sabbath."

That gave both Saturday and Sunday for study and contempla-
tion, and the fuller employment of Ben's wide-ranging mind. And
in his periods of free time he became a sort of two-faced Janus,
looking most interestedly within at his own mental, moral, and
spiritual faculties and tendencies, and outwardly at a physical
world that was yearly proving to be a more and more complicated
but still very fascinating place of residence.

On his way home the year before he had eagerly recorded
happenings in the world about him—one eclipse of the sun, a
moon-bow in the night sky, observations on that graceful swim-
mer, the dolphin, activities of minute objects of sea-life, a second
eclipse, this one of the moon, and even the practices of card-
sharpers. But he had also looked most earnestly within his own
mind and heart, found that he had been deceitfully used by
others to his hurt, and determined to draft a plan by which he
might direct his own conduct to better ends.

While the original of this plan was missing from the *Journal*
of the voyage, its ethical factors seem to have been recaptured
from a later manuscript that has, in its turn, disappeared. His resolutions were fourfold. First, he would practice frugality at all
times when he found himself in debt until the debt was discharged.
His obligation to Mr. Vernon, which fortunately had not been
demanded of him, preyed heavily upon his sensitive conscience.
Two, he was determined to "speak truth in every instance, to
give nobody expectations that are not likely to be answered."
Third, he would apply himself industriously to his means of live-

lihood. Fourth, he resolved "to speak ill of no man whatever, not even in a matter of truth; but rather by some means excuse the faults I hear charged upon others, and upon proper occasions speak all the good I know of everybody." His adherence to these principles "quite through to old age" was rather remarkable, yet perhaps not exactly unique when it is realized that the goals— material as well as spiritual—that he set up were always attainable. They might take effort and sacrifice, but they could be achieved. Throughout his life he was primarily interested in *the possible*. Each of his resolves would be put to the test, and probably the first that now came up for trial was industriousness.

Even though working for wages, he really exerted himself for Keimer, happy to be making a going concern out of what had been a rickety enterprise. But it soon became most apparent that Keimer's interest and civility were transient. Just as soon as the men were trained the new foreman would be dispensable. Relations gradually went into decay, and Keimer sought a cause that might be built up into a separation.

It soon came, rather unexpectedly, when a disturbance in the neighborhood caused Franklin to thrust his head out of the window in the upper story where the plant was located. Keimer, who had very likely run outside from the stationery store below, looked up, and crassly bellowed at his foreman to mind his own affairs and get back to work. It was an uncalled for and intentional insult, and if shouted at a somewhat more emotional person, might have cost the unstable Keimer a beating.

Feeling quite safe on this latter score, he bounded upstairs, continued his abuse, and claimed his chief regret was that their annual agreement still had so long a time to run. The man had suddenly become completely intolerable, and Ben told him briefly and candidly they were through, removed his apron, washed off his hands, and walked out. At the door he met Hugh Meredith, asked him if he would be good enough to gather together a few possessions left behind and drop them off at his lodgings. Ben had no immediate plans, but others did. Four weeks and more later the events were still deep-etched in the Franklin memory, and he then set down the following lucid picture of what happened.

"Meredith came accordingly in the evening, and we talked

my affair over. He had conceived a great regard for me, and was very unwilling that I should leave the house while he remained in it. He dissuaded me from returning to my native country, which I began to think of; he reminded me that Keimer was in debt for all he possessed; that his creditors began to be uneasy; that he kept his shop miserably, sold often without profit for ready money, and often trusted without keeping accounts; that he must therefore fail, which would make a vacancy I might profit of. I objected my want of money. He then let me know that his father had a high opinion of me, and from some discourse that had passed between them, he was sure would advance money to set us up, if I would enter into partnership with him. 'My time,' says he, 'will be out with Keimer in the spring; by that time we may have our press and types in from London. I am sensible I am no workman; if you like it, your skill in the business shall be set against the stock I furnish, and we will share the profits equally.' "

The proposition was highly acceptable to Franklin, and also to Meredith's father who, by good fortune, happened to be in Philadelphia. Sober Ben, while considerably younger, had had a favorable influence over the alcoholic tendencies of his prospective partner. An inventory of needs was turned over to a merchant-importer, and it was arranged to keep the matter secret. Hugh continued with Keimer, and Ben had a chat, but to no avail, with Bradford. So he very likely put the unemployed days that now occurred to good purpose in his studies.

But Keimer's choler proved to have been most ill-timed. New Jersey was about to turn out an issue of paper money. It was an exacting job, but correspondingly profitable. Franklin's skill was equal to it, and competitor Bradford might be just sagacious enough to pick him up and put him to work at the task. So Keimer pocketed his over-sized pride and sent peace overtures, perhaps through Hugh Meredith.

At least it was the latter who persuaded his friend to return, so that there might be further much-needed instruction before the partnership became operative. So a truce was made, and once more Ben was drawing wages.

As a mere youngster, his brother James' blows had seemed

both too frequent and too lusty. But in his present apprenticeship to life itself he discovered that chance was not above buffeting him about, and rather robustly at times, without too much evident justification. But he was learning, not only from books, but also directly from the pages of daily life. Did he miss more formal schooling than he had had? Not especially, at least there is no hint or suggestion in his later writings. He was now applying himself most earnestly to self-education, but felt the need of the participation and encouragement of others. And being very much the "self-starter," he did something about it.

About this same time some ultra-pious soul had testified in a letter to Bradford's *Mercury* that locally there were "no Masquerades, Plays, Balls, Midnight Revellings or Assemblies to Debauch the Mind or promote Intrigue." But men did seek social interchange even in still rather prudish Philadelphia. Where mere conviviality was all that was to be furthered, there were the "bottle associations" that met with great regularity in some of the taverns. With Benjamin Franklin it was *knowledge* that was to be furthered, and so he began the organization of a *scholarly* association. He gave it the name *Junto*, from the Latin root word meaning to join. Its direct descendant, still so called, continues to this day to provide adult education for thousands each year in Franklin's adopted city.

The kindred spirits which he gathered together were in wide variety with regard to age and background. One who aided him considerably in whipping the undertaking into shape was another native of Boston, Joseph Shippen. Yet he had left and come to Philadelphia two years before Ben was born, and was actually twenty-eight years older than his compatriot.

However, these discrepancies were no drawback, and in make-up and spirit the Junto was much like coffeehouse clubs with which he had had some contact in London. Other groups meeting regularly for reasonably serious purposes were by no means unknown in the Colonies, except that this one had a little stronger flavor of Cotton Mather's benefit societies, encouraged in his *Essays to Do Good*, than generally prevailed. It proved to be the first full-scale demonstration of the especial Franklin genius for initiating co-operative endeavor.

This Junto was also known as the "Leather Apron Club," since many members were mechanics or artisans. For a time it met on Friday evenings in the Indian King Tavern on the High Street near Third. But a little later it began holding its sessions in a room in the home of Robert Grace, a well-to-do member whose house faced on Jones' Alley, just off the High Street. Its discussions centered in the fields of morals, politics, and particularly natural philosophy, the latter area of knowledge being generally known today as *physics*. The rules required that each member in turn present one or more queries on any topic in these fields "to be discussed by the company; and once in three months produce and read an essay of his own writing, on any subject he pleased. Our debates were to be under the direction of a president, and to be conducted in the sincere spirit of inquiry after truth, without fondness for dispute, or desire of victory; and, to prevent warmth, all expressions of positiveness in opinions, or direct contradiction, were after some time made contraband, and prohibited under small pecuniary penalties."

It is perhaps deserving of emphasis that this had in no sense been an attempt to develop a forum for the exercise of the Franklin voice, for he had an inherent tendency to listen, rather than to talk. But if some trace of self-seeking is demanded as justification for the expense of effort in putting the Junto together, let it be found in the fact that this was an improved facility for picking the minds of carefully selected comrades, an activity which he had discovered could be an excellent aid to a liberal education.

Keimer had in young Ben Franklin the only person in the whole area capable of engraving on copper or of rigging a press to print from copperplates. Such refinements were required to print the detailed ornamentation necessary to prevent wholesale counterfeiting of paper money. Consequently, Keimer received the job of printing New Jersey's new issue of currency. As soon as plates and press were ready, Ben took them to Burlington, then the provincial capital, and spent a most pleasant and profitable three months there "making money." The committee in charge, some member or members of which had to be present when the press was run, included some of the leading men of the colony. And the young Franklin, rather than his "master," made friends of them all, and within a short time, and for many years to come, was Jersey's official printer.

Hardly was the task completed, and a return made to Philadelphia, when a ship came in with the type and other items from London. Before disclosing this fact, both Franklin and Meredith settled up affairs and left Keimer's. Finding a house on the High Street close by the market for rent, they took it, reserved enough space for their shop, and re-rented the remainder to Thomas Godfrey, glazier, mathematician, and member of the Junto, for his residence. Also it was arranged that Mrs. Godfrey would take them to lodge and board.

Today, when a new business feels it must start off with a great fanfare, it might be interesting to read Ben's own account of the opening day of Franklin & Meredith, Printers. Says he: "We had scarce opened our letters and put our press in order, before George House, an acquaintance of mine, brought a countryman to us, whom he had met in the street inquiring for a printer. All our cash was now expended in the variety of particulars we had been obliged to procure, and this countryman's five shillings [$1.25], being our first fruits, and coming so seasonably, gave me more pleasure than any crown I have since earned; and the gratitude I felt toward House has made me often more ready than perhaps I should otherwise have been to assist young beginners." And assist them he did, in case after case.

At sometime during this busy year of 1728 in which he began in business for himself he sat down and, jocularly rather than seriously no doubt, wrote an appropriate epitaph. Almost a lifetime later it was cut in his own tombstone, and is as typically Franklin as anything he ever wrote.

*The Body*
*of*
*BENJAMIN FRANKLIN*
*Printer,*
*(Like the cover of an old book*
*Its contents torn out*
*And stript of its lettering & gilding)*
*Lies here, food for the worms.*
*Yet the work itself shall not be lost;*

*For it will (as he believ'd) appear once more,*
*In a new and more beautiful Edition,*
*Corrected and amended*
*By the Author.*

It was also in the same important year in which he was twenty-two that this young man, often condemned for having been *irreligious* "composed a little Litany, or form of prayer." This was for his own use, and he had the commendable self-restraint to desist from any attempt to foist the beliefs upon which it was built upon others. That he did not achieve it out of indifference and disbelief must be apparent from this mere fragment of it.

"That I may be preserved from atheism and infidelity impiety and profaneness, and in my address to Thee, carefully avoid irreverence and ostentation, formality and odious hypocrisy—Help me, O Father!

"That I may to those above me be dutiful, humble, and submissive; avoiding pride, disrespect, and contumacy—Help me, O Father!

"That I may to those below me be gracious, condescending, and forgiving, using clemency, protecting *innocent distress*, avoiding cruelty, harshness, and oppression, insolence, and unreasonable severity—Help me, O Father!"

Careful throughout his remaining years to keep the well-defined religious aspects of his life a strictly personal matter, he was still sufficiently motivated by them so that they shine through in his writings, particularly in his letters.

One was his fine tolerance, as broad, as deep, and as sincere as that of the Quakers among whom he lived so long. A second was the value placed upon the here and now—the known, as opposed to the unknown. From this came his insistent belief that faith was best exemplified through works, by achievements to the glory of the Creator, for the benefit of one another in this life. This did not mean that he believed death was the terminus, for he surely anticipated a life after death, or else the sentiments in his epitaph were completely spurious. He felt strongly that the Author of us all was most directly concerned with daily human affairs, that, under His Fatherhood, we are indeed obligated to be brothers one of another and in the fullest and finest meaning of that term.

Since the close of the Silence Dogood essays in 1722, Ben had written very little that was broadcast. But from now on and for the balance of his life his pen would be busy. The occasion which again began putting his ideas into type came somewhat left-handedly. George Webb, a journeyman whom he had coached at Keimer's, managed to purchase the balance of his indentured time. Now free, he applied to Franklin for work, who had to turn him down temporarily. But he counseled patience, and told him in confidence he soon intended to start a newspaper.

Webb immediately hurried back to Keimer, divulged the secret, and was promised a place on a newspaper which Keimer suddenly decided to publish, and so announced publicly in October. Then on December 24, 1728, there appeared the first edition of this paper which bore perhaps the most ambitious title ever placed on a masthead—*The Universal Instructor in All Arts and Sciences: and Pennsylvania Gazette.* The scheme was in part rather a travesty. A fair share of the sheet was given over to reprinting material pirated from the recently issued Chambers' *Cyclopaedia.* There was some news, some verse, and a few leavening touches that rendered it less tedious than Bradford's paper.

Ben stood by for several weeks, then made some deal with Bradford to provide material for the *Mercury.* Beginning in February he started a series, a sort of weekly "column," titled the "Busy-Body." Its purpose was to focus attention away from the Keimer paper, and this activity vexed that gentleman no end. The Franklin satire struck home, and generated humbling but ineffectual replies. After continuing the attack for six weeks, Ben then withdrew in favor of his close friend and Junto companion, Joseph Breintnal, who kept up the lampooning for some months.

The *Universal Instructor* appeared in all for thirty-nine issues. By then its publisher's gross want of business ability had gotten him into dire financial difficulties, as Hugh Meredith had foretold. The plant was sold to David Harry, another Franklin trainee, but the newspaper went to Franklin. Keimer beat a hasty retreat to Barbados.

For a time Harry, because of influential friends, was considered

a sufficient threat so that Ben tried to join hands with him in a
partnership. Fortunately this spendthrift loftily turned the proposition down. He soon ran through and out of the business he had
acquired, and he, too, headed for the West Indies. Franklin and
Meredith had ridden out this somewhat cyclonic episode, and
the navigating had been almost solely Franklin's.

Bobtailing its name to *The Pennsylvania Gazette*, he became
a newspaper publisher and editor, the first edition appearing on
the second day of October in 1729. For a very long time to come
he would write the bulk of the words that appeared in its columns,
whether they reported news, gave relief through humorous
touches, framed advertisements, or composed the letters *to* the
editor as well as their replies. When a deceptive yarn or incident
was needed to point up a moral, or stress a public need, Benjamin
Franklin was ever equal to the occasion. Balzac maintained that
the *canard* had also been the discovery of the very same man who
gave us the lightning rod, the hoax, and a republic. Yet malice had
no part in his fine humanitarian nature, and the *Gazette* never
became a "scandal sheet," heaping detraction and vilification on
those it opposed.

The year 1729 also included two other accomplishments
worthy of attention. He began a career as a propagandist in which
he would one day make his influence felt on two continents. His
first pamphlet, *A Modest Enquiry into the Nature and Necessity
of a Paper Currency*, while anonymous, was his initial invasion of
the political arena. It was to foster business generally and the
economic good of the many, rather than, as has been contended,
to assure him revenue from the printing of the provincial money.

Such activity was nonetheless a profitable feature of his business. His kindness to Andrew Hamilton some years before was
paying off. Along with the printing for New Jersey, he was also
doing work for Delaware, and in 1729 ran off an issue of thirty
thousand pounds for Pennsylvania. By coincidence two thousand
pounds of these funds were earmarked for preparations for a new
State House, better known today as *Independence Hall*. In January of 1730 he was appointed public printer in the Penn colony.
With well-paying public work to stabilize their partnership
affairs, and the newspaper moving along nicely, the future looked

more favorable. But it was at that very moment another crisis blew in with the fury of a tropical storm.

Meredith's father had been able to meet but one-half of the two hundred pounds due the importer for their plant equipment, and a suit to recover the balance was brought. Hugh also had in a manner defaulted on his own obligations. He not only continued incompetent as a workman, but worse still "was often seen drunk in the streets, and playing at low games in alehouses," much to the firm's discredit. The situation seemed to border on disaster.

But Ben kept his head, and, without trace of solicitation on his part, was highly gratified to have two close friends, quite independently of each other, offer to refinance the business—providing Meredith be dropped overboard. Fearing he might appear vengeful in undertaking such a matter, Ben hesitated. But fortunately Hugh realized the jig was up, and proposed an easy means of erasing himself from the picture.

Thus the partnership was terminated in July of 1730, and funds needed to take the business over were borrowed in two equal installments from Ben's friends. And this incident pretty much wrote a termination to his apprenticeship to life, for, at age twenty-four, B. Franklin, Printer, was a full-fledged journeyman in the high craft of living usefully.

## IV. "And I Took Her to Wife"

### 1730–1732

*This affair having turned my thoughts to marriage, I look'd round
me and made overtures. . . . A friendly correspondence as neighbors
and old acquaintances had continued between me and Mrs. Read's
family. . . . I piti'd poor Miss Read's unfortunate situation, who was
generally dejected, seldom chearful, and avoided company. . . . Our
mutual affection was revived, but there were now great objections
to our union. The match was indeed looked upon as invalid, a pre-
ceeding wife being said to be living in England; but this could not
easily be prov'd, because of distance; and, tho' there was a report of
his death, it was not certain. . . . We ventured, however, over all
these difficulties, and I took her to wife, September 1st, 1730.—From
the* Autobiography.

BEN FRANKLIN, better read in the Bible than some of his
biographers liked to admit, was surely familiar with the next to
the last verse in the second chapter of Genesis. Thus he was fully
cognizant that a man should leave his father and mother, and mate
permanently with the wife of his choice. Anxious always to do
the right, as it was given him to see the right, this ardent, full-
blooded young man had been brought to the same conclusion that
Paul offered the Corinthians—"It is better to marry than to burn."
Whatever waywardness there may previously have been it had
best cease forthwith. He had marriage on his mind.

Mrs. Godfrey, who with her husband and family were his
tenants, had tried to act for him as a matchmaker with a daughter
of friends of hers. But when prudent Ben specified that a sizable
dowry must accompany the prospective bride, the deal fell
through, the Godfreys became nettled over the matter, and not
too long afterward moved elsewhere.

He still berated himself because of the cavalier manner in which he had treated Debby Read. His single letter to her from London had sounded a distinct note of finality, and on the rebound she had become involved with this Rogers person, from whom she separated almost immediately, refusing to bear his name. He was said to have a wife in England, which was hard to prove. And it was now all of two years since he had slipped off to the West Indies, and, some said, died there. Ben took to dropping by occasionally, and eventually the affection between him and Deborah began to smolder, then burst into flame.

Presumably this came about early in 1730, and while the marriage seemed desirable, there were a number of complications. He might be declared a bigamist if Rogers still lived, and even if he were dead, there was a chance of being saddled with his debts. Good judgment advised taking matters slowly. But there were circumstances with which Ben soon found himself face to face that demanded greater resolution.

While there was continual wrangling with Bradford over the use of the mails to distribute the *Gazette*, this was obviously not the basis of this newer pressure. Neither was it the final split-up with Meredith, nor the fact the Godfreys had taken their goods and chattels and left him, except for the print shop, with an otherwise empty house. The stern fact that impelled him to action came from quite another direction. Early in the following year *someone* was due to bear him a child. Who was the mother? That is still one of the best interred secrets in American annals.

This much is certain, however, and is testified to in the *Autobiography*, as quoted at the head of this chapter—six weeks following the break-off of the Meredith partnership, he took Deborah Read *to wife*. The date was September 1, 1730.

There were no civil formalities or record, no church ceremony. Quite bluntly, it was a common-law arrangement, very likely deemed the best solution under the dubious circumstances. There was some pressure involved, but it was surely no spur-of-the-moment affair, and "Mr. Prudence himself" very likely had legal advice from among his friends before taking this step. It is doubtful if any eyebrows were raised, and it was many years, and under

political stimulus, before this subject was hauled out for an airing.
But above all this one fact stands out stark and incontestable, this
marriage was satisfying and lasting.

Was the male child born early in the following year hers?
Since she bore two other children, it is biologically possible. In
private correspondence she was spoken of as this first child's
*mother*, and her mother in turn as the *grandmother*. There are
other shreds of evidence that seems to indicate her being the ma-
ternal parent.

However, as this child grew older, her attitude toward him was
not exactly what is customarily encompassed in mother love. Yet
on his part there was continuing deference and filial regard up to
the day of her burial. If this was not real, it was marvelous make-
believe. In after years Ben's political enemies would insist that the
mother was really a girl named Barbara who was later drawn into
the family as a sort of servant, and, about thirty years after this
mysterious event, hidden away in an unmarked grave.

This much is certain, none of the three principals, father,
mother, or offspring, ever went on record publicly in the matter
so far as is known. And neither the scandalmongers nor the
serious students of intervening generations have produced any
conclusive evidence.

The honeymoon cottage, such as it was, was available, and
into it that fall Franklin moved two widows. At least the widow-
hood of Mother Read was certain. That of daughter Debby, now
*Mrs*. Benjamin Franklin, had not been verified. But from then on
it made no difference.

The older woman seems to have been a resolute soul, who had
added to her income, at least since the husband's passing, by the
concoction of certain nostrums which had found some volume of
sales. She would continue their production at this new location
two blocks down the High Street, and dispose of them in the
store her son-in-law would shortly set up. The latter seems to
have always looked upon his wife's mother with dutiful affection.

But his affection for his wife was completely spontaneous. It
slowly settled down into mutual respect, deep understanding, and
full co-operation, and was a continuing affair years later when for
long periods an ocean divided them. She was no "bluestocking,"

had had little if any formal schooling, and was thus rather irresponsive to the broad intellectual phases so well developed in her husband. Handsome in a vigorous, robust sort of manner, she lacked the graces and subtleties which would have made her acceptable in the social world in which he moved in England and France. But she was a perfect match for him where prudence, persistence, and practicality were concerned. Out of their reciprocal admiration came a common purpose. They "mutually endeavored to make each other happy," and succeeded surprisingly well.

With his domestic affairs now so pleasantly ordered, Ben was able to give closer attention to other matters. A compositor, a friend of his London days, suddenly appeared, very likely on the annual ship in the fall of 1730, and was put to work in Meredith's place. This Thomas Whitemarsh was soon to have a part in a new endeavor in the Franklin scheme of things.

Except in Boston, there was not a real bookstore anywhere in the Colonies. The consequence was that books must be ordered from England, and were thus rather limited possessions even among those given to bookish pursuits. "The members of the Junto had each a few." It was Franklin's thought that if these volumes of his friends were gathered in one place, and arrangements made for their common use, all might profit the more. His enthusiasm was for a time infectious, and a library was set up in their meeting room in the Grace home on "Pewter Platter" Alley as the tiny street was often called. There they were usable during the Friday night sessions, or they might be borrowed for reading at home, and for a time this plan was satisfactory.

Philadelphia was growing far faster than the Colonies as a whole, and Franklin was now prepared to grow with it. Andrew Bradford's work he had always thought to be slovenly, and the *Mercury* apathetic. Even Keimer had been able to barge into the field, and in far less than a year's time increase his advertising until it occupied about one third the space given to editorial matter. Ben was not long in making the space sold equal in volume to that used editorially—and it was the advertising revenue even in those times that sweetened and sustained the profits.

Many printers today would consider the work passing through

the plant in those earlier times as so much trivia. It was principally *job work*, and ran strongly to sermons, tracts, pamphlets, much of it religious material. But such was the bread and butter of other printers in all the colonies, for it was an age when religious sentiment was being given a thorough airing. Also, Ben Franklin was not the man to deny an honest penny its right to be spent. On a little more ambitious scale, yet still religious, was the first hymnal of the Seventh-Day German Baptists—their *Göttliche Liebes und Lobes gethöne*—which he printed and bound in 1730.

Life was a bit snugger and more gratifying with a home of his own, and a bit more profitable with a business of his own. The two combined at about this time to foster an incident which he delighted in recounting years later with straight-faced raillery. Said he:

"My breakfast was a long time bread and milk (no tea), and I ate it out of a twopenny earthen porringer, with a pewter spoon. But mark how luxury will enter families, and make a progress, in spite of principle: being called one morning to breakfast, I found it in a china bowl, with a spoon of silver! They had been bought for me without my knowledge by my wife, and had cost her the enormous sum of three-and-twenty shillings [ca. $5.75], for which she had no other excuse or apology to make, but that she thought *her* husband deserved a silver spoon and china bowl as well as any of his neighbors."

Debby's opinion that her "Pappy," as she familiarly called her husband, was as good as his neighbors, was justified. Also her recent action was perhaps significant, for Ben Franklin was adding to his stature, and the year 1731 would embrace several highly important occurrences. Chief among them was easily the birth of a son. The date is indefinite, since there is no other record than the father's chance remark in 1750 that son William was then nineteen. The mother, too, as has been explained, continued to be something of an unknown quantity. But the child was excessively real, a great joy to his father, at least until years later when the younger Franklin chose the wrong side in the Revolution and the break between the two was never happily resolved.

It was early in this year that Ben joined the Masonic Lodge.

It had recently been imported from Europe, and he would play a prominent part in its affairs both here and in France. Also he would dispatch Thomas Whitemarsh south to Charleston, there to establish a print shop which, so it was arranged, would be his in a matter of a few years by purchase out of profits. While this fine sense of generosity would be imposed upon—but chiefly by relatives—he would in this way give printing facilities to a number of localities, and admirable opportunities to a number of deserving young craftsmen.

Some dissatisfaction having developed over the conduct of the book-lending scheme of the Junto, the members took their books home, and Franklin was faced with a challenge. Still certain that a properly organized and operated *lending* library would provide widespread benefit, he set on foot his "first project of a public nature." Working through the Junto, fifty subscribers were signed up who would purchase shares at forty shillings each (ca. $10), and pay annual dues of one quarter that amount. A list of books was drawn up by the provincial secretary, James Logan, and sent to London. By an Instrument of Association dated July 1, 1731, the Library Company of Philadelphia came into being, and served as parent of the host of subscription libraries that followed up and down the coast.

It was not too many years before non-subscribers were granted loan privileges, with rental charges of four, six, or eight pence per week, dependent upon the *size* of the volume. The venture throve, and thirty years later its shares were worth nearly ten times their original value. From this library its instigator benefitted in several ways. He had access to more and more books. His efforts were appreciated, and he moved up in general estimation. And he had served another apprenticeship, this one to subscription raising and the organization of public enterprise. His efforts in this respect would often be put to work in the days ahead.

Perhaps the year's most ambitious undertaking was the "bold and arduous project of arriving at moral perfection." This was no idle wish, no vapid hope, or mere good intention, but the determination to achieve a means of keeping a running inventory of his morality and his moral achievements. First he very carefully chose twelve essential virtues, and later, on the advice of an acquaintance, added the thirteenth. They were, together with his suggestions for their employment, as follows:

"TEMPERANCE: Eat not to dullness; drink not to elevation. SILENCE: Speak not but what may benefit others or yourself; avoid trifling conversation. ORDER: Let all your things have their places; let each part of your business have its time. RESOLUTION: Resolve to perform what you ought; perform without fail what you resolve. FRUGALITY: Make no excuse but to do good to others or yourself; i.e., waste nothing. INDUSTRY: Lose no time; be always employ'd in something useful; cut off all unnecessary actions. SINCERITY: Use no hurtful deceit; think innocently and justly, and, if you speak, speak accordingly. JUSTICE: Wrong none by doing injuries, or omitting the benefits that are your duty. MODERATION: Avoid extreams; forbear resenting injuries so much as you think they deserve. CLEANLINESS: Tolerate no uncleanliness in body, cloaths, or habitation. TRANQUILLITY: Be not disturbed at trifles, or at accidents common or avoidable. CHASTITY: Rarely use venery but for health or offspring, never to dulness, weakness, or the injury of your own or another's peace or reputation. HUMILITY: Imitate Jesus and Socrates."

In his scheme of operation each virtue in turn was to be on trial for an entire week. In a little book of ruled pages he kept score. Every offense against the virtue was chalked up. The intention was by concentrating upon it to make a *habit* of that virtue. Ultimately the system's author was forced to admit, "I soon found I had undertaken a task more difficult than I had imagined."

*Humility* apparently came easiest, while *Order* continued to be a concern. He was "fuller of faults" than he had thought, and carried on this idea of regularly checking on his tendencies for many years. While he does not wax enthusiastic himself over the results, perhaps restrained by modesty and humility, it must be admitted that much benefit may well have accrued from such practices.

The year 1732, in which another great American, George Washington, first saw the light, started off quite auspiciously for the twenty-six-year-old Ben Franklin. On January 8 Whitemarsh began the publication of the *South Carolina Gazette*, direct descendant of the Philadelphia paper of the same name. The partner in the South was just about to acquire the public printing in the colony, and the situation there was encouraging.

So it was in Philadelphia. Yet one might have had to grasp the fact from a not too prominent indication allowed to come to the attention of the public, which may have missed its full significance. The *Gazette* for May 11 dropped the Meredith name from the masthead, where *B. Franklin* stood alone as its publisher. Had he at last discharged his debts, even the one to Mr. Vernon which for eight years had been giving him bad twinges of conscience? It is to be hoped so, and from then on he appeared to be in full ownership and possession.

In this very same month he launched a German-American paper, the *Philadelphische Zeitung;* but, lest it come to look as though he had acquired the Midas touch, this undertaking was short-lived.

He was being very busy in a secretive sort of way about some other matter, giving it more and more of his time as the year wore on. He was honored by an office in the local Masonic Lodge; and he was most signally honored in October when his wife, without the least trace of uncertainty in this instance, presented him with a son, Francis Folger Franklin. Immediately little Frankie was "the apple of his eye."

Even this happy event did not, however, explain the partially undercover activities, and the month of December was wearing away before light was shed on the matter. In the *Gazette* of the nineteenth was an announcement—an *Almanack*, called *Poor Richard's,* and compiled by Richard Saunders, Philomath, would be printed and sold by B. FRANKLIN, at the New Printing Office near the Market.

Ben Franklin by this move was now distinctly on his way to fame.

# v. Franklin's Expanding Interests

## *1733-1737*

*I might in this place attempt to gain thy Favor, by declaring that I write Almanacks with no other view than that of the publick Good; but in this I should not be sincere, and Men are nowadays too wise to be deceived by Pretences how specious soever. The plain Truth of the Matter is, I am excessive poor, and my wife, good Woman, is, I tell her, excessive proud; she cannot bear, she says, to sit spinning in her Shift of Tow, while I do nothing but gaze at the Stars; and has threatened more than once to burn all my Books and Rattling-Traps (as she calls my Instruments) if I do not make some profitable Use of them for the Good of my Family. The Printer has offer'd me some considerable share of his Profits, and I have thus begun to comply with my Dame's Desire.—From the Preface to* Poor Richard, *1733.*

WHILE Franklin insists that "we kept no idle servants, our table was plain and simple, our furniture of the cheapest," his life with Debby was probably no more Spartan than that of many of his contemporaries. The husband had developed a reputation for working long hours, and the wife worked right along with him. Her mother perhaps saw to the affairs of the home, for Ben reported that Deborah "assisted me cheerfully in my business, folding and stitching pamphlets, tending shop, purchasing old linen rags for the papermakers, &c., &c." The shop she tended was in reality a store, which, since the chief business was printing, could well have been limited to stationery, and perhaps books. But its offerings, as advertised in the *Gazette*, will quickly set any such misconceptions straight. They included:

"Very good sack at 6s per gallon, glaz'd fulling papers and bonnet-papers, very good lamp-black, very good chocolate, linseed oil, very good coffee, compasses and scales, Seneca rattlesnake root, with directions how to use it in the Pleurisy, &c., dividers and protractors, a very good second hand two-wheel chaise, a very neat, new fashioned vehicle, or four wheel'd chaise, very convenient to carry weak or other sick persons, old or young, good Rhode Island cheese and codfish, quadrants, fore-staffs, nocturnals, mariner's compasses, season'd merchantable boards, coarse and fine edgings, fine broad scarlet cloth, fine broad black cloth, fine white thread hose and English sale duck, very good iron stoves, a large horse fit for a chair or saddle, the true and genuine Godfrey's cordial, choice bohea tea, very good English saffron, New York lottery tickets, choice mackerel, to be sold by the barrel, a large copper still, very good spermacety, fine palm oyl, very good Temple spectacles and a new fishing net."

The term *general* store hardly seems adequate, and it all sounds very confusing. It would have been, too, had these goods all been mustered in one spot. But those were the days when money, either coined or paper, was scarce, and barter the common means of exchange. Subscriptions, advertising billings, and charges for larger printing jobs were very likely often settled in kind.

Also, it was before the days of keying advertisements, and "enquire of printer" did not necessarily mean that he was always in personal possession of the item advertised. Ben was surely not above taking a commission for arranging and completing a sale. He was a straight merchant in relation to some items, and more probably a commission merchant in others. In any event, his middle name could well have been *Trader*.

There was also a sterner sort of traffic in the business affairs transacted in the store on the High Street, although it was an accepted practice of the times, and others in every good-sized town up and down the coast engaged in such activities. Franklin sold slaves, and also the unexpired time of indentured servants. At least there were many ads in the *Gazette*, beginning: "To be sold," and then offering "a servant woman, having three and a half years more to serve," or "likely negro woman, with man-child," or, "prime able young negro man, fit for laborious work, in town or country." Such ads usually terminated with the suggestion "enquire of the printer hereof."

It could have been a newspaper service of passing along inquiries to advertisers who preferred not to disclose their identities. It could also have been a commission arrangement. And it might have been—and actually was—slave trading. There may perhaps have been a scar on his conscience some years later when he informed his mother in a letter, "We do not like Negro servants." In his closing years Franklin took a firm stand against slavery, even to heading up an abolition society, yet some portion of his wealth came from this trading in human misery.

Although its first announcement had appeared rather late the previous year, the *Almanack* sold well, requiring three printings in all. This brought in added funds and provided capital for expansion. Also it left a little surplus for a trip to Boston, where he had not been since before starting for England nine years previously. He had probably returned from there before he had word of Whitemarsh's untimely death of yellow fever in September. Whereupon Louis Timothée, a French Protestant and "language master" who had edited the short-lived *Zeitung*, was dispatched to take over in Charleston.

Ben began a serious study of languages in 1733, and eventually acquired a passable reading knowledge of Spanish, Italian, German, and French, while he also wrote and spoke the latter, although somewhat imperfectly, even after nine years residence in France.

Moral affairs, and especially man's inhumanity to other men, were very much in the forefront of his mind as he swung into the following year. During it he established a firm hold on the public printing in both Jersey and Delaware, and began to try his hand at more book publishing, issuing a home medical text, and also the first Masonic book produced in America. He was elevated to Grand Master of this order before the year was out.

Also he had printed his second edition of *Poor Richard*, and with this character had struck a gold mine. While this unique character may not have been the exact likeness of its creator, it was still a substantial slice of the Franklin of that time. And if with it he courted and played up to the "prim people"—he preferred to speak of them as *middling*—it was because he realized they were the backbone of the land, and they thus made sense to the Philadelphia printer.

Not only was it his intention to make the *Almanack* "entertaining and useful," but he also felt the *Gazette* should be a medium of instruction as well as of news. Consequently he "frequently reprinted in it extracts from the *Spectator,* and other moral writers; and sometimes publish'd little pieces of my own, which had been first compos'd for reading in our Junto."

Also along these same lines was a letter, obviously written by the publisher, which appeared in the issue of February 4, 1735. It purported to be from an old man, and gave advice on the prevention and control of fires. Five years before, the city had been threatened with extinction by a blaze that started on Fishbourne's wharf, and was soon, because of the lack of organized forces to combat it, well out of hand. This fearful threat may have for a while promoted caution. But the time had come again when Ben felt further warnings were in order. Then, after this advance publicity had sunk in, he proposed to take positive steps to combat a possible conflagration.

He looked upon his newspaper as a public service, and thus something of a public trust, which should thus be kept free of "libelling and personal abuse." He even refused to sell paid space to be used for vilification and disparagement. There were occasions when he might have felt constrained to be a trifle harsh, yet he resisted them. Such was the case in connection with a religious incident that broke at about that time. A young Irishman, a Presbyterian minister named Hemphill, had started a program of remarkable preaching locally, and soon had the members of his own faith aroused. Since he stressed *good works,* Franklin not only approved of him, but began to champion him through the columns of the *Gazette.*

Unhappily it turned out at the height of the battle that the man was a plagiarist, delivering sermons of others, which, at a single reading, he had committed to memory. When it looked as though it might be a lost cause, Ben determinedly recorded as his parting shot in the affray that he very much "approved

of his giving us good sermons compos'd by others, than bad
ones of his own manufacture." The young publisher then quitted
the congregation where he had been fairly regular in attendance,
and where the preaching had occurred, although he continued
his subscription to the support of its ministers for many years.
His churchgoing days were pretty much over. Sunday more than
ever became his time for self-improvement—both mental and
moral.

A pleasant and profitable venture in this same year of 1735 was
his publishing of James Logan's rendering of *Cato's Moral Distichs*.
He was no doubt the leading scholar in the Colonies. At first this
very able Quaker and provincial secretary had misjudged the
earnest young printer with the inquisitive mind, considering him
and his companions in the newly formed Junto as tools of Sir
William Keith, and thus potential troublemakers. He had soon
revised his estimate, drew up the list of titles for the Junto's first
purchase of books, and came to value highly Franklin's real merits
and sincerity. Franklin in turn, as an old man, and long after
Logan's death, recalled vividly his visits to the scholar's lovely
country home, and the books shown him there, many of which
he no doubt borrowed.

His business seemed to be booming as he moved into 1736. At
least he made a purchase which would have been considered an
uncommon extravagance for a "middling" tradesman in those
days—he had a portrait in oils made of his little Franky. Of
course it could have been done to discharge a debt for advertising
or other service, but there was little question about it, the man
was prospering.

Music became a hobby, or perhaps another facet of his expanding interests. Earlier in our own century, the music indus-
tries were, among several other fields of endeavor, claiming him
as *their* patron saint; and he did ultimately play commendably
on at least four instruments, one of which, the armonica, he perfected.

Then suddenly a new and quite different phase of his life took
shape and began to develop. When the Provincial Assembly came
into session in October of 1736, B. Franklin, the printer, who for
several years had been busily making friends and influencing

people, found himself named *clerk* of this legislative body. He had indeed arrived! Politics then was for the gentry.

The thirty-year-old man, still "Ben" to his ever-increasing circle of friends, was naturally elated. But there were, unhappily, clouds on the horizon, and they rolled in in great depth within a month, for in mid-November little Franky, his especial pride and joy, contracted smallpox. On the twenty-first, the four-year-old child died, and the father was beside himself with grief. Once again his conscience seems to have stabbed him. A little more than fifteen years before, the first issue of his brother's *Courant* had ribbed Cotton Mather and his defense and advocacy of the newfangled idea of inoculation as protection against this dread disease. Mather then had been one of a tiny, but resolute, minority. And Ben, little more than a child really, had been amused as James and his friends heaped ridicule in keeping with the popular clamor upon the great preacher.

In the years since, a more mature Franklin had been thoroughly converted to this slowly growing medical practice. Yet his small son, on whom he set such store, had not been given this protection. Worse still, the gossips were very busily circulating the claim that Franky had died as the result of *being* inoculated. It was two weeks before he could do so publicly, but in the issue of the *Gazette* of December 6 he said in part, "I do sincerely declare that he was *not* inoculated but received the distemper in the common way of infection; and I suppose the report could only arise from my known opinion that inoculation was a safe and beneficial practice, from my having said among my acquaintance that I intended to have the child inoculated as soon as he should have recovered sufficient strength from a flux with which he had long been afflicted." Not only your outright sins, but those of omission, too, were likely to return at their pleasure and haunt you.

The memory of this child was engraved deeply on his heart, and long afterwards, when a man in his mid-sixties, he would indicate in a letter to his sister Jane that in recollection little Franky was still very much the "apple of his eye."

The immediate sting of this loss was perhaps softened somewhat by his heavy involvement in another public matter. The letter on *Protection of Towns from Fire*, which he had published under an assumed name the previous year had, he was happy to admit modestly, been "spoken of as a useful piece." But its author had had no intention of stopping there, and was determined to do something tangible about fire prevention and fire fighting. So he, and several of his associates, began to talk the matter up, proposing a scheme which has always been credited primarily to Franklin. Finally, on December 7, his group formed the Union Fire Company, a volunteer organization, and the first of many such to be formed in the next few years in Philadelphia.

For equipment, each of the thirty members to which the company was limited provided himself with six leather buckets, a hook, and four heavy linen bags, or baskets, these latter for packing and transporting goods. This gear he was required to carry to every fire. All members stood to be assessed a fine of two shillings (about fifty cents) for failing to show up at a fire or provide a suitable excuse, and a levy of twice that amount for not maintaining equipment in prime condition.

The company met once a month so they might spend "a social evening together, in discoursing and communicating such ideas as occurred to us upon the subject of fires, as might be useful in our conduct on such occasions." Upwards of fifty years later its originator described the results achieved by this most admirable enterprise, saying quite proudly, "The small fines that have been paid by members for absence to the monthly meetings have been applied to the purchase of fire-engines, ladders, fire-hooks, and other useful implements for each company, so that I question whether there is a city in the world better provided with the means of putting a stop to beginning conflagrations." Here was the nucleus of our modern fire fighting, and Benjamin Franklin, "patron saint" of other lines of human endeavor, is surely entitled to ride to fires in spirit on each and every piece of today's wonderful mechanized equipment, in which he would find unabashed pleasure and lively interest.

Along with his personal conscience he was also developing a civic consciousness, and expanding the means by which he might "live usefully."

His competitor Bradford, who had tried to debar the *Gazette* from the mails, was indeed lax. For several years he had failed to make up and turn in the post-office accounts, and Colonel Alexander Spotswood of Virginia, the deputy postmaster general dropped him, and made Franklin Philadelphia postmaster in his stead. This was no sinecure, and Ben lent it his best efforts. In addition, he agreed, in strong distinction to the selfish tendencies of his predecessor, to permit the competing *Mercury* to be carried by the post riders. But in this he was overruled by Spotswood until Bradford had rendered an accounting.

Having proved himself trustworthy and judicious, Ben was appointed a justice of the peace. But after hearing a case or two, he terminated this activity, feeling too greatly his lack of legal training. While he had a most admirable diplomatic mind, there would be a number of occasions in which he gave ample evidence that he was surely no lawyer.

It was at about this time that he was pursuing the study of architecture, some knowledge of which was one of the accomplishments of an eighteenth-century gentleman. The fact was pointed up by an advertisement in his paper, which reported, "Lent sometime since a book entitled Campell's *Vitruvius Brittanicus*, the person who has it is desired to return it to the Printer hereof." This four-guinea (twenty-one-dollar) volume evidently was wanted back for consultation. Many similar ads would seem to indicate that his loaning of volumes was done rather loosely, and that his memory for borrowers was highly defective. One wonders though if perhaps the lendee was well-recalled, and these ads were little tests in connection with the good intentions of others.

Now moving into his thirties, he was seriously involved in building up a competence in a sobersided community still dourly engrossed in achieving its destiny. But Ben, despite the fact that he had known some somber hours and suffered some hard knocks, had learned how much less tension is involved when life is approached in lighter vein, and humanity and its frailties are looked upon with tolerant good humor. This buoyant approach was to carry him far, and another ad in the *Gazette* gave a taste of its application:

*"Taken out of a pew in the Church, some months since, a*
*Common Prayer Book, bound in red, gilt, and lettered D. F.*
*[Deborah Franklin], on each cover. The person who took it is*
*desired to open it, and read the Eighth Commandment, and*
*afterwards return it into the same pew again; upon which no*
*further notice will be taken."*

In September that year, Thomas Penn reversed his father's effective Indian policy, and by the infamous "Walking Purchase"
so defrauded the native peoples in Pennsylvania that their invaluable friendship of more than fifty years was lost. Twenty-seven
years later Franklin would be called upon to patch up a peace in
a civil war among the white colonists which stemmed in part
from this hoax and swindle.

At about that same time the *Gazette* published an account of a
dinner given by Mayor William Allen, wealthy merchant-lawyer,
a brilliant contemporary, and, for a time, a patron of Franklin's.
It was held on September 30 to celebrate the completion of the
State House, which not until more than a century later came to
be known as "Independence Hall." It was claimed to be the "most
grand and most elegant entertainment that has been made in these
parts of America," and although the modest Franklin did not
admit it, he very probably was, as clerk of the Assembly, in attendance. When that body came into session again about two
weeks later on October 15, he was re-elected to this post, which
he held continuously until 1751, thereby making certain of retain-
ing the remunerative provincial printing, and of keeping in the
eyes of the more important men of the colony.

What a long way he had come since that day fifteen years before when he had surreptitiously gone aboard a sloop sailing from
Boston in the fall of 1723, headed he knew not where!

# VI. Developing a Civic Consciousness

## 1738–1742

*I began now to turn my thoughts a little to public affairs, begin-
ning, however, with small matters. The city watch was one of the
first things that I conceiv'd to want regulation. . . . About this time I
wrote a paper (first to be read in Junto, but it was afterward publish'd) on the different accidents and carelessnesses by which houses
were set on fire, with cautions against them, and means proposed of
avoiding them. This was much spoken of as a useful piece, and gave
rise to a project, which soon followed it, of forming a company for
the more ready extinguishing of fires. . . . After some time I drew a
bill for paving the city, and brought it into the Assembly.—From the
Autobiography.*

PHILADELPHIA, youngest of the larger towns on the continent, was rapidly growing up, and sloughing off some of its early
stiffness and hidebound ways. While the Quakers remained very
much in the ascendency, cosmopolitan influences were moving in,
as witnessed in 1738 by *Master* Hackett's announcements that he
was about to open a dancing academy. Not only was he prepared
to instruct in the popular steps danced in London, Dublin, and
Paris, but, to assuage the outraged feelings of the extremely pious
toward such seeming worldliness, he also promised to "give
young ladies, gentlemen and children the most graceful carriage
. . . and genteel behaviour in company." For years those seeking
to inject a little leaven into the doughiness of local life always
disguised their offering, and tried as best they could to make it
appear educational.

While Franklin, so far as is known, was never an enthusiastic
dancer, he could hoist a pot of ale or a liberal portion of Madeira,
and sound off on a spirited or rollicking song. It could have been

74 BEN FRANKLIN

that very spring that he and a group of friends sat one evening in a tavern, where the conversation worked its way around to poetry. Being customarily a better listener than most, he may have heard the others out, and then in mock solemnity bade them recall that they were middle-aged married men, and should lay aside their simulated "poet's mistresses," from which they supposedly received their inspiration, and get down to earth, and so give their efforts a better sense of reality. No doubt he took a heavy round of ribbing in return, and one of the company seems to have suggested that he compose a sample for their edification. At least there was handed to John Bard as he sat at breakfast the following morning a rather lengthy opus which began:

> Of their Chloes and Phyllises poets may prate,
> I sing of my plain country Joan,
> These twelve years my wife, still the joy of my life;
> Blest day that I made her my own.

It was an encomium of many verses to his "Debby," whom he had indeed taken to wife some years before, and the recipient was instructed to be prepared to render it feelingly at their next get-together. Ben had dashed it off before turning in the night before, and while hurried, it was rather typical, for poetry, even in his serious moments, was most certainly *not* one of his fortes.

But good humor and the lighter touch most certainly were, and he found them the ideal means of saving face, both his own, and that of an opponent who might need to be taken down a peg or two. A pleasant application of his deftness appeared in that year's *Almanack.* Like his competitors, he, too, included long-range forecasts of the weather. Yet he had no desire to pose as an alchemist or astrologer, preferring that Poor Richard's friends and followers realize these were mere guesses, and that any who offered such prognostications as dependable were crackpots and impostors.

So, he introduced "Mystriss Saunders," who had been reviewing the work of her husband, "poor Dick," and reported that, "Upon looking over the months I see he has put in abundance of foul weather this year, and therefore I have scattered here and there where I could find room some fair, pleasant, sunshiny weather, for the good women to dry their clothes in. If it does not come to pass according to my desire, I have shown my good will, however, and I hope they will take it in good part."

Some in Philadelphia tripped "the light fantastic" on their toes. Franklin had a way of making his words dance a merry reel, and of portraying a truth without hurting anyone's feelings.

A dedicated "do-gooder," he found a way in which the *Gazette* could extend its helpfulness to its readers, and also improve the postal services. Letters were then delivered only to offices on the main post roads, and there held until called for. Lists of such letters, which he now began to publish, made it possible for those in outlying areas to know of mail intended for them, and to arrange through friends and neighbors making the journey into Philadelphia to have it picked up.

Early in 1738 he was called upon to explain somewhat his unorthodox stand in religious matters. The situation came about in this way. In the previous year a burlesquing of the rituals of Masonry had resulted in the death of a gullible apprentice boy. This unfortunate incident in the Quaker City, in which there was a libelous attempt to implicate Franklin, was transmitted up and down the coast, bringing upon both him and the order undeserved censure. This news had badly disturbed his mother and father, who had written him an anxious letter opening up the whole subject of his beliefs.

In his reply he said in part, "I imagine a man must have a good deal of vanity who believes, and a good deal of boldness who affirms, that all the doctrines he holds are *true*, and all he rejects are *false*. And perhaps the same may be justly said of every sect, church, and society of men, when they assume to themselves that infallibility which they deny to the Pope and councils. . . . I think vital religion has always suffered when orthodoxy is more regarded than virtue; and the Scriptures assure me that at the last day we shall not be examined what we *thought* but what we *did*."

What seemed to bother Franklin, standing at the threshold of middle age, was not that he would miss finding religion, but that he had been quite unable to find the sort of spiritual expression in the churches of his time which satisfied his needs. Even the "Great Awakening," proclaimed a year or two before by Jona-

than Edwards, and which another mighty preacher would bring
to Philadelphia a little more than a year hence, would not alter
the situation. His attitude was not unlike that of another great
American of the following century, Abraham Lincoln, who was
not allied with any church, yet is not by any stretch of the imagi-
nation to be considered an irreligious man.

But in addition to spiritual dangers there were further physical
perils to be cared for. Something now having been done about the
hazard of fire, the next deserving consideration was the increasing depredations of night prowlers, burglars, highwaymen, and
the lawless generally. There was then no formal police organization, but a constable for each city ward, whose duties included
procuring assistance of the various householders in turn in his
bailiwick during the hours of darkness. Those who found such
duties burdensome could arrange to have substitutes serve for
them by paying six shillings ($1.50) a year.

The result had been the hiring of hoodlums and riffraff and the
enriching of the constables, with the complete decay of the
protection intended by this *city watch*. Franklin, working before
his sounding board, the Junto, proposed a "more effectual watch,
the hiring of proper men to serve constantly in the business; and
a more equitable way of supporting the charge, the levying a
tax that should be proportioned to the property."

What happened? "This idea, being approv'd by the Junto, was
communicated to the other clubs, but as [if] arising in each of
them; and though the plan was not immediately put into execution, yet, by preparing the minds of the people for the change,
it paved the way for the law obtained a few years after, when the
members of our clubs were grown into more influence." Such
was the genesis of a paid police system in Philadelphia, and Ben
Franklin was its advocate and herald.

One of the finest local exponents of practicality and learning
was John Bartram, the great Quaker naturalist, and a close friend
of Ben's. Thirsting for other kindred souls whom to exchange
observations and thus increase knowledge, he proposed early in
1739 the formation of an "association" which might act as a
clearing house of scientific information. Some of his friends
dissuaded him, contending the colonies had not matured suffi-

ciently. Yet the idea appeared sound to others, but needed more persuasive talents than the gentle Bartram possessed, such as those of his friend who had put together the Junto and the Library Company.

This latter enterprise was thriving, and had outgrown its first quarters, and found new space on the upper floor of the west wing of the State House. No doubt Franklin had a part in liberalizing its policies, so that from now on "any civil gentleman" was permitted to use the volumes on the premises, although subscribers only, plus the library's patron and mentor, James Logan, might remove them to their homes.

Hugh Meredith put in an appearance again, having failed in his land venture in North Carolina, and would now depend upon his former partner's bounty for several years. But the printing business he had left was still expanding, and new quarters for it were also in demand. So Ben rented another house, four doors to the east on the High Street, which John Wister the wine merchant leased to him for thirty-eight pounds ($185) a year.

By late fall of 1739 the city was all aflutter over the advent of the Rev. George Whitefield, famous Methodist missionary, who, tradition affirmed, had driven a dozen men crazy with the stirring sermon he had preached some years previously at his ordination. The man was truly a spellbinder, and so effective that the city's churches were shortly denying him use of their pulpits. He fascinated Franklin, at least his oratorical delivery did, if not his theological offerings, and soon printer and preacher were fast friends. Not only did the former print and distribute the latter's sermons, but he also lent his aid as a member of a group that purchased a piece of land and erected a tabernacle in which Whitefield was privileged to hold forth without let or hindrance. This was hardly the gesture of an infidel or agnostic, and neither this particular divine, nor a considerable number of other gentlemen of the cloth, would have valued the Franklin friendship—as they did—were he a blasphemer or an unreflecting renegade.

By his own admission he was a *deist*, and had been since that day as a child when a volume calculated to expunge deism from his mind had come into his hands. Singularly enough, the discerning youngster found its deistic arguments far more potent than the reasons given for their abandonment, and he was an immediate convert, and remained one despite liberal doses of dogma from without and much soul searching from within. This belief was accepted by a considerable share of the "founding fathers." While it was the very essence of godlessness, or even worse, to the orthodox, it now appears to have been little more than a "show me" attitude assumed by many of the ablest minds of that time, who found it highly unappetizing to sit at the tables of the past with their indigestible theological fare.

Whether or not he was truly a professing Christian is also subject to doubt, but if good works are in any sense a measure, he was surely a practicing one. He had a strong sense of responsibility, and was quick to recognize and cheerfully ready to fulfill his obligations. A current example at that moment could have been found in his response to the promises made some years previous to his ailing brother James that his son "Jemmy" should have an education and be taught a trade. The boy, now fifteen, had been brought down to Philadelphia, put to school, then served his apprenticeship, and finally was set up in business in his native Newport.

However, some who had dealings with Franklin were not as dependable. A dozen years before George Webb had disclosed the plans for a newspaper to Keimer, and kept Ben from that field for nearly two years. Now, in 1740, there was another almost identical incident. Even the names of the culprits were virtually the same, for the second was an attorney named John Webbe. He had been hired to edit a proposed magazine, spilled the plans to the Bradfords, who hurriedly prepared to publish one of their own. That winter of 1740–41 was notoriously bitter, in regard to both the weather, and the tumult and shouting between the two printing houses, each bent on having a magazine out soon after the new year.

And both did, yet neither survived. Bradford's *American Magazine* expired after three monthly appearances, while the Franklin offering, *The General Magazine and Historical Chronicle for All the British Plantations in America*, stuck it out through six. And at the risk of playing down what to Ben were great hopes and aspirations, let it be said that today, in an age of gaudy and out-sized periodicals, this effort would be classed as pretty much a mere pamphlet. It was even less than pocket-size. While there were sixty pages, they trimmed to a shade under three by six inches, which was anything but imposing. Nonetheless, the enterprise achieved one "first." It contained a six-line ad for a Potomac River ferry, the beginning of magazine advertising which, in these latter days, has swelled to huge proportions.

But the remainder of his publishing business was doing very well. Philadelphia with its thirteen thousand population was something of a metropolitan center, and was now supporting no less than eight printing offices. The printed word was indeed in demand, and 1741 saw the issuance of no less than three best-sellers, an achievement for a single year in Colonial America. In this fifth decade of the eighteenth century it took a sale of ten thousand copies within ten years to gain this designation, and the Rev. Horace Watt's *Horae Lyricae*, a book of not-too-dull juvenile poetry and hymnody, issued by Franklin, was one of the three.

It has been maintained that he was "instrumental in establishing eighteen paper mills in the American Colonies," yet such endeavors have not been too carefully documented. How much financial interest he had in any of them is doubtful. He did collect raw material for some of them, having handled about eighteen tons of linen rags during the six-year period then closing. There was a two-way advantage here—a profit on the rags, and very likely some priority in obtaining his full share of finished paper. And this latter may have had its benefits, since his own and his partner's plants formed collectively the largest paper-consuming group on this side of the ocean. In 1741 another branch was opened up when he launched James Parker in New York.

Because of his medical interest someone has claimed that Franklin was a frustrated doctor, needing only formal training to have been a peerless physician. Had he followed even a minimum of his varied interests through to final conclusion, he would have been the paragon of the ages, and required at least a half-dozen lifetimes for the accomplishment. His enthusiasm for things medical and those having to do with the promotion of health was both considerable and very sincere. He produced what was probably the first American medical treatise in 1741 for Cadwallader Colden, and it may have inspired him to a few endeavors of his own. At least, when *Poor Richard's* for 1742 appeared, it contained *Rules for Health and Long Life*. Without recourse to caloric values of different foods or other more recent refinements in medical knowledge, these precepts still seem capable of promoting comfort, well-being, and longevity.

There was a trace, too, of this same interest hidden away in an appeal for a public subscription featured in the *Gazette* for March 10–17. It solicited aid for the botanical activities of John Bartram. Ben not only loved the man for himself, and enthused in his botanical interests, but these latter tended to uncover new drugs and medicines and to expand the knowledge needed to improve agriculture.

Just at the moment he was highly enthused over the results of other studies and experiments conducted the past winter. He had long been disgusted with the inefficiency of conventional fireplaces, and also with certain shortcomings in the "airtight" stoves being brought in by the German immigrants. So he had perfected what he chose to call the "Pennsylvania fireplace," but which later generations rechristened the "Franklin stove." It was an apparatus of iron plates, with an open front, and connected by a pipe to the flue. Sitting out in the room, and well off the floor, air circulated freely about it, and the generated heat warmed the surroundings instead of escaping up the chimney. Feeling it was now perfected, he turned over his model in 1742 to his friend Robert Grace, who began the profitable production of these stoves.

Although the governor of the province offered Ben a patent for his enthusiastically received device, he staunchly refused it, reasoning that we should always welcome "an opportunity to serve others by any invention of ours; and this we should do freely and generously." How many of his contemporaries, and especially those who looked askance at his churchlessness, would have taken so charitable and unselfish a stand?

He did give one of his stoves to Bartram, who set it up in his home out across the Schuylkill River to the west. Quite likely he and Ben sat before it on the crisp autumn days that fall, drinking cider from the great stone press in the yard, and made further plans for the "association" the botanist had been advocating for a year or two. Peter Collinson, Quaker cloth merchant in London, and agent there for the Library Company, was one of England's leading botanists. Thus he had for some years been a correspondent of Bartram's. While at first he had tended to discourage a scientific society beyond the ocean, recently he had written more encouragingly. Local sentiment seemed to be increasing, too. But such a setup called for Franklin's organizing gifts, and at last he had become convinced the time was ripe. Now another task had been added to the well-filled months ahead of him.

It was nearly four miles in from Bartram's place in the country, and it is easy to picture Ben on a return trip at about this time, patiently waiting for Gray's ferry, which was always on the opposite bank when you wanted to cross, or ambling along the sparsely settled King's Highway on horseback deep in thought. Was the time approaching when his financial position would be such that he might detach himself from active participation in business? There were so many enterprises crowding in upon him, both those for his own edification and satisfaction, and others like this philosophical fraternity that were so very much in the public interest. How he longed for more free time to give to this host of worthy projects! Should he set a definite date for his "retirement"? Would it give greater certainty to his plans if he had such a goal?

This much was evident, he had better begin to locate a partner on whom he could lay some of the business matters that now consumed the lion's share of his waking hours. Yes, that was truly the next order of business.

And then, because he was still an intensely human creature, he very likely began to wonder what Debby had planned for her "pappy's" supper. He once boasted that he had little interest in food, but he was certainly not so indifferent that an afternoon in the country would fail to rouse his appetite somewhat. So urging the horse into a gallop, he pressed on along the road toward the clustered houses that now reached much further to the west than they had that Sunday morning nineteen Octobers before when he had first set foot in Philadelphia.

## VII.   Along the "Way to Wealth"

### 1742–1745

*Mr. Read has communicated to me part of a letter from you, recommending a young man whom you would be glad to see in better business than that of a journeyman printer. I have already three printing-houses in different colonies, and propose to set up a fourth if I can meet with a proper person to manage it, having all materials ready for that purpose. If the young man will venture over hither, that I may see and be acquainted with him, we can treat about the affair, and I make no doubt but he will think my proposals reasonable; if we should not agree, I promise him, however, a twelve-month's good work, and to defray his passage back if he inclines to return to England. I am Sir, your humble servant unknown.*—Letter of July 10, 1743, to William Strahan.

Young men suitable as partners, and particularly in the printing trade, did not grow on every bush. Ben's present partners were wanted where they were located. None of his own journeymen, nor those of others with whom he was acquainted, seemed suitable. And to take a likely lad and put him through an apprenticeship was rather unsatisfactory. It took customarily seven years, and unfortunate things could happen to any growing boy's interests and aptitudes in that length of time. He was very much on the lookout, but several months had come and gone without the least encouragement.

They had been anything but idle months, and much time had been given to thinking through this philosophical organization. It had been extensively discussed in the Junto, and opinions had been solicited from members of the Library Company, and among others. The ministers had for several years been preaching

the "Great Awakening" in the field of religion, and Franklin was
confident one was either due or actually upon them in the expanding physical world in which they lived. There was so much
*to know*, and so much more still *to be known*, and if men could
only be organized and thus encouraged to share their thinking
and their findings, there surely could be an awakening, and it
would be great indeed.

Things were better ordered in this respect in Europe, and
particularly in England, with which Ben was somewhat more
familiar. There had in the immediate past been no frontier there
to be tamed, no years of struggle while the wealth needed to
foster progress was being accumulated. By 1645 enough interest
had been manifest in subjects we today lump together as physics,
or science, so that some association for interchange between interested parties was called for, and a start made. By 1660 this group-
ing had resolved itself into the Royal Society, with a membership
made up of leading thinkers and practitioners in the various
segments into which philosophy of nature was already dividing.

Men and women in America were at that time still face to face
with an untamed Nature, and during the next several generations
would be in little need of a clearing house and sounding board
for their observations and speculations on what lay about them.
But vast changes had come to the narrow ribbon of settlements
draped along the seacoast since the turn into the 1700s, and with
the population doubling every few years, a new order of life
was evolving.

Even by the 1720s there had been budding "philosophers" in
towns all the way from Boston to Charleston. They were scattered, it was true, and the Philadelphia post-master believed the
fairly regular and quite dependable mail service the best possible
means of bringing them together. Centrally-located Philadelphia
was the very place for the headquarters. He would arrange, if
possible, to have such interchange carried free of charge by the
post riders because of its great intrinsic value, and, if justified, he
would start a monthly or quarterly publication to treat with the
"transactions" of such an endeavor.

The more he thought and talked about the matter, the more

enthusiastic he became. He had often wished his facilities were better for extending his acquaintance beyond his own local coterie of companions and friends. Some sort of inter-colony council—yes, one that would embrace all British-America—could be highly beneficial. So it was not too far into the year 1743 before he had drafted a pamphlet titled *A Proposal for Promoting Useful Knowledge among the British Plantations in America.* It was a call for interested Americans to set up an organization on the order of the Royal Society or the one achieved a little later by the French Encyclopedists. It would be "formed of *virtuosi* or ingenious men, residing in the several colonies, to be called *The American Philosophical Society*, who are to maintain a constant correspondence."

He had perhaps okayed proofs, or even seen copies into the mails before leaving on a journey. The winter had no doubt been rather confining, and travel would ever be his best antidote for a period of physical inertia. Just what else may have occasioned a trip to New England at that moment is uncertain, but scholars are now generally agreed he was a party to an important incident there in 1743, rather than four years later as he recorded it in his *Autobiography*.

A Dr. Adam Spencer, fresh from Scotland, was lecturing publicly on natural philosophy. His discourse embraced, along with a wide variety of other subjects, a rather sketchy treatment of a little-known force *Electricity*, together with some rather dramatic demonstrations. These latter, partly since they were new to him, and also because they tended to encourage personal experimentation in this intriguing field, took strong hold of Ben. Before he left for home it is quite likely some understanding had been reached that this Scotsman would bring his bag of tricks to Philadelphia after fulfilling his lecture schedule in New York that fall.

Just when Franklin arrived home again is not clear, but it must have been early in July, for it was then that he wrote a most significant letter, reproduced at the beginning of this chapter. Who the Mr. Read may have been with whom the London printer, William Strahan, had corresponded is not apparent. He could have been a Philadelphian, or someone whom Ben had encountered on his recent trip. But certain information contained in it was highly interesting, and on July 10 word was started to England to have this young Scots journeyman, so highly recommended, come over to America. There had been an intimation that another branch establishment was to be set up, but if this chap—what was his name, David Hall—was up to it, he would be kept right on here in Philadelphia.

The high spot of 1743, however, came without trace of doubt on the last day of August. It was then that a daughter was born to this man who had enough of the patriarch about him so that he would have thrilled as the parent of a dozen children quite as much as he did with but three. Early baptism seems to have been about as highly recommended in Philadelphia as it had been in Boston. Yet somewhat less resolute than his own parents had been, he and his wife waited until the tiny mite was five days old before carrying her around the corner to Christ Church to be christened. Ben maintained a pew there, but principally, it would appear, for other members of his family to use. The name chosen for the child was Sarah, but to the day of his death almost a half century later her doting father always thought of her as, and called her most affectionately, "Sally."

The fall before, as he had been compiling *Poor Richard*, he had noted with much interest the prediction of an eclipse of the moon in the evening of the following October 21. That would make it a Friday—a Junto night—and for months he had anticipated this coming event. But much to his chagrin, after a long wait and extensive preparations to profit by the occasion, a northeast storm roared in soon before it was to have started and clouded out the entire heavens. Fancy his astonishment when shortly afterward his Boston papers reported the earlier portions of this phenomenon having been observed there, and also the damage from a storm that raged in there toward midnight the very same evening. This was a "northeast" storm! Yet it had not hit Boston, four hundred miles to the northeast, until some hours later than its arrival in Philadelphia. At once he was the inquiring scientist, and dispatched letters of inquiry to friends far and near. It would be four years later, however, before he had satisfied himself, and was prepared to suggest the now well-proven fact that cyclonic storms which begin with violent winds out of the northeast are actually moving across country from the southwest.

Oh, if there were only more time! More free time! This feeling must have been much in his mind early in 1744 when Dr. Spencer arrived to start his *Course of Experimental Philosophy* in the Quaker City. Franklin acted as his manager, saw to it that he had ample advance publicity, and the series of lectures proved so popular they were repeated three times. Since his American tour was then over, Ben was delighted at the opportunity of buying the apparatus. But the weeks and months ahead were pretty tightly packed with other obligations, and these fascinating toys were forced to gather dust.

In April the American Philosophical Society was launched, elected Franklin secretary, held several meetings of its local members, consumed much of its founder's time, but, disappointingly, was for many years to come by no means the active, effective instrument anticipated.

James Logan had turned over to Franklin a second volume, *Cato Major*, to be published. Production on this text, which Ben considered his finest job of printing, may very well have served as a convenient excuse for numerous trips on horseback out to "Stenton," Logan's country place in Germantown. There he came to know, and be known to, Sally Logan, the provincial secretary's highly capable daughter, who divided her time between her spinning wheel, the dairy, and reading from the Old Testament in the original Hebrew as an after-meals diversion for her scholarly father. And she said of this now frequent visitor, "He was friendly and agreeable in conversation, which he suited to his company, appearing to wish to benefit his hearers. I could readily believe that he heard nothing of consequence himself but what he turned to the account he desired, and in his turn profited by the conversation of others."

Along with the *Cato Major* in which he took so much pride, he also was busily grinding out copies of a second best-seller, *Pamela*. This was not a one-man effort as had been the case with

Watt's book three years before, for Parker, his New York partner, ran an edition, while a third came from one of the Boston presses. His own advertisement of it read:

> "Just Published, And to be SOLD by the
> Printer hereof. PAMELA, *or* VIRTUE *rewarded.*
> *In a Series of* FAMILIAR LETTERS *from*
> *a beautiful young Damsel, to her*
> *Parents. Now first published, in order*
> *to cultivate the Principles of Virtue*
> *and Religion in the Minds of the* Youth *of*
> both Sexes.
>
> *A Narrative which has its Foundation in* Truth *and*
> Nature; *and at the same time that it agreeably*
> *entertains, by a Variety of* curious *and*
> affecting INCIDENTS, *is entirely divested of all those*
> *Images, which, in too many Pieces, calculated for*
> *Amusement only, tend to* inflame *the minds they*
> *should instruct.* Price 6s."

Today general opinion would consider this book downright silly. But that was not the valuation placed upon it by the audience Ben Franklin served. And able publicist that he was, he had his target well bracketed, and aimed his advertising copy accordingly. Because paper costs in those days were so high, white space in advertising was thought a needless extravagance. The acme of performance was to cram the greatest number of printing characters into a given space. It is interesting, therefore, in the ad above to see vertical, or Roman, type used for emphasis, in place of the sloping, or Italic, letters often used for that purpose, since the latter set just a trifle closer together.

In this connection, the question has been raised with reference to Franklin's scheme of capitalization and of punctuation, the opinion being advanced that it was somewhat eclectic, or even intemperate. Others, too, have commented that at times his spelling "wobbled." Regarding the latter, he followed common usage of the age with very few exceptions, and made fewer departures from rectitude than a whole host of prominent contemporaries.

Among the eight "creditable" usages of the Capital, or great Letter, set forth in a very popular *Grammar* of the mid-eighteenth century, is one prescribing its use to begin "any *W*ords, especially Names of Substantives, if they be emphatical." Herein was Ben amply covered for what may at times seem to have been vagaries. According to this same authority it was then customarily understood that "the Comma divides the lesser Parts of a Sentence, and stops the Reader's Voice till he can tell *One*. The *Semicolon* divides the greater Parts of a Sentence, at which the Reader must pause till he can tell *Two*. The *Colon* . . . three. The *Period*, or *Full-Point* . . . four."

Evidently he lived by the rules and the best usage of his time. Also it should be recalled that scholars widely experienced in Colonial American printing maintain that one outstanding feature of his output was its almost complete freedom from typographical errors. The man was meticulous as well as scholarly.

There was so much news to report, so many goods and services to advertise, that, during 1744, the *Gazette* found itself badly crowded, even on its enlarged page size of 7¼ by 11 inches. This necessitated the addition of inserted single-sheets to carry the run-over. These were spoken of as supplements, and thus was born a still-used newspaper term.

By contrast with other early American newspapers, the *Gazette* was superior editorially, and above the standard of most of its contemporaries typographically. Franklin's robust wit, at times a trifle broad or even bawdy by today's conventions, made its pages fairly scintillate when compared to other papers, the number of which was now increasing rapidly throughout the colonies.

Not only was his newssheet highly profitable, but so, too, was his book business, for which he now issued a catalog to boom the expanding mail-order business. Being the postmaster as well as the city's leading printer had its decided advantages. It is probable he was casting type, at least for his own purposes and to equip his new partnership ventures. Also he seems to have been experimenting with the casting of stereotypes, or printing plates involving blocks of type up to a whole page in size. Others, though, would perfect this latter process long after he had hung up his own leather apron and laid down his composing stick for the last time. But in this same busy year he did set up his "Dutch printing office" to handle work in the German language.

While his net in his more profitable years can hardly have run much above two thousand pounds, that was a tidy sum in those days, and would have been easily four times the profit of any other printer in all America. Why then did he desire to be done with a craft that had treated him so handsomely, and when he was so surely on the "Way to Wealth"? Probably no more logical reason can be given than that there was no real love of money in him. Money of and by itself he did not find completely satisfying. Other activities, those especially which contributed to the greatest good of the greatest number, brought him far richer rewards. One of the outstanding events of the year just past was that a most likely young Scot had arrived from London and had been put to work. He had high hopes of the purposes which this able David Hall could be made to fill. It might take two or three years to shape him up, but he looked promising.

And 1745 was another full year, although its happenings for the most part have little special significance. There was of course the sad news of his father's passing. Ben was not then certain of the old gentleman's age, except that it was well up in the eighties —eighty-seven it later proved to have been. Had this tendency to longevity been passed on to him, the youngest son? He hoped so, for one lifetime would, he felt, be quite inadequate for all the interesting things there were waiting to be attempted.

It was a war year, although Philadelphia had not been inconvenienced, and both the printing shop and the post office were continually overrun with folk awaiting the outcome of the siege of the French fortress of Louisburg in Nova Scotia. New England had furnished militia to back up British naval forces, and feeling ran high. The campaign called forth the publisher's ingenuity, and he put his skill as an engraver to work, turning out a map of the siege which appeared in the *Gazette*, and is said to be the first use of an editorial illustration in an American newspaper.

The local post office was coming to demand more and more of his time, and on those days when an outbound post was leaving it required his full attention. Then suddenly he was appointed comptroller of the entire American system, necessitating journeys of inspection, and to audit and adjust accounts of other offices. Rather than growing lighter, the press of affairs was becoming continually heavier. Would he never reach the point where he had better control of his time and efforts?

Surely 1745 was filled with a never-ending procession of affairs. Among them was the receipt of a set of tubes for use in electrical experiments sent by Collinson to the Library Company. It must have taken a strong show of will power by the aspiring scientist to resist laying all else aside and having another venture with this will-o'-the-wisp that crackled and snapped and gave off stabbing blue sparks whenever glass tubes and spheres were properly stroked or rubbed.

But at that moment Franklin was tied hand and foot by essentials which he could not, in good conscience, abandon. There was nothing for it at the moment but to let this bewitching subject of electricity incubate a while longer. Next year maybe, or if not, the year after surely. It, and dozens of other projects, beckoned. And they seemed so worthy of his attention that their time must certainly come.

## VIII.   Science Competes with Politics

### 1746–1748

*I think with you, that most Springs arise from Rains, Dews, or Ponds, on higher Ground; yet possibly some, that break out near the Tops of high Hollow Mountains, may proceed from the Abyss, or from Water in the Caverns of the Earth. . . . Now I mention Mountains, it occurs to tell you, that the great Apalachian Mountains, which run from York River, back of these colonies, to the Bay of Mexico, show in many Places, near the highest Parts of them, strata of Sea Shells; in some Places the Marks of them are in the solid Rocks. It is certainly the* Wreck *of a* World *we live on! We have specimens of these Sea Shell Rocks, broken off near the Tops of the Mountains, brought and deposited in our Library as Curiosities.*—Letter of July 16, 1747, to Rev. Jared Eliot.*

T*HE* foregoing is more illuminating than its writer had any intention that it would be. It was a typical Franklin letter, and typical, too, of many letters of that age. Jared Eliot, to whom it was addressed, was a Yankee preacher, living on his farm in Connecticut, where he dipped into medicine a bit, and could have qualified as a physician of his day. In a few years he would be considered the leading authority on agriculture in the Colonies, and for years Ben and he carried on an extensive correspondence in their interchange of general knowledge. At that particular moment they were exploring the field that was soon to become geology, seeing what they could uncover. For there were whole great expanses that as yet had been but little examined, and you had to dig to find. But such effort was often pleasantly rewarded by the new, unique, and stimulating information you picked up.

The body of knowledge that has grown to be so overwhelming

today, and so diversified that it sustains specialists in the less important phases of what are in themselves specialized subjects, was nowhere near that formidable two hundred years ago. Men with eager, active, retentive minds could become masters of several important fields simultaneously. Such versatility was relatively common, for it was one of the marks of a well-read and well-educated man, and here were two admirable samples of the genus.

Gentlemen were scholars in those days, much as they are golfers today. The pursuit of knowledge was a highly approved occupation, and the coffeehouses in London, and the taverns here, were the country clubs of that other age, where you went for divertisement, and to play the rousing game of hunting knowledge. Sometimes it got to be almost an obsession.

While the motives behind acquiring an ever-broader understanding of the surrounding world could be somewhat mixed, they grouped principally about two major reasons. One of these activated the wealthy, who found in this search a means of filling their idle time with activities that could be justified before the court of conscience. They thus tended to be dilettantes, obtaining their satisfactions chiefly from applause of their accomplishments. There was far more of this type of approach in England, and it tended to characterize the Royal Society, with which the American tradesman-printer would soon begin to have dealings. Its members still lived and had their being in the spirit of Isaac Newton, dead but twenty years, and they liked to feel they followed after natural philosophy for its own sake alone, and were thus more in the nature of what are today termed "pure scientists."

Great wealth was relatively uncommon in America until the following century, and a much more extensive practicality forced itself into men's thinking on this side of the ocean. Here knowledge was more frequently sought after for the direct benefits it might yield than for mere amusement or idle commendation. Nonetheless, you were certain to get a real thrill from passing on a tasty morsel of undiscovered knowledge to a friend, or correspondent, and, if the truth be known, Printer Franklin seems to have been drawn to electricity by those same invisible forces that bring a child and a new toy together. Even to his eminently practical mind the magic "fluid" cannot at the very first have

promised much in the way of results other than quenching the
thirst of curiosity. But it would not be many months before a
chance remark in a letter disclosed that, as extensive experiments
were being carried on, one part of his mind was monitoring the
whole subject, and seeking means by which the expended effort
would be recompensed through tangible results.

David Hall was proving to be a find indeed. But then, he had
worked at Watt's fine plant in London, as had Ben, and, despite
the beer guzzling there, the place turned out excellent craftsmen.
Fortunately this canny Scot was also a good organizer, and gave
promise of becoming a tiptop businessman. It might take a year
or two to "blood" him properly, but the best way to do that was
to load more and more responsibility upon him. By such means
Franklin was soon enjoying greater freedom than he had known
in years. But it must not be idle time. So Spencer's equipment was
hauled out, and electrical experiments were underway once
again.

A neighbor on the High Street, Ebenezer Kinnersley, a Baptist
minister, but without a pulpit at the time, was one of his earliest
associates. He was, according to Franklin, "ingenious," and contributed much time and effort. Another who was very close to
these activities was Thomas Hopkinson, first president of the
American Philosophical Society, and first, too, of three generations of eminent Hopkinsons. A third member of this inner circle
was Philip Syng, skilled artisan, who devised the lovely inkpot
for the chairman's table in the Assembly Hall in the State
House, and into which at a later time the signers of the Declaration, and the Constitution, dipped their quills.

Franklin's home was at the very center of the town in those
days, and it is probable that the tubes that Collinson had sent
from England the previous year were brought over from the
Library's quarters well out on Chestnut Street. And there the
work went on, Franklin either experimenting alone or assisted by
one or more members of the group. Separated by a broad ocean
from others working with similar equipment and in the same
little-known area, these Philadelphians had to start virtually from
scratch, and master the very rudiments first. Then, as they began
to get their feet more firmly on solid ground, they came to cer-

tain definite conclusions, coined terms with which to label their findings, and perfected and amplified their equipment. Both Ben and Phil Syng were able mechanics, and the latter especially contributed some effective contrivances.

William Franklin, between fifteen and sixteen, had grown restless, and wanted some part in the war then in progress, which had so far managed to pass Philadelphia by. He had attempted unsuccessfully to enlist for a cruise on one of the local privateers, so arrangements were made for him to accompany one of the four companies of militia heading for the campaign in Canada. There was a pause in matters electrical while the youthful ensign was being outfitted, and marched away in June, only to spend the balance of that year in Albany.

The program of experimentation was also broken into long enough at another time during the same year for Ben to produce a treatise titled *Reflections on Courtship and Marriage*. Three years later, it chanced to be the first of his books to find its way into type in Europe.

But the interest in electricity continued, and Ben and his associates acquired much skill with their demonstrations. In fact, their proficiency seems to have become town gossip, and brought them a handicapping audience. The house, close by the market, was altogether too convenient, and sometime in the fall or the early winter of 1746 the traffic to it had become so heavy that years later the *Autobiography* recorded recollections of it as follows. "My house was continually full, for some time, with people who came to see these new wonders. To divide this incumbrance among my friends, I caused a number of similar tubes to be blown at our glass-house, with which they furnished themselves, so that we had at length several performers." But whether concentrated in Franklin's home, or scattered in the homes of others and in the meeting rooms of the Library Company and the Junto, the work was evidently intensified as the turn was made into 1747. Ben was still the leading participant, pressing forward himself, and guiding and encouraging the others, ever willing to accord fullest recognition of their contributions.

Collinson not only maintained a lively interest in things American and had sent over a tube for what he had perhaps thought

might be merely the casual amusement of members of the Library
Company, but he was also a member of the Royal Society. Ben
thought the kindly gentleman's present should have proper
acknowledgment, especially now that it had been put to such
profitable use. He was positive as well that other experimenters
might be fully as interested in what had been uncovered in Philadelphia as the group there was in turn anxious to know what
progress was being made in Europe. So a detailed letter of results
to date was sent off to Collinson in March. This was the first in a
series of letters on the subject of electricity drafted during the
next several years, which, when later collected and published,
made the name of Benjamin Franklin well known in Europe almost as soon as it became familiar in the several colonies in
America. With this earliest missive went an appeal for the latest
advices on what other experimenters were accomplishing in Britain and on the Continent.

Almost as though this request had been anticipated, a very
fine and complete set of equipment arrived in July, a present of
the Penn family to the Library Company. But about the same
moment a fleet of Spanish and French privateers appeared in Delaware Bay, braved the shoals in the river, sailed up and attacked
riverside farms just below New Castle, and threw unprotected
Philadelphia into turmoil and then consternation. The City of
Brotherly Love had suddenly waked from its lethargy and feeling
of false security to find itself face to face with the uncertain
fortunes of war.

Thus for the time being the proprietor's thoughtful gift—and it
seems to have included one of the brand-new condensers that
came to be called Leyden jars—would have but cursory attention,
for one of the crucial moments in the life of Benjamin Franklin
had arrived. In a colony racked with political cleavage, although
having its full complement of capable men, he seemed the one
person capable of formulating a plan to remove the threat to
their safety. Also he had the complementary ability to reconcile
the various factions at loggerheads, and thus give the plan a fair
chance.

Did circumstances sweep him into this situation, or did he seek
it ambitiously? A yes, or no, either way would be no more than

opinion. Accused of self-seeking, he could have pled "duty," for he had a penchant for doing good, for contributing unselfishly to the commonweal. On the other hand, the forty-one-year-old man was fast becoming a pillar, and a power, in the community. Also he had innate political skill and know-how—and such talents, in some manner, almost always seem to find employment.

The metal of the various groups which he was called upon to weld together was so unlike that it seemed impossible to find a flux to bond them. The Quakers, in control politically, leaned heavily toward pacifism, and even a small schism in their ranks did not prevent the majority from opposing any participation in this so-called "defensive" war. They felt the proprietors should defend the province in which the now non-Quaker Penns continued to hold so substantial a stake. The proprietors, however, were certain such responsibility devolved upon the colony itself, and sent governors over primarily to see that their great holdings were not taxed a single farthing more than could be avoided under any circumstances. The wealthy and important group composed of other than the Quaker members wanted both that sect and the proprietors to contribute their full and fair share of both taxes and effort to the common defense; while the common people, called upon for manpower, were necessarily exercised as to how their contribution would be spent.

Early in November Jemmy's apprenticeship of seven years was up. The indenture which had bound him had stipulated that when his term was complete he was to have "one good new suit of clothes, besides his ordinary apparel." But a generous uncle, who had developed a strong liking for James's orphaned son, was prepared to add much more, such as new type and other items. After the young man had been started for Newport, Ben turned back to his problem of preparedness.

Its controversial points had been well aired in the *Gazette*, and on November 17 he began distribution of a pamphlet titled *Plain Truth; or, Serious Considerations on the Present State of the City of Philadelphia and Province of Pennsylvania. By a Tradesman of Philadelphia*. In its shrewd assessment of the overall situation the politically able "tradesman" had found the common ground on which the opposing factions could draw somewhat closer together. Rumors seeping up from the West Indies that French privateers were about to rendezvous there for a mass attack in the early spring aided his efforts. It was not too long before he had an *Association* set up, backed by common approval, if not by legal enactment of the Assembly, and one that would not court the antagonism of the proprietors. Under it some ten thousand militia were quickly recruited in the province, and formed into units. Those in the Philadelphia area chose the free-lance organizer for their colonel, but since he was totally without military aspirations, he turned down this proffered honor. At times he could summon up a most becoming humility.

Somewhere along the way he had found time to edit and write the almanac for 1748, which, when it went into distribution, proved to be an enlarged volume, and bore the altered title *Poor Richard Improved*, which would be its name on remaining issues.

As 1747 drew to a close, the man whose religious attributes were sometimes questioned proposed a "fast day," the first such event to be celebrated in Pennsylvania. Ben himself drew up the proclamation, which set aside Thursday, January 7, 1748, in which to acknowledge "dependence on the Divine Being, to give thanks for the mercies received, and no less to deprecate His Judgments and humbly pray for His protection."

Military and political matters were sufficiently pressing so that electricity was, as far as Franklin was concerned, in abeyance. In March he was one of a group which made the trip to New York to borrow cannon from that colony, and in April this artillery was received and set up in a fort built below the city on the bank of the Delaware. Evenings that might have been spent perhaps more pleasantly, this organizer of civilian defense gave to guard duty, walking his post as a "common soldier." He would have been named for a seat in the spring term of the Assembly, in which he had for a number of years served as clerk, had he not refused. He feared, no doubt, that the loss of his independent position during the emergency might be most unfortunate. But he was now plainly a public figure, and, irrespective of his preferences, from now on and for the remainder of his life, the common good would have first call on his time, thought, and efforts.

In May he journeyed up and across the Delaware River to Burlington, New Jersey, where he had recently acquired a three hundred acre farm, and on which he was currently expending time, energy, and funds. Agriculture to him was both a business and a science, and he and his great friend, the Rev. Mr. Eliot up in Connecticut, poured a stream of letters back and forth dealing with its fine points. These letters seem to indicate rather frequent visits to his New Jersey domain.

In the late summer a somewhat fantastic picnic was planned, although whether it was carried out is uncertain. An electrocuted turkey was to be roasted on a spit turned by an electric jack, over a fire started by an electric spark, and toasts in "electrified bumpers" drunk to famous electricians, to the accompaniment of a salute of guns from an "electrical battery." This could have been by way of celebration of Ben's withdrawal from sole ownership of the printing business, which came in September. David Hall— "Edinburgh Davey"—was sold a partnership interest, and took over active management. At once Ben moved around the corner and up a couple of blocks to a new home at Second and Sassafras Streets. This latter would soon be renamed Race Street, when it came to provide the best road to the race track laid out in Central Square, now the center of the modern city. To one expecting to give the bulk of his time from then on to study and experiment, this withdrawal to a far quieter neighborhood must have been a pleasant relief.

Before stepping aside he had managed to get Thomas Smith off to establish another partnership at Antigua, in the West Indies. But these partnership arrangements from here on were less and less with intent to a profit for Franklin, and more to encourage able journeymen and provide suitable localities with printing facilities.

Was the time now ripe for a return to the experiments so rudely interrupted in the middle of the previous year? There were still some business involvements, but they were comparatively few. The war scare was over, and peace merely awaiting the signing of a treaty in October. The time seemed propitious indeed, but public service would make a few more levies. This man who had been focused so sharply in the public eye, particularly for the past year, could not be permitted to hide his

political talents under a bushel in the seclusion of his library. In
October he was chosen to a place in the city government, a seat
on the Common Council. True to the gentlemanly code of the
age, which demanded that he who had time and talents at his disposal must put them to use for the public good Franklin accepted.
Politics seemed unmistakably to be stealing a march on Science.

## IX. In the Public Welfare

### *1748–1751*

*I think with you, that nothing is of more importance for the publick weal, than to form and train up youth in wisdom and virtue. Wise and good men are, in my opinion, the strength of a state far more so than riches or arms, which, under the management of Ignorance and Wickedness, often draw on destruction, instead of providing for the safety of the people. And though the culture bestowed on many should be successful only with a few, yet the influence of those few and the service in their power may be very great. Even a single woman, that was wise, by her wisdom saved a city.*—Letter of August 23, 1750, to Samuel Johnson, D. D.

FRANKLIN was at his electrical experiments again in earnest as soon as conditions were back close to normal in the late fall of 1748. There were far fewer interruptions at the new home on North Second Street, and the winter days, passed before the cheering fire in one of his Pennsylvania fireplaces, were most profitably spent. The magic bottle now added to his equipment, and in which charges could be "condensed," or stored and built up in intensity, was a fascinating device, yet one that needed to be treated with some caution and care. When "charged" it could lash out at you with a biting, searing flash, and strike you a blow that would hurl you reeling across the room, and leave you numb and partly paralyzed for hours afterward.

One or two fairly medium shocks, and the frequent snap and crackle of the peculiar blue sparks set the experimenter to wondering. There was a limit to the amount of "fluid" that could be induced to enter one of the Leyden jars. But as more of them were built, and linked together, or a battery contrived of a series of panes of glass covered with lead foil, a far greater charge could be built up that might be released with one of these lightning-fast tongues of bluish light. Lightning-fast? Yes, and lightning-*like* as well!

Could there be any connection between these electrical sparks being generated right here in his library and the destructive lightning that flashed out of the boiling clouds of a summer "thunder-gust"? Were electricity and lightning one and the same natural phenomenon, different only in degree? This ardent researcher, working pretty much out of touch with kindred souls in Europe, was soon convinced that the small flames he produced and the far larger ones generated by Nature in a stormy moment were identical. The thought itself was not original with him, but the proof, soon to be formulated, was.

By April he was sending more data to Collinson, but withholding his new beliefs until there was better certainty of his position. And almost instinctively he was searching all the while for practical applications. Years later it would seem to him that the august body of natural philosophers in England scoffed at his reports read to them by his correspondents, and Dr. Michael Pupin, great electrical scientist of our own times, explains how it came about that Ben's attitude was perhaps justified. Says he, "No natural philosopher of that century could expect to attract much serious attention who in his inquiries departed from the rigorous mathematics of the Newtonian school. The Franklin stove, the Franklin rod, the Franklin electrical plate, had nothing in common with the Newtonian school of natural philosophy, and that may explain why most of Franklin's communications to the Royal Society relating to his electrical researches, were not considered sufficiently important to find a place in the *Transactions* of that Society." Far more interested in activities, practices, needs and their fulfillment, than in mere speculation and theory, the American's practicality seemed beneath the concern of these "pure" scientists.

During the early part of 1749 he had begun again to talk up the launching of a school of higher learning. Finding supporters, many of them from among members of the Junto, he decided the time had come to open up subscription lists to found an academy.

An explanatory pamphlet would be needed, and he produced one with the title *Proposals Relating to the Education of Youth in Pensilvania*. Franklin's own motivation in the matter was summed up in a single sentence, "For doing good to me is the only service to God in our power; and to imitate his beneficences is to glorify him." The purpose of the proposed school was briefed in another sentence, "An ability to serve mankind, one's country, friends and family, which ability is (with the blessing of God) to be acquired or greatly increased by true learning . . . should indeed be the great aim and end of all learning."

The purpose of the colleges so far founded in the Colonies had been primarily to train ministers, despite strong protests to the contrary in launching the last among them. Franklin saw a need for advanced education in other activities as well, notably business and politics. Surely it was most essential as a sort of normal school to provide proper teachers for elementary education sharply on the increase. Also he doubted whether the strong adherence to classicism and the past was desirable in these days of awakening knowledge. Was the extreme emphasis upon Latin, Greek, and Hebrew justified? Was it actually outmoded? Ben proposed stressing English, and including training in the great economic foundation of all wealth—agriculture. And as if that was not radical enough he even sang the praises of athletics.

His hard-hitting pamphlet he distributed at his own expense. While it was having its impact, he perfected his solicitation procedure, and soon contributors were signing up. The promises ran to something like five thousand pounds, and on November 13 a board of twenty-four trustees was selected, which elected Franklin their president. There was still something like fourteen months of preparation before sessions could begin, however.

Just what the occasion was is not clear, but it is supposed that it was in this year that the first real census was taken in Philadelphia, presumably under the supervision of Franklin. It seems to have been sponsored or occasioned by William Allen, the wealthy merchant-lawyer, later to be chief justice of the province, currently Ben's political patron, and later rather a bitter opponent.

Back in the summer, when the school activities were first getting under way, the Masons had further honored Ben by electing

him Grand Master for Pennsylvania. But these other activities did
not, as in the previous year, mean that his researches were terminated. Just a week previous to becoming president of the Academy, he had made an interesting entry among the minutes he kept
of his experiments. It reads: "Electrical fluid agrees with lightning
in these particulars. 1. Giving light. 2. Color of the light. 3.
Crooked direction. 4. Swift motion. 5. Being conducted by metals.
6. Crack or noise in exploding. 7. Subsisting in water or ice. 8.
Rending bodies it passes through. 9. Destroying animals. 10. Melt-
ing metals. 11. Firing inflammible substances. 12. Sulphureous
smell. The electric fluid is attracted by points. We do not know
whether this property is in lightning. But since they agree in all
particulars wherein we can already compare them, is it not probable they agree likewise in this?"

Not far from this same time he seems to have forwarded to
Dr. John Mitchell, formerly of Virginia, and now returned to
London, a series of no less than fifty-six observations and supposi-
tions having to do with "thunder-gusts." These dealt with thunder
and lightning storms, that often wreaked so much havoc, and
were perhaps the result of notations made as he had watched these
summer disturbances. Since the letter was evidently read to the
Royal Society, this data, still to be conclusively proven, may have
been the material that was laughed at. Many serious-minded
people at the time were convinced that lightning resulted from
the mysterious explosion of poisonous gases in mid-air.

Given time in which to do so, he proposed to prove lightning
and electricity to be one. But he had already found that an electric
current created a magnetic effect. If he wound a wire about a
piece of iron and passed a current through the wire, the iron became magnetized. This fundamental was the one from which the
telegraph, the telephone, and the electric motor were later developed.

The census figures collected the previous year began to give
Ben some concern as the half-century mark was passed. Philadelphia was growing apace. There were now seven thousand tax-
able citizens, evidence of great expansion of wealth. These people
owned about two thousand dwellings, most of them three-storied.
There were about one thousand other structures such as ware-

houses, breweries, stables, sheds, etc. And every time a single one of them burned down the owner suffered a total loss. In the largest city in America not a single structure was covered by a penny's worth of insurance. Vessels and their cargoes were so protected, and a good Quaker underwriter here in Philadelphia that wrote such marine coverage always began his policies most prudently, "By the grace of God, amen!"

But in England people were insuring their homes and places of business against loss by that universal ravager—fire. Why not in Pennsylvania as well? And why was it not logical for the men associated to extinguish fires to associate also to protect themselves from excessive loss? At their meeting on February 26, 1750, the members agreed to raise among them a sum equivalent to one thousand dollars "for an Insurance Office to make up the damage that may arise by fire among this Company." Another enterprise in which Ben would play a conspicuous part was opening up.

About two weeks earlier young William Franklin's name had been registered in the Middle Temple of the Inns of Court in London. His father, contrary to his usual frugal tendencies, was bringing up his own son as a "gentleman." He would be trained for the law. In a long letter to the boy's eighty-three-year-old grandmother in Boston, written in April, his father had said, "As to your grandchildren, Will is now nineteen years of age, a tall proper youth, and much of a beau. He acquired a habit of idleness on the expedition, but begins of late to apply himself to business, and I hope will become an industrious man. He imagined his father had got enough [wealth] for him, but I have assured him that I intend to spend what little I have myself."

Of Sally, not seven until the end of August, he wrote, she "grows a fine girl, and is extremely industrious with her needle and delights in her book. . . . She goes now to dancing school."

By an early spring packet came word from Collinson, explaining that letters of his, particularly the one on "thunder-gusts," had "been read before the Society & have been Deservedly admired." This was encouraging, but more so was his Quaker friend's intention to collect Ben's written materials on electricity up to that time and "putt them into some Printers Hand to be communicated to the Publick." There had been an article in the

January issue of the *Gentleman's Magazine,* stimulated by the reading of Franklin's papers before the Society. There would be another in the May edition, made up of his material on lightning rods.

But post office and other affairs seem to have been competing with electricity that spring and early summer of 1750. The Academy was badly in want of a first-rate educator to bring it into being and make it into a worthy endeavor. Perhaps his comptroller's duties took him to the north, but at some time after the weather warmed he stopped in Stratford in the Connecticut colony to make a personal appeal to the Rev. Samuel Johnson. There was a follow-up letter after the return to Philadelphia. But while Johnson and Franklin saw eye to eye on some points, the gentleman four years later became the first "Reverend President" of King's College (later Columbia) rather than of the institution out of which grew the University of Pennsylvania. Nonetheless, this reverend gentleman, who had shaken his colony to its very foundation after his graduation from Yale by swinging over to the Anglican communion, retained his regard for Franklin; and of the latter's plan for the Academy had admitted that "nobody would imagine that the draft you have made for an English education was done by a Tradesman. . . . A true genius will not content itself without entering more or less into almost everything, and of mastering many more in spite of fate itself."

Dr. Johnson's son William, also a president of Columbia, would be an associate of Franklin's in London twenty years later; and the carefully kept records of his stay there as agent of the Connecticut colony have furnished many fill-ins of missing details of Franklin's concurrent residence as Pennsylvania agent at the British capital.

By late summer he was making slight revisions in some of his assumptions, and readying himself for the big step, proof that lightning could be drawn from thunder clouds. Having proposed fire insurance earlier in the year, he began to be hopeful of overcoming one of the leading causes of fires, by conveying the huge sparks harmlessly from the sky into the ground. Since he then lacked a structure tall enough and suitably situated in Philadelphia, he submitted suggestions on how a test should be made to Collinson. Franklin was far less concerned with who completed the proof than that there be positive proof on which to build further, and usefully. In this connection he assured his friend in London that it was not "of much importance to us to know the manner in which nature executes her laws: 'tis enough if we know the laws themselves. 'Tis of real use to know that china left in the air unsupported will fall and break; but how it comes to fall, and why it breaks, are matters of speculation. 'Tis a pleasure indeed to know them, but we can preserve our china without it." Here was the reasoning of the "applied" scientist.

The long draft of his accomplishments having been sent off to London, other matters began to demand his attention. Dr. Thomas Bond, leading local physician, had been doing his best to raise money sufficient to build a hospital. After many of his best prospects for funds had demanded to know what Franklin's attitude toward such facilities might be, the physician finally sought out and laid his problem in the lap of the promoter. The whole idea was new to America, and needed much explanation, but probably no one in Philadelphia at the time was better equipped to put the idea across effectively.

The electrical equipment came back into use for a time in December. Possibly some new pieces had been completed and were to have something of a dramatic testing before a group gathered for the purpose. Ben speaks of "two large [Leyden] jars, containing as much electrical fire as forty common phials." With much patient effort they had been fully charged, and their power would be demonstrated on this second day before the holiday, when their discharge would be used to dispatch the Christmas turkey.

And then something unforeseen happened. "The company present (whose talking to me, and to one another, I suppose occasioned my inattention to what I was about) say that the flash was very great and the crack was loud as a pistol." Ben had been struck senseless by a tremendous shock. He felt properly ashamed for his notorious blunder, but was quickly back to normal again.

After the holidays it was lack of leisure time, more than any fear of electrical potency, that occasioned his scientific pursuits being laid aside again.

A curriculum having been arranged and a house rented, the Academy was opened on January 7, 1751, with a Mr. Dove as master. The quarters soon proved too small, and a deal was made for the use of the structure built ten years or more before for the Rev. Mr. Whitefield's preaching. Among other considerations in this transaction was the operation of a "charity school" for the education of poor children, which came about in September that same year. Thus the enterprise, not quite as its chief sponsor had visualized it, moved ahead, but presumably consumed much of his time.

So, too, did the hospital matter. The subscriptions came rather too slowly from private sources alone, and a petition for a public grant was readied right after the turn of the year. Other matters, too, were bubbling up. King George's War had been over now for going on three years, and there was a strong "westward movement" in progress, which promised some day soon to precipitate a contest between Britain and France in the Ohio Valley. The colonies were growing rapidly, filling in to the point where "elbow room," at least by standards of that time, was at a premium, and the demands of the land-hungry were focusing attention beyond the Alleghenies. The Indians in the area were growing restless, and the customary Franklin curiosity had been stimulated by these western affairs when he had been appointed a member of the Indian Commission the previous year. His mind began to range over the whole American scene, and the scientist for the time being became the statesman and sociologist. Visualizing a growing need, he outlined in early 1751 his first suggestions for a *union* of the colonies. It would be three years before he would introduce it in greater detail, and twenty-five before he would see it as a reality. Seeds had been sown that would sprout in union, blossom in independence, and ripen as fine fruit of freedom.

About the same time, and as a sort of rebuke to the imperfect knowledge Parliament displayed in legislation for America, Ben also drafted his *Observations concerning the Increase of Mankind, Peopling of Countries, Etc.* While it was then shown to but a few close friends, and not published for another four years, it indicated new trends of thought which would go far to pattern the next quarter-century of his life.

Then a post rider heading north brought word that briefly gave him pause, but soon had him checking among his friends, and sitting down to write a letter to be hurried to England by the first ship to sail.

# x. Mr. Deputy Postmaster General

## *1751–1753*

*I have just receiv'd Advice that the Deputy Post Master General of America (Mr. Elliot Benger residing in Virginia) . . . is tho't to be near his End. My Friends advise me to apply for this Post. . . . I have not heretofore made much Scruple of giving you Trouble when the Publick Good was to be promoted by it, but 'tis with great Reluctance that I think of asking you to interest yourself in my Private concerns, as I know you have little Time to spare. The Place is in the Disposal of the Post Masters General of Britain with some of whom or their Friends you may possibly have acquaintance. . . . I have heard £ 200 was given for this Office by Mr. Benger and the same by his Predecessor. . . . However the less it costs the better as 'tis an Office for Life only which is a very uncertain Tenure*—Letter of May 21, 1751, to Peter Collinson.

WHEN he had disengaged himself almost three years previously from private business, Franklin had felt that "by the sufficient tho' moderate fortune I had acquir'd, I had secured leisure during the rest of my life for philosophical studies and amusements." Much as he had anticipated such "leisure," it perhaps fell short of his hopes. Active by nature, he seems to have always grown restless when his life became too sedentary.

There may also have been moments when he mistrusted both the sufficiency or durability of his "fortune." To so provident a character, the acquiring of further regular income would hardly be taken amiss, and he was trader enough to "take a risk" to gain any such added revenue.

But beyond these considerations there was the great delight he found in promoting the common good, and, now that he had begun to think of America as a unit, rather than as thirteen separate colonies, he saw the postal facilities as a needed instrument in their uniting. Thus when word reached the postal comptroller that one of the two colonial deputy postmasters general was desperately ill, he found political backing through the new provincial chief justice, William Allen, and sought further aid in obtaining the post through Collinson in London. He had in this way taken the first step in a sequence of events which would make of him by the outbreak of the Revolution the most widely known American.

In April of 1751 the editor of the *Gentleman's Magazine* had issued a pamphlet made up of Franklin's writings on electricity; and about as Collinson was receiving the plea quoted at the beginning of this chapter, William Watson, English electrician, was reading an "account" from it to the Royal Society. Ben's name was becoming more widely and more favorably known at the seat of empire. Thus in the midst of his new-found leisure he continued to find much to take up his time and efforts.

The local post office had grown to the point where separate quarters were needed. So the Read homestead on Market Street was taken over, and in January 1752 its operations were moved from the Franklin & Hall printing office. Deborah often assisted there, and soon it had a full-time clerk.

Connections with the *Gazette* had by no means been terminated, for Ben often wrote much that appeared in it. In the issue of May 9 he had attested his enlarged spirit of Americanism by roundly condemning the British government for still exporting criminals to the colonies. His counter-proposal was to ship rattlesnakes to London in repayment.

Sometime during the summer he seems to have sandwiched in a brief return to things electrical. He planned and perhaps wrote, but at least aided in developing, a series of lectures with Ebenezer Kinnersley launched in Philadelphia later that year, and which he repeated very successfully in Boston, and the next year in New York and Newport. By the spring of 1753 he had given them as far afield as Antigua, in the West Indies. What is more, they continued sufficiently popular so that he still found eager audiences for them in Philadelphia in the years 1754, 1760, and 1764.

The hospital matter, too, tended to drag along and consume

no little time and thought. In January Ben had proposed to the Assembly that if that body would vote two thousand pounds to the project, a like amount would be obtained from subscribers. Assembly members were soon convinced that no such substantial amount could be equalled through subscriptions, and were thus persuaded to approve this liberal grant. The act actually gave a filip to the Franklin-Bond endeavors, and they were soon able to claim the public funds. To the very end of his life he still found amusement at his ingeniousness in this instance, claiming, "I do not remember any of my political manœuvres the success of which gave me at the time more pleasure, or wherein, after thinking of it, I more easily excused myself for having made some use of cunning." This political acumen was soon to have ample employment.

For fifteen years he had sat as the muted and none too influential clerk of the Assembly. Now, in August 1751, he was chosen by the citizens of Philadelphia as a burgess to represent them in this provincial legislature. And he would be re-elected ten times, by his own avowal, without ever kissing a baby, handing out a twist of tobacco, or clapping a constituent upon the back and asking for his vote. The hustings would have been a frightful bother to Ben, for he spoke in public most reluctantly, and preferred to feel that he had put forth services that justified his being inducted into, or returned to, public office.

His last official act as clerk was to record his having qualified as a member. The first act of his successor was to enter a petition of twenty-year-old William Franklin to be awarded the vacant clerkship. And the new member, his father, saw to it that the opening went to the son. Ben would be called a nepotist many, many times in the years just ahead. And if filling public offices with his kinfolk was all that was required to deserve the epithet, he was entitled to it. However, being a completely logical man, he had his own reasonable explanation for this practice.

Almost as though he anticipated the criticism and the mudslinging he might now expect as a working politician, he wrote the Rev. Eliot as follows just a month later, "What you mention concerning the love of praise is indeed very true; it reigns more or less in every heart; though we are generally hypocrites, in that respect, and pretend to disregard praise. . . . *Being forbid to praise themselves, they learn instead of it to censure others; which is only a roundabout way of praising themselves.*" Being given but little to vanity, jealousy, envy, or contumely himself, his words were rather significant.

On the first day of October he was made an alderman in the city government, and his political cup indeed seemed to be running over. Long afterward he recollected that, "I would not, however, insinuate that my ambition was not flatter'd by all these promotions; it certainly was, for, considering my low beginning, they were great things to me; and they were still more pleasing, as being so many spontaneous testimonials of the public good opinion, and by me entirely unsolicited."

He now stood at the entrance to a year that would be full to overflowing. This 1752 was also a time in which many people, especially in Europe, began to look upon him as something of a wizard and magician. It would also complete nine years of acquaintance with electricity, first encountered as very much of a mystery, and now, by his ministrations, on its way to becoming a science. Yet the year began for him on quite a different note.

Almost two years previously an insurance pool had been arranged to protect the holdings of the thirty members of the Union Fire Company. In 1751 Ben, tempering big-heartedness with the caution of wider-distributed risk, had proposed extending this coverage to others, and he and Philip Syng, the silversmith, had been appointed to work out the details. At a meeting held in September five other volunteer fire companies had agreed to go along in the formation of a permanent association that would be open to the general public. In the *Gazette* of February 18, 1752, appeared an ad inviting any and all who might be interested to participate in this scheme in which the policy-holders would insure each other's houses "upon the most equal terms and apart from all views of separate gain or interest." A meeting of subscribers was held on March 25, and, with leading citizens as its directors, there came into being the famous old *Philadelphia Contributionship for the Insurance of Houses from Loss by Fire.*

Heading these directors was B. Franklin, who was later "desired to get a sufficient number of policies printed." He had played a major role in bringing fire insurance to America.

There would be a return to matters electrical in April, when Ben and Dr. Cadwallader Evans sought to relieve suffering by the introduction of this mysterious fluid into the medical field. A young woman that had been the victim of frequent convulsions consented to undergo tests. While unsuccessful as far as such spasms were concerned, and in no way advancing electricity, the trial had this oblique benefit, a report of this case rapidly awakened European interest in the activities of Philadelphia physicians.

The Franklin mind was wrestling with other philosophical matters as well. Almost at this same time he was writing to his New York friend, Cadwallader Colden, on the subject of air and light, protesting that "I must own I am much in the dark about light." Who could help loving a man with the fine faculty of making levity express humility?

But this light-heartedness would dim for a time when word came from Boston of the passing of his mother in her eighty-fifth year. Said he of her to his sister Jane, "She [was] a discreet and virtuous woman."

Over the ocean, and consequently unknown to him at the time, momentous things were happening. Three of the leading scientists of France had determined to carry out Franklin's proposed experiment of drawing electricity from the clouds of a thunderstorm. On a hillside about eighteen miles outside of Paris a one-inch iron rod, forty feet high, was set up. And there in the midst of a tremendous hailstorm on the afternoon of May 10, 1752, and in the presence of a priest and a handful of peasants, a watchman drew off a host of crackling blue sparks from the base of the rod into a small Leyden jar. Three days later the report was made to the Académie Royale des Sciences that the Franklin theory had been proved beyond a shadow of doubt—electricity could be drawn from the storm clouds.

Eight days later came verification when another thundershower passed above a similar rod set up within Paris itself. At once word was sped across the Channel to the Royal Society. The King of France desired to commend Franklin warmly for his understanding, and Collinson for his thoughtfulness in publishing the brilliant American's investigations. Then in July an experimenter in England confirmed the findings in France. There would be still further proof handed in that same summer; and, as Carl Van Doren so aptly comments, "He was famous in Europe before he knew it in America."

But what was he doing all this while back home here on this side of the Atlantic? Tradition maintains he was flying a kite in the open fields several blocks west of his home on Sassafras Street. And well he may have been, although as far as he was concerned he seems to have kept it a complete secret for many weeks. In fact the more positive account of such an episode came from the pen of the budding young preacher-scientist, Joseph Priestley, who incorporated it fifteen years later in his work on the *History and Present State of Electricity*. Franklin is supposed to have read his manuscript before it went into type.

Surely Ben was aware that Christ Church was intending to erect a steeple—the first in the city—to hold a "ring of bells," for he had been appointed one of the managers of a lottery to raise the funds. He had no doubt visualized this vantage point for a test of his reasoning as soon as it was completed. Evidently though he was very eager to announce his scheme of protection by lightning rods in *Poor Richard Improved* for 1753. But to advocate erection of an unproved device was a little too risky a procedure. There must be some way out, and presumably the kite as an alternative suggested itself. There is every probability also that it was tried out, and that the "dread of ridicule" in connection with it, which Priestley mentions, may have made Franklin withhold the recounting of his experiences. The sparks received from a brass key at the end of a wet kite string probably satisfied *him*. But this was, at least in the eyes of the uninitiated, quite a different conductor than he would advocate, or that would be seen in the stout iron rod he was readying for erection beside his own home, and which would be in place in September. By that time, however, the European papers began to arrive telling "of the success of the Philadelphia experiment for drawing the electric fire from clouds by means of pointed rods of iron."

By October 19 he was ready to advertise in the *Gazette* the forthcoming 1753 edition of *Poor Richard*, which was to contain the article *How to Secure Houses, etc., from Lightning*. While the evidence flowing in from Europe might be conclusive to some, there had better be some semblance of proof from America as well, and so data in connection with the kite experiment appeared in this same issue of the *Gazette*.

The inventor very likely had reason to tread cautiously, for it would be folly to believe that humanity without exception was awaiting his lightning rod with open arms and unquestioning approval. It was long a bone of contention, particularly by the ignorant and prejudiced, and one feature of Kinnersley's lectures was to explain away opposition by the superstitious and the excessively religious wary of withstanding "acts of God." While many of the rods came to be erected, the device still had its detractors years later. During the devastating visitation of yellow fever in 1793, when the cry of "Bring out your dead" echoed along Philadelphia streets, one of the city's leading citizens, and an ex-Postmaster General, was convinced that the considerable number of lightning rods, "by imperceptibly drawing off the electric fluid from the clouds, and thereby preventing thunder," were in large part responsible for the virulence of the epidemic.

But the air just then was filled with other things besides electricity, for violent protests would be made over "stealing" eleven days from the calendar. At long last the Gregorian scheme of reckoning had been adopted by Britain. The year henceforth would begin officially on January 1 instead of March 25, and eleven days must be dropped from the calendar to accommodate to the rest of Europe. Ben's birthday would come on January 17, rather than the sixth. The shift over was made by declaring the day following September 2 to be the fourteenth, and mobs in some places rioted and demanded, "Give us back our eleven days!"

About the first of December he may well have paused outside the State House to watch the hanging of the bell which had cracked some months before when it was tested following its arrival from England. The American copper, added during its recasting, had made the tone very indifferent, and this bell—which would ring out for Liberty twenty-four summers later—had just been melted and recast a second time.

There had been a letter from Boston early in this final month of 1752, describing the critical illness of the eldest of his own brothers, John Franklin. Quickly designing a device which might relieve his suffering, he managed to contrive the first flexible catheter known in America. "I went immediately to the silversmiths"—undoubtedly Phil Syng's—"and gave directions for making one (sitting by till it was finished) that it might be ready for the post" on December 8. In London, a fortnight later, the Royal Society would be listening with increasing deference to how this able, erudite man had flown his electrical kite.

For nearly ten years Ben had kept up a lively interest in Hudson Bay and neighboring cold-water regions to the north of Canada. During about half that period there had been a parliamentary reward of twenty thousand pounds waiting to be paid to the discoverers of a Northwest Passage. This had brought heightened interest, even in America, and early in 1753 he aided Chief Justice William Allen in raising nine hundred pounds for the equipping of the schooner *Argo*, in command of Capt. Charles Swayne, which sailed off to the north in April. The skipper returned safely in November, after being held back by the extra-heavy ice of that season in Hudson Bay. But the subscribers listened intently to his account of the trip at a banquet in a private room in the Bull's Head Tavern, felt he had made worthwhile contributions, and agreed to dispatch him again the following year. Thus Franklin played a leading part in the first of many American attempts to penetrate the Arctic.

In May he was corresponding with an English barrister with whom he would be intimately associated in the years ahead. His name was Richard Jackson, and because of his extensive knowledge, Charles Lamb, years later, dubbed him "Omniscient" Jackson. The purpose of the letter was to convey Franklin's disgust at the quality and character of the German immigrants of that day, also at what he thought to be such completely unwarranted welfare expenditures, which ran counter to his close-grained sense of thrift. Some of his biting comments of this nature were soon due to be used against him politically.

Although he was no longer faced with the day to day problems of the printing office, he had by no means lost interest in ways of improving its processes. Better equipment and methods were much in his mind during the remainder of his life, and he managed at this time to send off specifications for alterations to be made in the construction of a press which seem to have had much merit.

Also the subject of religion came to the fore again, and his position on certain phases of this controversial subject had to be restated in a letter to Joseph Huey, written early in June. While the insufficiency of "good works" seemed so clearly apparent to some, and was so readily subscribed to by others, Franklin boldly maintained that "the worship of God is a duty; the hearing and reading of sermons may be useful; but, if men rest in hearing and praying, as too many do, it is as if a tree should value itself on being water'd and putting forth leaves, tho'it never produc'd any fruit." He wished to see works, "real good works, works of kindness, charity, mercy, and public spirit; not holiday-keeping, sermon-reading or hearing, performing church cere-monies, or making long prayers, filled with flatteries and com-pliments, despis'd even by wise men, and much less capable of pleasing the Deity." Short on theology, he ran way long on humanitarianism.

Leaving instructions for the inauguration of a local "Penny-Post," he set off to the north on a ten weeks' survey of post roads, offices, and carriers. Although as yet still only comptroller of the system, he was already making distinct improvements in this com-munication service, which would prove to be one of the larger contributions toward eventual Independence. This new idea be-ing tried out in Philadelphia was but one small example of his many contributions, and was described briefly in the *Gazette* of July 5, which made the following offer: "Whatever Letters, for Persons living in Town, remaining uncall'd for, on those Days they are brought to the Post Office, will the next Morning, be sent out by a Penny-Post provided for that Purpose." Three weeks later it was necessary to announce: "*Note*, That the Penny-Post would have delivered those [letters listed, and] directed to Persons living in Town, if he could have found their places of Abode." Evidently there were discrepancies in addresses even in those days.

The colonial postal system reached from Portsmouth, New Hampshire, to Charleston in South Carolina. From the north to Philadelphia it was very regular and fairly fast for that time. From Philadelphia south to Williamsburg it depended upon volume, for the carrier waited before a start was made in either direction until there were sufficient items to defray the cost of a trip. From Williamsburg on down to Charleston the service was both erratic and infrequent. It was due for further overhaul and marked improvement during the next few years.

By July, Ben was in the Boston area. Harvard, at which he had aimed a few venomous darts as Silence Dogood in the columns of the *Courant,* had long since forgiven the enmity of the raw printer's lad and member of that struggling newspaper's "Clan of Honest Wags," and now graciously awarded the famous electrician and philosopher its Master of Arts degree. Had either the college, or the recipient, been aware of happenings current at that very moment in London, this act would have seemed doubly appropriate and timely.

Naturally taciturn and given little to small talk, it was perhaps on this journey that he perfected a device to relieve him of a grilling at every inn at which he sought to put up for the night. This ruse, as he explained it, was to preserve his own "tranquillity." Entering a hostelry, he would announce, "I am Benjamin Franklin. I was born in Boston. I am a printer by profession, am travelling to Philadelphia, shall have to return by such a time, and have no news. Now, what can you give me for dinner?" Mine host's long interrogation was thus avoided.

In New Haven, early in September, Yale honored him in the very same fashion that its famous contemporary had done a few weeks before in Cambridge. Honor was indeed flowing, and to him to whom honor was due.

He was at home but little longer than it took to resaddle his horse, and then off again for a stay at the Widow Piper's Tavern in Carlisle, one hundred twenty miles to the west. Together with Richard Peters, and Isaac Norris, he was chosen to act in place of the governor of the province in treating with certain chiefs of the Six Nations returning home to Ohio country from a powwow with Governor Dinwiddie in Virginia. This raw and but recently settled frontier town was thus the scene of Ben's entrance into the field of diplomacy.

It took four days to make the journey, and commissioners and Indians both arrived on September 26. The Philadelphians were somewhat at a loss to know what was expected of them, but they fell into the competent hands of George Croghan, shrewd Indian trader, and the halfbreed Andy Montour, who had been at the Virginia conclave at Winchester. Also present was the "Holder of the Heavens," that great and good friend of the Indians and chief interpreter for Pennsylvania, Conrad Weiser.

The program was laid out with their invaluable aid, and run off under the guidance of these three men fully familiar with Indian protocol. The proceedings dragged on for several days, held up by the delay of a wagon train from Philadelphia bearing gifts needed to bind the savages to any treaty that was made. Finally, after a couple of days of time-consuming ceremonies, satisfactory arrangements were arrived at, and the rum promised the natives as part of the bargain was turned over to them. Thereupon the savages staged a night of fantastic orgies that the ex-printer never forgot.

It was a revealing experience indeed, and he would write, and Franklin & Hall would print later that same year, a full account of the conference in book form, titled *A Treaty Held with the Ohio Indians at Carlisle in October, 1753.* And thirty years later, as he rested from the greatest mission of his long diplomatic career, he would write again about these native American peoples. His *Remarks concerning the Savages of North America* seemed almost to point back to this first diplomatic encounter in a tiny frontier village, from whence a trail that was destined to lead to the winning of the West, and to empire, swung south down the great Piedmont Plateau.

But one of the principal things Ben brought away from Carlisle was his friendship for Croghan, and especially for Conrad Weiser. He would be allied with this latter most colorful gentleman in further equally colorful enterprises shortly.

It was surely late October, or early November, before his extensive travels were over and he was back in his library in the house at the southeast corner of Sassafras and Second Streets. But he returned to find the most cheering of news awaiting him. During his more recent absence word had at last been received of his appointment, back in July, as the Deputy Postmaster General. He was certain he could make himself especially useful in this post.

And while he was receiving the congratulations of his family and friends, still other honors were being conferred on him across a broad ocean. That very same Royal Society which he had thought tended to withhold recognition at the outset of his electrical experiments was now awarding him the Sir Godfrey Copley Medal for work in the field of "Lightning and Electricity." It would be well into the new year before word reached him—a year in which he would lay one of the deeper foundation stones of federal union and American Independence.

## XI.  For an Indestructible Union

### 1754-1755

*I mentioned it yesterday to your Excellency as my opinion, that excluding the people of the colonies from all share in the choice of the grand council [of a Colonial Union], would probably give extreme dissatisfaction, as well as taxing them by act of Parliament, where they have no representative. In matters of general concern to the people, and especially where burthens are to be laid upon them, it is of use to consider, as well what they will be apt to think and say, as what they ought to think. . . . That it is supposed an undoubted right of Englishmen, not to be taxed but by their own consent given through their representatives. . . . That compelling the colonies to pay money without their consent, would be rather like raising contributions in an enemy's country, than taxing Englishmen for their own public benefit.*—Letter of December 18, 1754, to Governor William Shirley of Massachusetts.

ONE rather vivid recollection that Franklin may well have brought back with him fom his journey beyond the Susquehanna would be that of whole families in transit to new homes. If his trip was made via Lancaster, it would have taken him through the Conestoga Valley, whose carpenters and smiths were already busily turning out that famous "vehicle of empire," the Conestoga wagon, chief goods carrier of early frontier days and ancestor of the prairie schooner.

Had it been four years earlier, he might by chance have ridden along for a time beside just such a wagon, bearing the effects of a family leaving their farm in Berks County. They were heading west, and then south, into new country—and thus into Indian country—which ultimately meant a struggle for possession of any land on which they "squatted." A gangling sixteen-year-old, his long rifle resting lightly on the horn of his saddle as he jogged along ahead, would be a prominent figure within a few years, and today personifies this whole eighteenth-century trek of the land-hungry. His name was Daniel Boone.

And while Franklin surely never encountered Boone, he was fully conscious of his kind, and filled with the realization that destiny lay in the western reaches to, and over, the Alleghenies. A contest for empire was building up there. It would be engineered by the French, but implemented especially by their Indian allies, and there was dire need of a strong union of the highly independent American colonies to oppose this threat.

In fact there had been disturbing news exchanged at Carlisle. The French were building a line of forts in the Ohio Valley. And shortly after his return from that parley, the Governor of Virginia sent a young twenty-one-year-old militia officer to warn the interlopers out of what the Virginians very definitely considered their territory. The youthful major's name was George Washington, and Franklin was due to meet him within a year or so, and under quite unexpected circumstances.

In fact by early 1754 the Virginians were considering military measures in the country to the west, and soliciting aid of the Pennsylvania province. But Quaker hesitancy toward embroilment in "aggressive action," and a feeling by the proprietary party of "let's wait and see if anything beyond Virginian interests are threatened," resulted in no aid being extended. Then in May came the unsettling news that a Virginian fort had been taken, and the Indians were stomping out war dances and getting ready for scalping sorties all along Pennsylvania's unprotected borders. While even these fearful threats brought no immediate action on money bills or military preparations, they did suggest the advisability of sending commissioners to a congress of the northern colonies long scheduled to be held in June at Albany.

Despite the fact that invitations to attend had been issued in London the year before by the Lords of Trade, the colonial response had been cautious and delayed. While its immediate purpose was to appease and hold in line the powerful Indian confederacy, the Six Nations, there was suggestion of some sort of colonial union, which seemed to promise the stifling of independent action by the several colonies and the surrender of certain rights. But even with Indian threats looming large and the benefits of concerted action quite evident, it was late May before Pennsylvania named its representatives and signed their commissions. They were John Penn, good-for-nothing grandson of founder William Penn, and stuffy, hidebound Richard Peters from the Common Council, together with Isaac Norris and Benjamin Franklin from the Assembly.

Franklin, surely the most ardent advocate of union among the four, had been busily broadcasting its advantages through the pages of the *Gazette*. Whether or not he was familiar with the Chinese proverb setting forth the comparative merits of a picture as opposed to a thousand words is not certain. He did feel very intently the need of driving home certain truths, and came forward with the first American newspaper cartoon. It was a drawing of a snake cut into eight sections, each labelled with the initials of one of the colonies, and bore the caption, "Join or Die."

It was June 17 before the Pennsylvanians arrived at Albany, three days after the congress was to have assembled. Yet they were in ample time, for members of the Six Nations with which they were to treat, were purposely more tardy. While the program for dealing with the savages was being worked out, it was resolved among the delegates that some form of colonial union appeared essential, and a seven-man committee, of which Franklin was a member, was appointed to suggest suitable arrangements.

Immediately the gentleman from the Quaker City was right in his element. For several years, three at least, he had been devising means to such an end, and while others present had ideas of their own, the Franklin "hints" seems to have predominated. In early July he was asked to draft the *Plan*, which had been agreed upon after debate. His proposals were accepted, and then transmitted for approval to the assemblies in all of the colonies.

On the surface at least, the Albany sessions seemed to have been highly successful. A promise of loyalty to the English had been exacted from the savages in return for wagonloads of presents, and the delegates had favored putting up a united front in opposition to French infiltration and connivance. Yet while the natives were being appeased and lip service was being paid to joint action, an incident in southwestern Pennsylvania had touched off a war that would spread across the ocean to Europe and on to India. A Virginia officer, George Washington backed up by a handful of militiamen, had surrendered a small log stockade he had dubbed "Fort Necessity" to the French. In the Old World the long-drawn-out hostilities that resulted were called the Seven Years' War. In America the name would be the French and Indian War. But in reality it was the "war for empire," which strengthened the British hand in North America, and was in a manner a prelude to the Revolution.

While every colony would soon be involved, not a single one of them had the foresight to approve of the *Plan of Union*. Said its author long later: "Its fate was singular: the assemblies did not adopt it, as they all thought there was too much *prerogative* in it, and in England it was judg'd to have too much of the *democratic*."

Home again briefly after the Albany Congress, Ben seems to have found at least one relaxing evening, as he joined with his many Scots friends in the Assembly Room on Hamilton Wharf at the foot of Walnut Street. The local chapter of the St. Andrews Society was having its summer outing, and there was much singing and gaiety.

Not too long afterward he felt the necessity of being about his enlarged postal duties, and he set off on a four months' trip to New York and New England, during which he would visit every office in the northern colonies. Whether it was while he was still at home, or during the early stages of this trip, he drafted a *Plan for Settling Two Western Colonies in North America*. As was not infrequently true in Franklin proposals, there was an immediate and well-stressed purpose, which might be termed the principal ax to be ground. And besides there was customarily a less apparent but equally real need, a sort of smaller hatchet wanting to be edged up a bit.

This plan was such a bifurcated proposition. It aimed primarily at enlarging the number of settlers in the West, as an offset to the growing French strength in that area. But it appears the Indians had sold to a Connecticut syndicate "clear" title to an area in the Wyoming Valley in central Pennsylvania, presumably within the Penn grant. Settlers from several of the New England colonies had been encouraged to buy farms in this section, and were streaming in, fully prepared to sustain their belief this land had been granted to the Connecticut colony before it was handed to the Penns to quash the Admiral's sixteen thousand pound claim against the Crown. It was Ben's intent "to divert the Connecticut emigrants from their design of invading this province and so induce them to go where they would be less injurious and more useful." But the secondary design was not especially successful, and, by a strange quirk of fortune, the author of the pamphlet thirty odd years later would be called upon to clear away the results of a "war" that ensued over the Connecticut settlers' claims.

William Franklin had been made postmaster in Philadelphia to succeed his father, and had then given up that office to one of his mother's relatives when he was moved up to comptroller of the whole system. In Boston, Ben appointed his ailing brother John to handle the local office, which the latter carried on until his death two years later. He in turn was succeeded by his wife, which is believed to have been the first instance in America of a woman holding public office.

But Ben's stay in New England, which continued on through the winter, gave him many contacts with a most zealous supporter of *Union*, Governor William Shirley of Massachusetts. Yet the plan his excellency advocated would have given the colonists but little say in their community affairs. Franklin astutely criticized it in a series of letters, and thus managed advance training for the sort of problems he would soon be facing up to in London. The quote from one of his missives at the beginning of this chapter contained the selfsame arguments he would be pouring into the ears, and he hoped the minds, of his majesty's ministers through the years ahead. In fact these very letters would be published when the need came for all Britain to have a clear and unequivocal statement of the American position. But the fact of his being favorably known to Shirley would be a godsend of quite another order, as far as Franklin was concerned, in less than a year's time.

As he started back toward Philadelphia after the turn into 1755, he kept to the coast road, as was his custom. Perhaps at this season there was promise of less snow along shores swept by salt-laden breezes. Stopping at Newport, or perhaps it was at Westerly, he met a stunning, highly intelligent young woman, less than half his own age. Her maiden name was Catherine Ray, and at once he was truly smitten. After spending a number of days in her stimulating company, he regretfully put her aboard a small vessel to cross the sound to her home on Block Island. As Franklin headed on into Connecticut himself, she was very much in his mind, and it is possible that, before he reached home, letters from her, a trifle indiscreet she later thought, may have caught up with him. He had been back in Philadelphia but a few days when he replied, and thus began a friendship, sustained principally by correspondence, that lasted for the remainder of his life. Yet even after she married into the prominent Greene family, the Greenes and the Franklins were much in each others thoughts, and homes, during the years ahead.

He had sought for any news of the tense situation in the Ohio country and along the Pennsylvania frontier as he made his way south, but reassurance did not come until he was back in home territory again. Word had either recently arrived, or was soon handed in by his post riders, that a shipload of British dragoons had landed at Hampton Roads. They were under command of an officer of the Coldstream Guards, a General Edward Braddock. Their momentous objective was to put an end to the threat of the French and Indian allies in the Ohio Valley and ultimately drive these Gallic intruders out of North America entirely.

Ben very likely was much interested in the fact that the governors of the four major colonies, Massachusetts, New York, Pennsylvania, and Virginia, together with the head of the Maryland colony, were to confer with Braddock at Alexandria on the lower Potomac River in April. He may even have talked with Governor Shirley as that gentleman passed through to the south for the meeting.

He would also have been interested in a somewhat different enterprise, a move of his partner James Parker. He had become printer not only to New York and New Jersey, but for Yale College as well, and was just then launching the *Connecticut Gazette*, which Franklin had considered on his stop at New Haven. But things nearer at home now began to boil up. There was much to-do in the Assembly over the voting of funds to support this British army headed for the frontier. And then suddenly Franklin found himself on the way to confer with Braddock, whom he was to meet at Frederick, in Maryland. With William as his aide, but in his capacity of Deputy Postmaster General, he rode off for his rendezvous. Presumably his chief purpose was to arrange with this stubborn and opinionated commander-in-chief of all American forces for a special postal service that would keep him in the most rapid communication possible with the tidewater sections.

Once in contact with the Britisher, he found that the mission had a dual purpose. Braddock had acquired a strong antipathy for Quakers, and thus for Pennsylvanians, and the diplomatic Ben Franklin had been dispatched to soften the attitude of this important personage. They got on very well, and then most admirably, after Franklin mortgaged his whole financial future by obtaining wagons and trace and pack horses in the Susquehanna Valley to help move the army into western Pennsylvania, where the French were to be decimated, or driven into Canada.

Ben rode back to Philadelphia, perhaps observing along the way the whirlwind of which he would write so full an account to Collinson that fall. He had neglected this good friend most shamefully, and he took time out now to get a very long letter off to him in June, covering unanswered questions from the correspondence of the former year, finishing up a "philosophical packet" long promised, and assuring the gentleman in London that he was "sick" of politics and of being a go-between for the governor and the proprietary faction on the one hand and the Quaker bloc on the other. He would, he claimed, refuse election were it not that he felt that now and then he influenced adoption of some worthwhile legislation.

He was on hand for the dedication ceremonies of the new Masonic Temple, and had some time to give to a new clerk or secretary, whom he had promised, "Diet at my own Table, with Lodging and washing and £25 per annum." This Daniel Fisher worked for the Postmaster General only briefly, but long enough to leave a somewhat raffish picture of Deborah Franklin protesting in violent language about the people who troubled her "Pappy" by their everlasting demands upon him, and remarking of son William, "There goes the greatest villain upon earth." The implication was that the father much preferred the son to her; and Fisher records in his diary that she was turbulent, jealous, and proud by nature. The incident, nonetheless, tended to raise again the question of William's rather dubious maternity.

This young Virginian was still in Franklin's employ on July 18 when, about mid-afternoon, an express galloped into town bearing the prostrating news that the obdurate General Braddock and his forces had been wiped out in an ambush in the hills in southwestern Pennsylvania nine days before. Ben's heart must have skipped several beats, for the commander-in-chief, on whom he was dependent to make good the repayment pledges he had given in person for horses and wagons garnered from upstate farmers, now lay in a grave beside a lonesome trail in the wilderness. The local Assembly had agreed to foot the costs of special postal services, but not this other obligation. Franklin faced financial ruin, the summer heat that year he found prostrating, and the aroused populace, threatening the persons and property of the pacifist Quakers, made life highly uncomfortable. Assembly affairs, too, were extremely abrasive, and in a letter in August he protested, "I abhor these altercations, and if I did not love the country and the people would remove immediately into a more quiet government, Connecticut, where I am also happy enough to have many friends."

It was not until October that he breathed easily again. His friend Governor Shirley of Massachusetts had been appointed as commander-in-chief to succeed Braddock, and considerately ordered payment of the obligations Franklin had, in an excess of patriotism, incurred. They amounted to nearly twenty thousand pounds.

Relief from this worry merely made room for other concerns, for fear and apprehension soon stalked the province from end to end. Where would the now unopposed French—or their savage allies—strike next? One especially vulnerable spot would be the northeast, close to the more populous sections, and in the area where, eighteen years before, the Delawares had been so treacherously dealt with in the nefarious "Walking Purchase." While not a powerful or warlike tribe, they would willingly contribute to retaliation for the manner in which they had been so roundly cheated. There would be bloodshed in the western reaches as well, with a threat to Philadelphia itself from at least two directions. But the city seemed less vulnerable, and the refugees from outlying areas began to head in its direction.

The lines of cleavage in the Assembly—with loyalty to the non-resisting Friends, or to the governor and proprietary group —became even more marked. Because Franklin esteemed the Quakers generally, and even respected their religious scruples against bearing arms or participating in armed conflict (although he did not share them), and because he demanded the proprietors bear their full share of the burden of defense, Franklin soon had the proprietary contingent hurling their choicest epithets at him. Actually he held the balance of power in the Assembly, and letters were dispatched to Thomas Penn in England reporting what a malefactor he was.

It was a busy fall, calling up all his conciliatory abilities, but by November he was able to draft a military bill with sufficient compromise so that it had support from both sides and became law. It provided for a state militia, while granting to the Friends the right to refuse service because of their conscientious objections. There was also a companion bill providing funds to equip the fighting men and prosecute a war if need be. A committee of seven, with peaceably disposed Franklin at its head, provided a sort of war department. And this action came none too soon, for the night before the legislation became law, the Indians struck, and wiped out an isolated German mission settlement at Gnadenhuetten about seventy-five miles to the north of Philadelphia.

This incursion set up a mad scramble of the "Dutch" settlers from the back countries, and a mob surged down to the Quaker City and drew up before the governor's residence on Second Street, bearing scalped corpses as gruesome and incontrovertible evidence. "What," they demanded to know, "were the Proprietors doing, or prepared to do, for their better protection?" Governor Morris assured a deputation from his unwanted guests that the Penns had put up some five hundred pounds, and the Assembly much, much more. So why didn't they take themselves up Chestnut Street to the State House and there consult with Mr. Franklin?

That middle-aged philosopher, into whose somewhat reluctant hands the safety of the province had been thrust, was now on duty "every day, Sunday not excluded." It happened that on that particular afternoon, November 26, the Assembly was in session, and the naturally taciturn Franklin was forced to make a speech. Facing the protesting host, he was convincing enough that the throng dispersed peaceably, and, in view of his promises, returned to their homes. But something constructive had to be done, and promptly, too, and it became clearer daily who the one person in the province seemed to be that was capable of bringing order out of threatening chaos.

Governor Morris, who had taken over from the unwilling Hamilton, was forced to act, and swallowing his pride as best he could, summoned the chairman of the Committee of Defense. It was necessary, Morris explained rather haltingly, that he attend a conference in New York. So, would Mr. Franklin take such of his fellow commissioners as he felt might be necessary, and repair to Bethlehem and Easton and make provision for the security of that imperiled section of the province? There would be a full-scale meeting of all the commissioners on New Year's Day in the little frontier community of Reading, by which time, the governor gave assurance, he would have returned from New York and be on hand. Philosopher Franklin was about to become "General" Franklin.

Preparations were hurriedly made, and at sunup on December 18 a contingent of some fifty cavalrymen, and three Conestoga wagons of supplies, left by the Bethlehem road for the important

Moravian settlement in the Lehigh Valley to the north. The cavalry was in part an escort to three gentlemen of quality. First among them was the Honorable James Hamilton, ex-governor, and son of Andrew Hamilton, a former Franklin patron. There was also Joseph Fox, Quaker chairman of the Assembly's potent committee of accounts, and the other, the rather portly Co-deputy Postmaster for America, as some official papers named that office. But this wintry morning he was not launching out upon postal matters, but the martial business of defense. The Moravians whom he was about to visit would insist on calling him "General" Franklin, and as though to carry out the role, an aide rode deferentially behind him as they left the city. This was of course his son William. Of the four, this latter was in fact the only one who had had any first-hand military experience.

On the second evening, December 19, the party, its cavalry escort, and at least one of its baggage wagons arrived at Bethle-hem, fifty-five miles away over one of the most frightful stretches of road imaginable. But Ben, long used to the saddle, came through in top form despite a fit of illness that had had him in bed for a week the previous month. Travel so stimulated him that he could, until his final years, always make light of its incon-veniences and excessive demands. The night was spent in the Crown Inn on the south bank of the Lehigh River, opposite the novel Moravian monastery. The band of "quietists," or religious mystics, that had planted this spiritual outpost in the wilderness, had been a powerful influence in the area for the past fourteen years.

There had been a persistent rumor that attacks would be made along this frontier on Christmas Day, and the settlers had deserted their outlying cabins, and swelled the little town to three times its customary five hundred inhabitants. But a stout stockade had been thrown up about the principal buildings of the Brotherhood, and things seemed reasonably secure, so the military party pressed on the following day to Easton.

Here Ben was overjoyed to find William Parsons, one of the early Junto members, who had been laying out this new town-site at the junction of the Lehigh and Delaware Rivers. It, like Bethlehem, was overrun with settlers from roundabout, but lacked the stabilizing influences of the mission in the larger community to the west. The tiny "town in the forks" was destitute of food and any sense of order or military preparation. An attempt was begun to enlist a regiment from among the townspeople and refugees and to make the settlement less vulnerable to a surprise attack. But the enlistments were very sluggish, contrary to Ben's hopes, yet much to the gratification of the proprietary member of the group. That whole faction had been basically opposed to this militia act which Franklin had pressed through the Assembly.

Theoretically, at least, Hamilton, an ex-governor, was ranking member in this three-man junta sent to buoy up the sagging fortitude of the border towns. But his amusement at Ben's difficulties in encouraging men to bear arms in their own defense perhaps terminated the latter's sense of compliance during their ten days at this outpost. On the last day of their stay Franklin took over, began issuing orders, commissioned Parsons a major, put him in command of the inductees, and did his best to whip the community into some manner of security before he left. If he was worthy of being called a "general" by the common folk up here at the edge of the wilderness, perhaps he had better get down to playing the part.

The Christmas they had spent in Easton had been neither cozy nor especially merry, although the savages had not struck as had been expected. There was perhaps little more to be expected from the New Year's Day to be put in at the cluster of log houses about a muddy central square fifty-five miles to the west. But be there they must, and on December 30 they started off, stopping that night in Bethlehem. This gave Franklin an opportunity to meet the head of the Brotherhood, Bishop Spangenberg, and Ben and "Brother Joseph" became fast friends.

Early on the morning of the last day of the year the group was off again, heading for "Redding town" over the King's Highway laid out three years previously. But it was more than a single day's journey, and New Year's Eve would have to be spent along the way. While there is no definite record, it is thought they put up at the hospitable tavern of Dan Levan in Maxatawny township.

Was there anything by way of celebration? Surely the two top men in the party were both convivial gentlemen, and they can hardly have allowed such an evening to pass without laying aside their paltry differences and assuaging their cares while draining a festive bowl.

For Ben Franklin it had been a fantastic year indeed. And actually something more than just the year was drawing to a close. Within less than three weeks he would be having another birthday—his fiftieth. A half-century—a rather remarkable half century, too—had been lived. It had been an accomplishment in which one might take reasonable pride. Still, the best years of a lifetime were, in many respects, yet to come.

## XII. The Colonial Agent in London

### *1756–1758*

*Our Assembly talk of sending me to England speedily. Then look out sharp, and if a fat old fellow should come to your printing-house and request a little smouthing [job work], depend upon it 'tis your affectionate frieind and humble servant, B. Franklin.*—Letter of January 31, 1757, to William Strahan.

NEW YEAR'S morning, 1756, Ben was up betimes, and, with his companions and escort, cantered off down the still rather rugged King's Highway toward Reading. As Dan Levan bid them good-by, and they swung out from the tavern yard, the unbroken wall-like mass of Blue Mountain that lost itself in the horizon to the northeast and southwest frowned down a bit ominously at the horsemen. Was the enemy really lurking right now just behind this huge rampart a dozen or more miles to the north?

By early afternoon they reached Reading, reined in their mounts in the town square, and were welcomed by the governor and his party, who had arrived about an hour before. The conference went into session the following morning and continued through that day and into the next, when a courier from Bethlehem burst in upon them with the perturbing news that the Indians had struck again at the mission outpost at Gnadenhuetten in the narrow valley of the Lehigh, the only passable defile through the unbroken mass of Blue Mountain. A detachment of soldiers sent to hold this important pass after the first attack had been thrown back, and the country from Easton to Reading was once more vulnerable.

Governor Morris had agreed to treat with important Indian

chiefs at Harris's Ferry on the Susquehanna, fifty odd miles further west. Feeling this would prove less arduous—yes, and less dangerous, too—he designated Franklin to be the preserver of the neighboring "back counties." Drawing a *dedimus* that virtually granted the "general" the powers of a field marshal, the governor retained most of the officials, including crafty old Conrad Weiser, and half the cavalry escort, for his own purposes, and on the morning of Tuesday, January 6, bid Ben and his shrunken party godspeed as they set out for a return to Bethlehem. His excellency would go on toward the west the following day.

For a man who some years later would resolutely maintain that "there never was a good war or a bad peace," this assignment might seem a bitter pill. But Ben took it in stride and in good part, consoled, no doubt, because it was decidely in the public welfare. For variety's sake he toasted his shins before the fire at Peter Trexler's hostelry that evening on the way back, and the next afternoon, Wednesday the seventh, was again in Bethlehem.

There he would stay among the Brethren and the still increasing refugees for eight days, and leave enviable evidence of organizational ability and military know-how. On Saturday the Bishop arranged a musical evening that was a real treat to Franklin, who also took a profound interest in the church service the following morning, and in the Moravian mores, religious and secular, throughout his visit.

On the morning of the fifteenth the "general" was at the head of a considerable party of soldiers and axmen, heading north to establish a substantial fort in the Lehigh gap at Gnadenhuetten in place of the former, but ill-fated, "Huts of Grace" now totally destroyed. It was only twenty miles, but the going was slow and the weather wretched. The printer-philosopher-soldier spent his fiftieth birthday in a fair tavern run by a resolute soul, Nicholas Uplinger, waiting for a freezing downpour to cease.

But the skies finally cleared, the party reached the site, the men worked willingly, and on the twenty-fifth Fort Allen, named in honor of Ben's present arch-enemy, the chief justice, was completed and christened. There had been a few desultory shots fired from considerable distance by Indian scouts lurking high above the valley as the work progressed. This was "General" Franklin's baptism of fire. During the next fortnight two less pretentious stockades were erected, one fifteen miles west along the escarpment that is Blue Mountain, the other a similar distance east of the break-through of the Lehigh River. One was designated Fort Norris, the other Fort Franklin.

There was now a hurried call, however, for the soldier to give place to the statesman. The meeting date of the Assembly had been capriciously advanced a full month to February 3. By the time the word reached Ben at Fort Allen deep in the wilds he would have to hurry. Fortunately a military adventurer from New England, a Colonel William Clapham, hove in sight at about this time seeking employment for his Indian-fighting abilities. Said Franklin, "I gave him a commission and, parading the garrison, had it read before them; and introduced him to them as an officer who from his skill in military affairs was much more fit to command them than myself; and, after giving them a little exhortation, took my leave."

This civilian had, however, done very well by this frontier area with his soldiering. Enlistments at last caught hold, and there were now five hundred or more men under arms. Fortifications had been erected, and, better still, a fair measure of confidence restored. Wednesday afternoon, February 4, the ex-general appeared in Bethlehem, had his horse shod, his bridle mended, and put up for the night. The next day he and son Billy pushed their horses hard, and late that night were bedded down at home in Philadelphia, his fifty concentrated days of military life behind him. He maintained this late arrival was intentional, having been determined to ward off a grand entrance amid a cavalcade of horsemen, which his friends had secretly planned to give him.

Father and son had missed the opening sessions of the Assembly, and also a most remarkable performance when the self-complacent governor took complete personal credit for the securing of the frontier. Being in disrepute with the proprietors, the hard pressed Morris appropriated the Franklin accomplishments to shore up his own sagging fortunes. But there would still be ample fireworks, many of the displays involving the now highly influential leader of the anti-proprietary forces. One was the outcome of the militia bill he had fostered.

Patriotism being perhaps more infectious here in the city, the ranks of the newly formed Regiment and Artillery Company of Philadelphia had been fairly well filled before he left for the "wars." He had had some intimation that the associators were demanding he be made colonel. When Governor Morris had hesitated in confirming their selection, a considerable contingent had flowed down Second Street and raised such a "rumpus" as to threaten blowing the stone shingles from the "Slate Roof House" that was the executive mansion. In view of this tender of their determination, the appointment was agreed to, although the commission was held back until late in February.

However, being a legally constituted military officer produced certain complications. Highly ambitious as well as patriotic, the members of his regiment drilled nightly in the broad High Street. The young ladies found it very exciting, while young gentlemen not members of this group found it distasteful, and soon organized a competitive regiment of their own and began to cast aspersions. This anti-Franklin regiment came to offer a real challenge, and finally on March 16 his original body of troops held a review on Society Hill that climaxed anything of its kind ever seen in the province. The applause and huzzahs of the crowds left its members feeling pretty cocky. They insisted on escorting their colonel to his home, and in front of it fired off a volley that smashed window panes and some of his choice electrical equipment.

The following day, as he was starting off for Virginia, twenty regimental officers galloped before his house, prepared to act as an honor guard as far as Gray's Ferry, three miles southwest of town. There was much stir and clatter as they moved off, and "to the end of the street, which is about two hundred yards, the grenadiers took it in their heads to ride with their swords drawn."

Embarrassed, yet more than a little titillated by this demonstration, their colonel bid them adieu at the ferry, and rode off to the south. But in the Quaker City consternation reigned among the opposition forces. Such gestures were reserved only for princes of the blood, so this was most tangible evidence that the man Franklin was bent on treason or becoming a dictator. Archsycophant Richard Peters, who found special satisfaction in depreciating the leader of the opposition to the Penns, now had a heyday. Already looked upon as dangerous and hostile, the very person who had possibly saved the Penn's province from invasion was now adjudged to be their certain enemy. Penn even went so far at one time as to attempt to have this leader of the opposition stripped of his postmastership.

But it was April in Williamsburg, and in an atmosphere of peace and serenity the College of William and Mary conferred the third honorary Master of Arts degree upon Mr. Deputy Postmaster General. A week later the borough of Norfolk made him a "freeman and Burgess." Perhaps, too, the fifty-year-old *Colonel* Franklin met again with the twenty-four-year-old *Colonel* Washington, with whom he had talked in February in Philadelphia, when the younger man, disgruntled with the manner in which he was being used by his native Virginia, had sought military employment in the colony to the north. He and Franklin were much interested in a joint project involving the two colonies, a post road from Philadelphia to Winchester.

He returned in time to take his place in the May session of the Assembly, and was totally unaware when the twenty-ninth came and went that some three thousand miles away a venerable body of natural philosophers had voted him in as a fellow of the Royal Society. The pleasant news of this induction would take a month of more to arrive. It was at about this time that he stepped out as president of the College, Academy and Charity School, although continuing as one of its directors. But this educational facility had come under control of a group utterly opposed to his own views, and one of the most vocal of his enemies, the Rev. William Smith, was now made its provost.

In June he hurried to New York with a formal "address" to Governor Shirley, retiring as commander-in-chief, and bid his friend good-by as he sailed home to England. But Ben was soon back, and embroiled afresh in Assembly matters. In August came a new governor, William Denny, and with him, in a handsomely velveted case, was the Copley medal, awarded to Ben three years previously by the Royal Society. The exceeding promptness with which Denny presented this token on the night of his own welcoming reception made the gesture appear to be part of a program engineered by the proprietary faction. Their opponent was being subjected to persuasion in the hope that a new flow of honor and preferment in his direction might make him more amenable. Denny even offered to commission Franklin a general and send him off at the head of militia forces to capture Fort Duquesne on the site of the present-day Pittsburgh, feeling it could keep him away from Assembly affairs for months, or perhaps permanently. The gentleman, however, was sufficiently astute to see through this ruse.

In September came an urgent plea from Aaron Burr the elder, head of the college just then moving into its new buildings at Princeton. Would Mr. Franklin very kindly bring his "electrical globes" with him and come and minister to New Jersey's Governor Belcher sinking into complete paralysis? Ben, forced to beg off in a crisis over a money bill, sent along equipment and instructions in the hope "Brother Jonathan" might be helped, but to no avail.

Collinson had written him that rumor had it that the Franklin-Penn relations were at a new low ebb, but in November he was almost jovially suggesting to his English friend not to worry. But his levity soon gave way to earnest concern. The French threat to the province again became both real and immediate. He and Governor Denny left hastily for Easton to make a treaty with the Delawares, and they had little more than arrived, when Fort Allen, built but ten months before in the Lehigh Gap, together with the little village that had sprung up about it, were wiped out.

Denny, back home in December, and under heavy bonds by the proprietors to play their game of evasion of taxation, soon locked horns with the Assembly, and a showdown became inevitable. It was not long delayed, and at the end of January Speaker Isaac Norris and Franklin were appointed to take the matter of proprietary non-co-operativeness to England for decision by the Crown. But the former begged off, and was excused from the journey because of ill health.

An attempt to coerce the issue and vote a money bill was unsuccessful, and the new British commander-in-chief, Lord Loudoun, hastened to Philadelphia and sought to force accession to the proprietary will. In the face of a perilous impasse, Franklin managed to effect a compromise. But on April 4, he and William, who had just resigned from the Assembly clerkship, set off for New York, on the first leg of an extended and, so it later proved, debilitating trip to London. Pennsylvania's battle with her landlord was shifted to the latter's home grounds in London. An able lieutenant, Joseph Galloway, would be called upon to hold Franklin's popular party together.

Father and son were to take passage on a packet that was to be one ship of a sizable convoy, for it was wartime. They made haste in the belief the fleet was about to be off. But Lord Loudoun, who proved to be another master bungler, managed by his dilly-dallying to keep the ships in port until mid-June. Thus there was an opportunity for an excursion into the Passaic Valley country in New Jersey, and two to three weeks at partner James Parker's home at Woodbridge, where Deborah and Sally joined the party. This stay afforded ample time in which to coach Parker in his new duties as comptroller of the postal system. He would be in complete charge for several years, for William Hunter, the co-deputy, was in England for medical treatment, and was never again active in postal affairs. Ben had perfected a highly simplified bookkeeping procedure which had made the records far easier to maintain, and had done so excellent an organizational job that the system soon began to operate for the first time at a profit.

At long last they were away, and the American who had viewed more of, and was known by more people in, his native land than any other single person, was now about to spend many years in Europe, where he was already the most widely known citizen of the New World.

With an abundance of time at his disposal, he laid himself out in preparing the copy of the 1758 issue of *Poor Richard Improved*, the last of the Almanacs he would personally edit. Also he found time for his studies of things having to do with the ocean, which had had to be neglected for the past thirty-one years since his trip home from England as Mr. Denham's clerk.

But despite his employments, it was to prove a grueling voyage, topped off with a threat of shipwreck in its final days. Landing at Falmouth, just inside the Lizzard's Head, almost at Land's

End, the two Franklins made the final two hundred fifty miles overland by chaise, stopping "a little by the way to view Stonehenge on Salisbury Plain and Lord Pembroke's house and gardens, with his very curious antiquities at Wilton." Finally, on July 26, they were warmly welcomed by Peter Collinson at his home on Mill Hill in London, with whom they lodged briefly.

Soon, however, the father and son were ensconced, along with their two Negro body servants, in a four-room suite in the home of the Widow Stevenson at 7 Craven Street, just off the Strand. These quarters, while not exactly "regal," were proper, comfortable, convenient, and decidedly in contrast to those Ben had occupied in Little Britain so many years before.

His first important conference was with Lord Granville, head of the Privy Council. But it proved rather disturbing to find that important minister so partial to place and prerogative, rather than to democracy and justice. Charles Pratt, the attorney general, astonished him by foreseeing a day when the colonies would seek their freedom from Britain. Within the month there was a civil but thoroughly frigid meeting with Thomas Penn, at his home in New Street, Spring Garden. The relations between the proprietors and the Pennsylvania Assembly began to appear virtually irreconcilable, and what had been expected might be a stay of only a few months quickly promised to run into two or three years. Actually about sixteen and a half of the next eighteen years would be spent in England.

And then quite suddenly the several strenuous years just lived through, the recent exacting voyage, and the London weather, to which he was as yet not acclimated, laid Franklin low. He speaks of the ailment as a prolonged cold, but it seems to have been much more serious. There was a relapse after his attempt to be up and about too soon, so that the illness had him incapacitated through much of September and October. In fact it was well into November, despite the admirable care of a long admirer and now fast friend, the Scottish physician John Fothergill, before he had his strength back again. By the end of that month he made a call on ex-Governor Shirley perhaps to explore possibilities of a federal union between colonies and mother country, a sort of imperial arrangement directly under the king, and with regular

American representation at Westminster. Now that he was in circulation again, he began a letter home to which he added afterthoughts during a period of two weeks.

By December he was back in stride again, had his own coach, leased by the month, and the world's foremost electrical authority, not too heavily burdened with political matters at the moment, fairly reveled in philosophical interests which more mundane affairs had in late years crowded aside. Also, since he was to be abroad for some time, he had an Irish artist, John Dixon, do a miniature in oils, which he sent home to Deborah. An entry in his account book shows he paid him £6 6s, or about $30.

Advance copies of *Poor Richard* had arrived, containing the novel preface he had concocted on shipboard, which seems to have found immediate popular response in England. In it the prudential philosopher had taken a selection of the pithy sayings culled from former issues and strung them together in a mono-logue as though spoken by an ancient countryman, Father Abra-ham. This choice bit, variously known as *Father Abraham's Speech, The Way to Wealth,* or *La Science du Bonhomme Richard,* was destined to be reprinted countless times down to the present day in all principal languages, and to achieve world-wide fame. It has proven perhaps the most widely popular of all quotes from American writing, and at once began to increase its author's fame and popularity.

Between his illness and the thought of a prolonged exile, his letters for a while expressed a strong dislike of his surroundings, but this died away as he was caught up in a whirl of social affairs. In February he was heavily engaged in a shopping spree in which he amassed a tremendous store of presents promptly hurried off to the home folk. There was a purchase of electrical equipment for Harvard, the packing of which he supervised. In one of the boxes he tucked a copy of the handsome and unique Baskerville printing of Virgil for the college library. There was an oppor-tunity, too, to serve one of his early loves, the Library Company having asked him to be its purchasing agent.

During the spring he and a newly made acquaintance were busy perfecting a three-wheeled clock the versatile American had thought up. Evenings were usually spent in most congenial company at one or more of several coffeehouses that served various groups as club headquarters. There was noticeably more formality in most associations here in London, and, while he was treated with great cordiality and respect, there were none of the close, long-known Philadelphia friends on hand. Thus B. Franklin, Esquire, was now less familiarly addressed as "Franklin," rather than as "Ben" or "Benjamin," while the increasing use of "Mr. Franklin" by the younger men gave an occasional disturbing reminder that the years were indeed piling up.

Just when is not certain, but fairly soon after arrival he made something of a sentimental journey, visiting the Watt's plant near Lincoln Inn Fields where he had once worked. Stepping up to a press, he inked his form and ran off a few sheets as an indication his hand had not lost its craft. Then he sent the pot-boys scurrying off to neighboring alehouses for refreshments so all might join in a toast of "Success to Printing."

It was perhaps in the late spring of 1758 that William satisfactorily completed his legal studies and was admitted to the English bar. In any event, the two Franklins set off in May for a holiday at Cambridge. There the father got in touch with a former correspondent, Professor John Hadley, with whom he now performed some fascinating experiments in evaporation. So great was the sincere regard shown the American philosopher and diplomat at the University, that he returned to enjoy more of its agreeable atmosphere during the commencement exercises in July. And then, being conveniently located to do a little family research, he explained away his impulse in a letter to Deborah by saying, "I found the journey advantageous to my health, increasing both my health and spirits and therefore as all the great folks were out of town and public business at a stand, I the more easily prevailed upon myself to take another journey."

Turning into Northamptonshire immediately to the west, he and Billy were soon in Wellingboro, where a relative, Mary Franklin Fisher, was found who remembered Josiah Franklin's departure for America seventy-five years previously. In the next town, Ecton, they located the remains of the family's small freehold, the data for two centuries on births, marriages, and deaths, and the graves of several generations of Franklins in the yew-shaded churchyard. In Birmingham, fifty miles further west, they uncovered traces of Deborah Read Franklin's forebears. There, too, the Philadelphia craftsman visited one of the foremost printers and typefounders of those times, John Baskerville.

Back in London in September, he was better reconciled to both the city and the tight little island that contained it. There was a moment of sadness and retrospection when he found word of the passing of two old Junto friends—William Parsons, geographer and major of militia at Easton, and Stephen Potts, humorist, former employee as a bookbinder and erstwhile doorkeeper of the Assembly. Here was unmistakable evidence that time was truly marching on.

But the jaunt of the past several weeks had paid the liberal dividends he always garnered from travel, and his renewed energy began to demand employment. By November he had found it as he started making contributions to a "war of propaganda" that extended through several years. His first endeavor aimed at convincing the British populace that the mountainous military budget of the current war, primarily against the French, was justified. This latter nation formed the main threat to the American frontier.

However, politics would have to share his interests with matters philosophical, and his efforts in this field were not by any means all theoretical and speculative. Visitors at Craven Street that December of 1758 could well have encountered a portly gentleman, down to his waistcoat, somewhat sooty in spots, and on his hands and knees fitting a new false front to his sea-coal grate. He was working out a scheme which had occurred to him, and which he was happy to find yielded more heat and comfort from less fuel, and also cured smoky fireplaces.

He was adjusting to life in England, and beginning to enjoy himself thoroughly. Yet he was surely not going British, for— while there had been rumors back home a twelve-month before that he had been made a baronet, and governor of Pennsylvania —he was still plain Ben Franklin, and American to the very core.

# XIII. A Scottish Holiday

## *1759–1761*

*After we took leave of you, we spent some weeks in Yorkshire and Lincolnshire, and at length arriv'd at our House here in good health, having made a tour of nearly 1500 Miles, in which we had enjoy'd a great deal of Pleasure, and receiv'd a great deal of useful Information. But no part of our Journey affords us, on Recollection a more pleasing Remembrance, than that which relates to Scotland. . . . I enclose you one of our Philadelphia Newspapers supposing it may give you and my good Lord Provost some Pleasure, to see that we have imitated the Edinburgh Institution of an Infirmary in that remote Part of the World. Thus they that do good, not only do good themselves, but their Examples are the Occasion of much Good being done by others.*
—Letter of January 3, 1760, to Sir Alexander Dick.

BACK in Pennsylvania the battle between the popular and the proprietary factions still continued unabated. The Rev. William Smith, provost of the College, Academy and Charity School, had gotten into the fray, was arrested at the order of the Assembly for alleged libel of that body, and suddenly in January of 1759 appeared in London to plead his cause with the higher powers. Quite naturally his antipathy toward the agent of the Assembly at which he was so aggrieved was very real, and he launched into a scurrilous attack quite out of character with his dual functions of clergyman and head of an educational institution.

A commentary on this episode by one of Franklin's most able critics is rather illuminating. Says William Cabell Bruce, who was not above giving Franklin the back of his hand when he felt him deserving of such treatment, "It must be admitted that anyone who quarreled with such a social, genial, well-balanced being as Franklin cannot hope to escape a very strong presumption that the fault was his own." The Agent had his own explanation for Smith's defection, contending in a letter to Polly Stevenson that, "I made that Man my Enemy by doing him too much Kindness. 'Tis the honestest Way of acquiring an Enemy."

But there were much more interesting happenings in London than this little man who persisted in reviling his former friend and patron. At the moment the Envoy was again enjoying the theater, with which he had had little experience since his former visit in England. He had even felt constrained to deprecate play-going back home as a gesture to the Quakers, who looked askance at stage performances.

The previous year he had brought over and propounded certain questions to Thomas Penn, and in February an answer was made direct to the Assembly, Franklin being bypassed as unmistakable evidence the proprietors did not recognize him as the colony's agent. But this slight was offset by a most unexpected and highly gratifying occurrence. He suddenly received from the Scottish University of Saint Andrews a diploma conferring upon him the honorary degree of Doctor of Laws, the award having been in recognition of his work in the field of electricity.

This was indeed a pleasant diversion from the Smith darts, the proprietary snub, and the war tension. He had no doubt been an occasional visitor at the British Coffee House, rendezvous of the expatriate Scots in London, and he very likely now increased the frequency of his visits there, both to show appreciation of the honor their countrymen had paid him, and also to try on the new title of "Doctor." It seemed ideal in style and fit, and, with ever increasing use, lent dignity to the man, and through him to the cause of the American Colonies which he espoused and for which he was looked upon more and more as the London spokesman. This appreciated incident, too, very likely suggested a pleasant employment of the summer holiday ahead.

The death in March of Richard Partridge, his associate in the colonial agency, may have turned his thoughts to a return to America. He recommended the appointment of a correspondent and friend of several years, Richard ("Omniscient") Jackson, as the permanent agent. But there was something of an upheaval back in Philadelphia. Governor Denny approved a revenue bill which included taxes on proprietary holdings. While the Penns did not start suit against him under the bond they exacted from all their appointees to the governorship, there was certain to be a showdown when the bill came up in England for consideration by the crown. So the envoy stayed on, cheered somewhat by the fact that Thomas Penn falsified testimony in connection with a case involving the proprietors and the Delaware Indians, and thus may have prejudiced the ministry. He now had better hopes of the revenue bill being enacted in a manner beneficial to Pennsylvania when up for hearings some months hence.

By late spring the English coastal towns were much alarmed, each of them expecting to be raided momentarily by the French navy and privateers. Also there were a few taut and gloomy days right at home on Craven Street, the reasons behind which are not too clear. Mary Stevenson, the highly intelligent and eligible daughter of the household, ever known as "Polly," was being sent to live at an aunt's in the country. It may have been that the move was merely to please the wealthy relative and guarantee the niece a considerable legacy. Some have thought there may have been complications because of William, then twenty-eight, unattached, and rather warm-blooded. Also his doting parent was a most willing matchmaker. Yet there seem to have been no further involvements as respects William Franklin, if, indeed, there ever had been any. But the elderly ambassador missed the girl who had virtually adopted him as a father, and soon began a correspondence with her that is one of the most remarkable of its kind. By her own choosing the subject matter of his letters was to be natural philosophy, and they are very much a testimonial to the high regard in which he held the able and affectionate Polly.

Then, in June of 1759, the James Ralph who had accompanied him to England so many years before, and used a shallow pretense to break off their friendship, was prepared to do him favors. Now one of the ablest propagandists in Britain, he aided in getting a text in which Franklin had a considerable interest into type. It was titled *An Historical Review of the Constitution and Government of Pennsylvania*, and was a documentation of the case of the Assembly and people against the proprietors. The Agent had gathered the data, and it had been written by Richard Jackson, now, and for some years to come, associated with Franklin in colonial representation.

Strahan, who was then preparing to leave for Scotland to close a profitable deal in book publishing, may have refocused the Doctor's wavering thoughts regarding a journey there himself. He had gained the impression that Scotland and Ireland, as well as America, were treated somewhat as stepchildren in empire matters, and a trip for political exploration might be justified. Also he may have felt the educational facilities which had honored him should be better known by a generation back home across the ocean just then seeking higher education.

But tourism, definitely in the Franklin blood, may have been sufficient in itself, for by late June or early July tailors were hurrying through new garments for both father and son, and the diplomat's impressive wig went off to the peruke maker's shop for overhaul and refurbishing.

There was a settlement with Mrs. Stevenson, a payment to the liveryman who delivered a heavier traveling vehicle, and on August 9 the Doctor and Billy headed northwest to Birmingham. Visits were made there, pottery picked up in nearby Stafford-shire, and there was further visiting outside of Derby in the next county. In neighboring hills the philosopher had the novel experience of digging out bits of rock in which seashells were embedded, after the fashion of specimens that had been given the Library Company in Philadelphia.

From Derbyshire they swung west through Manchester to Liverpool. Here the travelers had hoped to find late word of how the war went in America. But shipping was almost at a standstill, and the city was still very apprehensive lest the French ships suddenly pay the port a most unwelcome visit. Also, as letters which had arrived in London since his departure would indicate, the fighting, with respect to the French, was just then moving into its final stages on America's northern frontier.

On the twenty-ninth of August they left Liverpool and headed north, and with the promise that indifferent roads already nego-tiated would now deteriorate rapidly. Keeping up along the west coast, they passed through Preston, Lancaster, and Carlisle, to the Scottish border. There they pushed on over the stark hills of Roxburgh and Selkirk to Edinburgh on the Firth of Forth. But as rough as the roads may have been, as dour the countryside, or as deplorable the inns, the thousand and one new things to see, talk about, and note down for further thought brought a thrill. The Pennsylvania Agent was having a wonderful vacation.

And he would have a priceless time during the next two weeks in Edinburgh. He and William would be made Burgesses and Guild-Brethren and given the freedom of the city, and both father and son would meet many people that would be friendly and helpful in the years ahead. It was somewhat reluctantly that they left well along in September, heading west toward Glasgow. After a few days there, they turned north to Stirling, and on along the lower edge of the Highlands to Perth at the head of the Firth of Tay, turning east to St. Andrews on the coast. Striking back to Stirling around the upper reaches of the Firth of Forth, they followed its south shore into Edinburgh. Then, after completing "six weeks of the densest happiness" ever experienced, they took the road through Lothian and Berwick, and followed the east coast down to Hull, where they ferried over the Humber, and on due south into London. About the first of November they were back again at Craven Street. By the most direct roads, and without side trips, they had covered a minimum of twelve hundred miles, little more than two days by car over contemporary American highways and turnpikes, but in those days it was a real accomplishment. Franklin, who had kept score, and was most meticulous in such matters, claimed they had covered fifteen hundred miles in all. Thus it was indeed the grand tour, although it would no doubt have proved a terrifying experience to many of the Doctor's acquaintances.

London had had, like most other larger centers of the time, its summer visitation of smallpox, and with his interest in human welfare still unabated, the Pennsylvania Agent did something about it. Passing the data along to Dr. William Heberden, he kept at this competent but very busy physician until the latter had produced a pamphlet with the thoroughly explanatory title *Some Account of the Success of Inoculation for the Small-Pox in Eng-*

*land and America Together with Plain Instructions, by Which
Any Person May Be Enabled to Perform the Operation and
Conduct the Patient through the Distemper*. To the medical doctor's text the doctor of matters philosophical added a substantial
preface. He was still much interested in, and ambitious for, ex-
tension of the benefits of the healing arts.

This moment, when his trip had surely restored him in body
and spirit, is perhaps when he chose to sit for a portrait, for
Benjamin Wilson painted him sometime during this year. Also
he would have been much elated over news of the success of
arms in America. Wolfe had defeated Montcalm on the Plains
of Abraham while Franklin was at the height of his round of
pleasure in Edinburgh, and France was virtually through in
Canada.

Immersed again in his ever-growing circle of friends and in his
British-American problems, the winter of 1759–60 passed pleasantly and rapidly. In January he was selected a trustee of Dr.
Bray's Associates, and for a year seems to have acted as chairman
of this fund for the education and conversion of Negroes in
North America. Although there is no record of their having sat
together in meetings of this enterprise, it is presumed that he
must surely have encountered another Associate then on his way
to fame, the moralist and dictionary builder, Dr. Samuel Johnson.

There may have been one discordant note at about this time,
although there is a possibility that son William did not confide
his indiscretions to his father, despite the fact they were very
close and the father most lenient and understanding. It can be that
Strahan, excessively fond of the younger Franklin, as he was also
of the elder, was his confessor, and aided in covering up a sorry
business. On the last day of February 1760 some woman, whose
identity has never been disclosed, bore William a son out of
wedlock.

Had two generations of Franklins transgressed the commandment that makes marriage a necessity as well as a sacrament? The
evidence regarding the younger generation is conclusive. It hardly
seemed a propitious business for an ambitious young man just
then doing his level best to work his way into the good graces of

some prominent politician at whose hands he might expect to be awarded a snug berth. Yet while it in no way condones this serious breach of morality, such incidents were sufficiently frequent in eighteenth-century London as to have caused little adverse comment—providing they were carefully covered up. And this sordid affair, by someone's competent connivance, was well hushed up. There are some grounds for believing that Benjamin Franklin did not know that he had become a natural grandfather until the child was seven or eight years old. For it was at about this age that the child came into the keeping of the grandparent, who for a time called him William Temple. He began to shower affection upon him, ultimately added the Franklin surname, and treated the youngster as though he were as legitimate as careful observance of every injunction of law or ritual could have made him.

Along with political problems forwarded by the Assembly, the spring packets also began to unload the first contingent from a perennial crop of young men who would take their first decisive step toward fame and fortune by appearing in London, and seeking aid from Agent Franklin. Earliest to arrive that year seems to have been John Morgan, in search of a medical education. Franklin started him off at once to Edinburgh. A second prospective student had to be reclaimed from incarceration in France as a prisoner of war, while a third had to have his finances replenished after nearly being lost with all his shipmates at sea.

In the war of propaganda and empire politics, his chief contribution for 1760 came with the publication in April of his tract *The Interest of Great Britain Considered, with Regard to her Colonies, and the Acquisitions of Canada and Guadaloupe.* In it he spoke as a British subject, vitally interested in the building of a world-wide empire, yet as an American determined to rid the thirteen coastal colonies of restrictions or subjugation at the hands of France. In January that same year he had assured his Scottish friend Lord Kames that he had "long been of the opinion, that the foundations of the future grandeur and stability of the British empire lie in America." For the next twelve or thirteen years he would hope and fight for such an Anglo-American imperialism.

He had wished to visit Kames and other Scots again in their native heath, but the money bill passed in February of the previous year was up for hearings and the Agent was apparently doomed to spend the summer in the city. In the prolonged hearings before the Privy Council's Committee for Plantation Affairs, Franklin had stoutly maintained that the estate of the proprietaries would not suffer in any manner by the provisions of the questionable act. This contention so impressed the chief justice that he called the Doctor aside and said if he were willing to enter into an engagement to guarantee this point the bill would be approved. The necessary assurances were given, and on September 2 the king in council allowed this revenue act to stand as written. It was a victory for the Assembly, and for their London representative, and while the decision came too late for the Doctor to set out for Scotland, it seemed quite worthy of proper recognition.

It took perhaps a fortnight to get straightened around, but about the middle of September the father and son were again in the chaise, and heading west. But few details respecting this holiday have even been uncovered. It is thought they went first to Bath, both out of curiosity and to try the waters, and perhaps on the off chance it might in some manner aid William's political ambitions. Evidently they went on to nearby Bristol, and from there may have ferried the Severn, for they seem to have taken quite a turn through Wales. Franklin says they also went to Liverpool and to Glasgow, and that he stopped in Birmingham for some electrical experiments with one Matthew Boulton. Some years later this latter wealthy philosopher would be experimenting with compression steam engines, a model of which would one day appear in Craven Street.

Perhaps it was when he returned that he found a letter from Dr. Kinnersley back in Philadelphia. It told of a house in the city that had definitely been saved that summer from lightning damage by one of the Franklin rods. It had taken some years, but at last there was one clear-cut case of their protective value now on record.

Also he would have received word that he had been appointed Provincial Grand Master of Pennsylvania by the Masonic Lodges.

Right there in London were further honors that were accorded him in November. He was appointed to the Council of the Royal Society, a distinction that would be given again in 1766, 1767, and 1772.

During the winter months, when a fire on the hearth was an inducement to work at his writing table, may have been the time when he drew up one of the most famous of his several hoaxes. While he was no churchgoer, he had learned to read from the Bible at five, and had been something of a student in it for fifty years past. Thus he knew its style well, and now employed it most deceptively to turn out what he called *A Parable against Persecution.* He not only memorized this bit in its entirety, but even went so far as to have it printed and bound into a Bible of his own as though it were the fifty-first chapter of Genesis. For some years he would either quote, or pretend to read, from this spurious section, to the great confusion of all but a few close friends in on the secret, but much to the amusement of the wily Doctor.

It was at about this time, too, that he first met a young schoolmaster, Dr. Joseph Priestley, whose interest in politics he would sharpen, and whose predilection for chemistry he would foster, but in whose becoming a Unitarian minister he evidently took no active part. Thus began a friendship which would last for thirty years, and from which both men would derive great benefit and pleasure.

As the weather warmed, there was a return of interest in Scotland again. But the probability now was of a termination of the agency arrangements and a recall to Pennsylvania. Just when was not certain, but he had perhaps best continue in London. Also he had another hoax up his sleeve, and proceeded to write it out. It professed to be a chapter from a book on the Spanish monarchy by a Jesuit of the previous century. The artful propagandist titled it *Of the Means of Disposing the Enemie to Peace,* and had it published and distributed in August of 1761 as an aid in combating a pacifist and defeatist attitude he felt to be dampening British support of the efforts needed to build an empire.

A rather unexpected letter arrived from Holland, from Pieter van Musschenbroek, whose Leyden jar Franklin had put through its paces in America fifteen years before. The Dutch scientist had thoughtfully listed and sent to him a complete record of all European writings on electricity to date. It was perhaps this letter that decided the destination of the holiday to be fitted in during the summer pause in political affairs. Sometime in early August father and son were again on their way, this time to Holland and Belgium.

Although not as long either in weeks or miles as the Scottish vacation two years before, it was an interesting and stimulating journey, and the pair were back in London in time to witness the coronation of the new king, youthful George III. Neither His Majesty nor the good Doctor could have had any idea on that joyous occasion how much of a thorn each would prove to be in the side of the other in the years ahead.

At about the time of his leaving for the Continent, Franklin had received reappointment as Deputy Postmaster General. Fortunately the American system was now furnishing him an income, for he had been the chief means of moving it over onto a profitable operating basis. It might be well to be at home, at least long enough for a thorough check of its current facilities. This need was soon re-emphasized by the death of his co-deputy, William Hunter. Then to add to these business demands came a sentimental pull, centering in the sad news of the death of his mother-in-law, Mrs. Read. There had always been a strong sense of affection and mutual respect between them since that day, so many years before, that he had gone as an immature seventeen-year-old to live in the good woman's home on the High Street in the Quaker City. And for the past thirty-one years she had been a member of his own household as his wife's widowed mother.

The sobering word of her passing set him to weighing London against Philadelphia in the balances, and the result seems to have been a determination to get back home with all possible speed. However, it was still wartime, and he would have to be patient until he could find a safe place in an American-bound convoy, which he presumed might leave early in the spring.

# xiv.  The Temporary Return to America

## *1762–1764*

*Dear Straney:—As good Dr. Hawkesworth calls you, to whom my best respects. I got home well the 1st of November, and had the happiness to find my little family perfectly well, and that Dr. Smith's reports of the diminutions of my friends were all false. My house has been full of a succession of them from morning to night, ever since my arrival, congratulating me on my return with the utmost cordiality and affection. My fellow citizens, while I was on the sea, had, at the annual election, chosen me unanimously, as they had done every year while I was in England, to be their representative in Assembly and would, they say, if I had not disappointed them by coming privately to town before they heard of my landing, have met me with 500 horses. . . . Mrs. Franklin and Sally desire their compliments and thanks to all for your kindness to me while in England.*—Letter of December 2, 1762, to William Strahan.

THE winter of 1761–62 was a period of rather impatient waiting, never knowing when the admiralty might decide to start a convoy off to the west. January passed, and so did February, without any particular happenings, and then about the first of March the Pennsylvania Agent received rather pleasing word, not of a ship about to sail, but of a handsome parting tribute. Oxford, "at a meeting of the Heads of the Houses," had decided that Mr. Franklin, "whenever he shall please to visit the university, shall be offered the compliment of the degree of D.C.L., *honoris causa.*"

Would there be time in which to arrange for a trip there and back? At that moment the roads were bottomless mud, and, though but sixty miles away, Oxford was out of the question.

By April, however, the immediacy of sailing had pretty much vanished, and toward the end of that month the Doctor and his handsome son set off by way of West Wycombe. On the last day of April another honorary doctorate was conferred upon the father, while William, building quite a reputation on his own, received the Master of Arts.

This was the university that three years previously had awarded a Doctor of Divinity degree to the abusive William Smith, almost as though in commendation of his vituperation of the Pennsylvania Agent. And, by rather unpleasant coincidence, Smith reappeared in London from America at about the time of the return from Oxford. One of his first malicious acts was to dispatch a letter filled with bitterest animosity to the president of one of the colleges at the university. It was turned over to Franklin, who encountered its author at Strahan's home, and exacted an apology of sorts, and a promise of full retraction of the missive's charges. But the reverend gentleman failed to make good on his promise, and began once more to spread false rumors of wholesale defection among the Agent's supporters and friends back home.

While Franklin awaited transportation, his London acquaintances, and Strahan in particular, did their utmost to keep the American permanently among them. Although there were moments of wavering no doubt, affairs at home did demand his personal attention, and the delay became somewhat burdensome. It was perhaps to help fill the time that he perfected a musical instrument which he called an armonica. It consisted of a series of glass hemispheres, each ground to give off its individual tone in a scale of musical intervals when struck, or rubbed, with the finger tips. These were fixed in sequence on a long shaft which could be revolved by a foot treadle. By sitting before the device, fitted into a case like a tiny spinnet, the performer pumped with one foot, and stroked the whirling glasses in proper order, and brought forth any tune he wished in a succession of pleasing tones. Franklin had several of these instruments built for his friends, and the best among those still in existence dates from 1762.

Finally the host of British cronies, along with William, who was staying on for the time being in London, bid the Doctor good-by, and in July he hurried down to Portsmouth on the Channel. The convoy reputedly had been about to sail, but the days, and then the weeks, dragged by, and he wavered, and almost gave up and returned to London again. But sometime about August 23 he went aboard ship and was at last on his way.

No more than a day or two before, with the benefit of the father's influential friends, but in no small part by his own able and astute lobbying, William had been rewarded with a most juicy plum—governorship of the New Jersey colony. While the elder man had been fairly certain the appointment would be made, there is doubt that confirmation reached him before sailing. He was perhaps aware, too, of the circumstances behind the notice which appeared shortly afterward in "Straney's" *London Chronicle*, giving the details of the marriage of the Honorable Mr. Franklin to a Miss Elizabeth Downes, late of the West Indies. But the gentleman whom the ministry had perhaps thought to make more tractable by his son's appointment was, especially at the time of the wedding, far out on the broad Atlantic.

At sea the Doctor was soon back again at his oceanography and particularly interested in the influence of a skim of oil on wave action. It was a rather poky voyage, part of the convoy having to furl sails almost daily to allow the slower ships to catch up, but afforded one most pleasant interlude when a stop was made at the island of Madeira. There fresh food could be picked up for the balance of the ten weeks' trip, and especially great bunches of luscious wine grapes then ripening. About the first of November his ship slipped up the Delaware, and he was at home before his arrival could be heralded about. Once again, as on his returns from the war on the frontier, he had, as the letter quoted above explained, frustrated the plans of his host of well-wishers.

It was good to be home, to be called "Ben" once again by close friends, and to realize that Philadelphia was growing less and less a provincial town, and rapidly becoming the colonial metropolis. But for all that, England had fitted him culturally and intellectually like a glove, and he cannot have been long at home before he was heaping inducements upon Deborah to pull up stakes and go with him to London—permanently. But in that quarter he encountered resistance that withstood all his persuasiveness. His wife, not at all an ardent traveler, had an especial aversion for the sea that could not be by-passed. Also she perhaps realized that, since she had been no particular asset to her husband socially in Philadelphia, her contribution in London might even tend to be a liability. In any event she refused to be influenced by Ben at home, or by Strahan's persuasive suggestions made to her from England.

Catching up the loose ends of his affairs after the longer-than-expected stay abroad consumed the colder months. In February the Assembly, of which he had been continuously a member, met again, gave him formal thanks for his efforts, which his opponents maintained had been nihil, but had actually been considerable. His pay and his expense account were adjusted, and on a total cost basis that completely belied the claim of his enemies that he had been recklessly squandering public funds.

At about this same time he made a snowy trip, probably on horseback, to New Jersey to welcome son William, being settled in his new duties at the alternate capital of the colony, Perth Amboy. A little later on the governor would make his home more permanently at the other seat of government, Burlington.

There must have been a real thrill when news was received, perhaps in March, of the Treaty of Paris, which had been signed on February 10, and had put an end to a conflict, thought of in this country principally as a long tussle with the French and the Indians, but which was, without a trace of exaggeration, the first "world war" of modern times. The good Doctor may well have chatted enthusiastically about the peace provisions before the Franklin stove in his library, for the treaty's conditions were quite in keeping with his own philosophy of British-American empire and with suggestions made in some of his propaganda pamphlets of the past several years. He would be unpleasantly surprised very shortly to realize that French secret envoys were infiltrating the colonies and doing their best to advance any latent sentiment for separation from Britain. Fourteen years later he would welcome such interest, and cultivate it fully in achieving American Independence.

As soon as the roads would permit, he donned his mantle of Deputy Postmaster General and was on his way to Virginia. His purpose there was to settle with the estate of his late colleague, and to meet his new co-deputy, John Foxcroft. Together they soon set out to visit the principal offices from Williamsburg to the edge of Maine. Those in the southern area having been called upon by the end of May, the two deputies were in Philadelphia on June 1, and a day or two later they attended a public dinner for son William and wife at Elizabeth Town, New Jersey. Their next long stop was close by at Parker's home in Woodbridge, where the accounts for several years were gone over.

When Franklin had first received his appointment ten years before, the system had shown an annual deficit of some seven hundred pounds. In the interim it had increased in size, and in acceptance and efficiency, so that it not only paid its way but yielded a sizeable surplus. It was an accomplishment to be proud of, and overwhelmingly a Franklin achievement.

By June 27 the deputies were in New York. Three new colonies were about to be added by proclamation to the original thirteen. The largest of them was Quebec, and preparations were now made to extend the postal service to it by a route north to Montreal, and thence down the St. Lawrence to Trois Rivières and Quebec City. Also a mail packet service at frequent intervals was inaugurated between New York and London. Ben's old friend, Cadwallader Colden, had become New York's governor, and some time was spent with him and Jeffrey Amherst discussing the serious Indian troubles then harassing the frontier. Daughter Sally had joined the party during the New York stay, prepared to accompany her father into New England.

At last they pressed on through Connecticut, where Franklin had the misfortune to be thrown from his horse. At Warwick, in Rhode Island, they put up at Catherine Ray Greene's for several days while he obtained some relief from his injuries. But they had quite a schedule ahead of them, and were soon on their way once more, via Providence to Boston.

On their return from Portsmouth to the Bay City about the first of September the fifty-seven-year-old man was again thrown from the saddle, this time dislocating his right shoulder. He was a month or more in the city of his birth recuperating. Yet his stay was anything but a dead loss. His residence in London as a colonial agent would have been of extreme interest to Josiah Quincy, whom he had done a considerable favor in Philadelphia several years previously, and to many others among the group in Massachusetts who would in a short time now begin proudly to think of themselves as "patriots."

It was toward November first before he and twenty-year-old Sally arrived at home. He had covered some sixteen hundred miles, a little more than in his Scottish tour four years before, but had not come through in such good condition, nor had the journey yielded quite the same intense pleasure. By December 10 he took his place regularly again at the Assembly sessions, and perhaps heard for the first time the details of the king's proclamation of October 7. It definitely limited colonial expansion to the west, and this the Doctor disliked heartily. However, he laid the restriction to the king's ministers rather than to the young sovereign himself, who was still highly popular, not only with Franklin, but generally throughout the colonies.

But while peace may have come to Europe, it had not arrived along the American frontier, and Indian outrages had matters in a turmoil. In the Susquehanna Valley, where danger was rife, a group from the vicinity of Paxton, lashed into a frenzy by the fanatical preaching of their sanctimonious parsons, had fallen upon and virtually exterminated the handful of harmless and partially civilized natives living in their own small town about fifty miles down the great river. This most contemptible instance of unprovoked slaughter took place about daybreak on December 14. The sheriff prudently hurried the few survivors to Lancaster and, at their insistence, secured them in the workhouse. Moravian missionaries in the vicinity, merely as a precaution, sent some one hundred forty friendly Indians that were their charges off to a place of refuge just outside Philadelphia. John Penn, irresponsible son of one of the proprietors, and recently appointed governor, then issued a proclamation, on the advise of his supporters, calling upon all officers within the Colony to maintain peace.

But the zeal of the "Paxton Boys" had been strongly inflamed by their taste of blood, so they saddled up, filled their powder horns and shot pouches, and set off for Lancaster to wipe the

red-skinned affiliates of Satan that had escaped them from off the
earth. The sheriff was overpowered, the jail breached, and the
luckless remnant there dispatched. Then considering their pious
crusade for the moment complete, they returned to their homes
amid the rather general plaudits of their neighbors. And not only
was there local approval, but some of the province's "leading"
citizens, whose viewpoint was limited to the ends of their own
noses, endorsed such frightful vindictiveness. Even the ineffectual
governor found it convenient to go along with such an attitude.

However, the late agent at the Court of St. James, who was an
"expansionist" at heart and determined the frontier would be
pressed ever further back into the interior, realized the full import of this heedless act and its unprincipled support. With his
penknife he sharpened and split the tip of a fresh quill, and began
to set his thoughts down on paper. Not too long after the turn
into 1764 he had published a stirring, hard-hitting pamphlet,
*Narrative of the Late Massacres in Lancaster County*. It was not
only an answer to arguments in support of the Paxton Boys, but
a stinging rebuke to all mob violence, and a condemnation of any
and all such "Christian white savages."

While this brochure added to the number of Franklin enemies,
and perhaps started the Paxton Boys on their march on Philadelphia, it also solidified the stand of the more level-headed citi-
zenry, and even encouraged a fair share of the Quakers to take
up arms to quell this threatened insurrection. In addition, it made
the unmilitary Dr. Franklin once more the man of the hour, and,
as the upstate mob approached Germantown, the well-frightened
governor fled to the Franklin home at midnight, prepared to defend the province from behind the great philosopher's coattails.

A riot act passed by the Assembly had been in force for some
days, and finally the former "general" swung into the saddle, and
led a committee of Assembly members and clergymen out to
parley with the hotheads, who had ridden into the area perhaps
as much to impress, and even intimidate, the government as to mo-
lest the Indian refugees. The "fighting face" he put on, and the
"reasonings" he heaped upon the leaders had dispersed the mob
"within four-and-twenty hours." He had, however, to eat a little
crow himself during the proceedings, but law and order were

maintained. To while away the time as these discussions were under way, the rank and file of the Paxton Boys had practiced marksmanship on the weathervane at the tip of a church spire in the Germantown market place, as the well-riddled relic testifies. When their leaders reappeared and gave the orders, they very likely straggled off for home a hundred odd miles away, sorely disappointed that their powder had not been put to more sanguinary purposes.

The incident had done much to point up the political animosity in the province, and Franklin sagaciously appraised the situation. There was a clash of religious beliefs and adherences that made for cleavage. Also there was under-representation of "back county" interests in the legislature, and neglect of frontier problems. But by no means least among major causes of friction was the split between the middle and lower classes and an American aristocracy of privilege in the making. A dozen years later he and other "Franklin democrats" would have to preserve the rights of the "middling people" by writing unqualified protection against aristocracy into Pennsylvania's first constitution as a state.

An insurrection almost at his own doorstep having been so ably put down, John Penn hastened to discredit the conciliator's performance by posting a liberal bounty for Indian scalps, male or female. The proprietors must act like petty despots, whether peace was served or not.

George III also suffered somewhat in Franklin's estimation that spring of 1764, when a tax program and other restrictive legislation was aimed at the colonies. Yet the king still seemed far more preferable to deal with than the proprietors, and relations between the Assembly and the Penns had fallen to the lowest stage ever, and were very close to the breaking point. So much heat was involved in fact that in April the Doctor turned out a tract titled *Cool Thoughts on the Present Situation of Our Public Affairs.*

For some time there had been mild agitation to petition the king to take over Pennsylvania from the Penns and operate it as a royal colony. When a money bill for fifty-five thousand pounds had to be finally put through pretty much on Penn terms, there was a sudden demand to draft such a petition and press it through to a successful conclusion. Toward the end of May Franklin slipped

into the speaker's chair to be in better control of the battle royal
that loomed ahead.

But there were other things, too, begging for attention. He had
recently broken ground for a home in Oriana Street just back
from the south side of Market Street, between Third and Fourth.
Postal affairs also claimed his time, for a regular packet service
from London to Charleston was being established for the benefit
of the southern colonies, while "night riding" was tried out in
the north, where it so speeded up the transmittal of mail that a
Philadelphia businessman could write to New York with a chance
of a reply back in his hands within two full days. This seemed
phenomenal, but before the summer was over the speed-up had
been extended to Boston, from which point an exchange of
letters dropped from three weeks to six days.

While Franklin & Hall were no longer the public printers,
"Davey" was still publishing *Poor Richard Improved*, and right
in the middle of political fireworks that lasted through the summer the old master tried his hand by writing the preface to the
1765 edition. In it he prophetically forecast the fact that if Britain
laid heavy taxes upon the colonies, British manufacturers could
expect to lose their American market. It was by such an embargo
a few years later that the colonists sought to dissuade British stub-
bornness, and avoid the Revolution.

In September the proprietary, or *New* Party, distributed an
anonymous and highly scandalous pamphlet attacking the Doctor,
the *Old* Party leader. The mother of His Excellency, the Governor of New Jersey, was held up to question and scorn, and
declared to be an oyster-house wench, but lately deceased after
having been kept secreted for many years in the Franklin home.
Obviously, the battle was in its final stages, for no holds were
barred.

At the October election there was an unexpected upset, and
both Franklin and his right-hand man in the Assembly, Joseph
Galloway, were defeated. However, the older, anti-proprietary
party as a whole won pretty much its customary support, still
maintained an easy majority in the legislative body, and was determined to put the province under the direct care of the Crown.
On October 26 there was a vote to send the former agent back to

London again, bearing the petition he himself had drafted and had signed on the day he took over as speaker six months previously.

Was he pleased with this sudden turn of events? Obviously the thoughts of being in Britain again cannot but have quickened his pulse. Since, as he then reasoned, he would of course be gone but a very few months, Deborah might possibly reconsider and go with him. And when that idea proved futile, he thought to take Sally so she might, as it were, top off her education with a few months in England. But stubborn Deborah refused to subscribe to this suggestion as well.

Thus his first feeling of elation at going may have tapered down materially before he finally set off early in November. It was necessary to pick up his ship at Chester, seventeen miles down the river from Philadelphia. And while there were no drawn swords this time to add to the already excessive choler of the proprietors, there was a huge party of no less than three hundred friends and well-wishers that rode along with him on horseback down the King's Highway.

But he was fully deserving of such honoring, for Dr. Benjamin Franklin was advancing to ever greater and more far-reaching experiences. And it would be much, much longer than he had anticipated before he would ride through the Delaware Valley again. Had someone told him it would actually be just a few months short of eleven years, he would have thought the man daft, yet such proved to be the case.

# xv. The Repeal of the Stamp Act
## 1764–1766

*We at length, after a long and hard struggle, have gained so much ground, that there is now little Doubt the Stamp Act will be repealed, and reasonable relief given besides in our Commercial grievances and those relating to our Currency. I trust the Behaviour of the Americans on the occasion will be so prudent, decent, and grateful, as that their Friends here will have no reason to be ashamed, and that our enemies, who predict that the Indulgence of Parliament will only make us more insolent and ungovernable, may find themselves, and be found, false Prophets.—*Letter of February 27, 1766, to Charles Thomson

ON DECEMBER 9 he wrote to Deborah from the Isle of Wight, across the Solent from Portsmouth, and thus opposite the point from which he had sailed home twenty-seven months before. Said he of the friends recently parted with in America, "The kind prayer they then put up for thirty days' fair wind for me was favorably heard and answered, we being just thirty days from land to land." It had been a rather rough but fairly short crossing, and he hurried on to London, where he most pleasantly surprised his other family-by-adoption on Craven Street. His letter to his wife telling of his safe arrival set the bells back home to joyously pealing out the good news.

Once again the London climate clutched at the Pennsylvania Agent, and he was for a time house-bound. Richard Jackson, who had acted for the province in his absence, brought him up to date on the local political situation, and Franklin went to work as soon as possible, presenting his protests to Grenville along with other colonial agents, and lobbying against passage of the Stamp

Act. By February it was conceded that this revenue bill, to which the colonies were so uniformly opposed, would pass, and in March it was enacted, with provision to go into force on November 1 that same year. George III was at that moment having his first attack of insanity, and his assent was given by commission. Yet this latter incident, if its significance was fully understood by the Doctor, does not seem to have shaken his confidence in the Crown.

In London the Agent considered this tax measure a sad mistake, but accepted it as an accomplished fact, and, at the request of the government, proposed John Hughes, a friend back home, as stamp officer for Pennsylvania. He even went so far as to order a large supply of paper on which to publish the *Gazette*, of a size that would have saved money by lowering the tax that reached even to newspapers.

Then for a time the "rich man's disease," the gout, confined him to his quarters on Craven Street. Little did he then realize how badly he had underestimated the violent reaction of the colonists to the Stamp Act. Perhaps nothing was further from his mind than that Deborah was standing siege for nine long days at home, while mobs threatened to burn the house down over her head in retaliation for her husband's presumed support of this despicable legislation. Hughes, totally innocent of previous knowledge or intents in connection with this stamp affair, received threats to his life, and promptly resigned from an office he had never sought.

A shipment of seeds came in from John Bartram, but they had left early enough so that the word that accompanied them gave no hint of how upset opinion was back home. As the items were being unpacked it was pleasant to realize that the Quaker scholar was just then being named King's Botanist. These little political chores for friends took time, as did some non-political ones as well. Such was the current attempt to procure through his Scottish friends a degree for Ezra Stiles, later to be president of Yale College. On the score of diversions, the Agent seems to have found time to listen to a little music, and to testify to the fact that "modern" music left him rather cold, while he delighted much more in "a plain old Scotch tune."

By summer the new house back in Philadelphia was completed. And as reports of the adverse reaction to the stamp tax, from Boston to Charleston, began to mount, there may have been moments when it appeared the Franklin political career might also be finished. Resolutions passed in Virginia and Massachusetts seemed, when put in type, to be close to treasonable. He protested from England how resolutely he had fought against this revenue measure, but he was resigned to it as law, in decided contrast to his countrymen who were determined to kill it off at any expense.

By the time he received word of colonial groups organizing as the "Sons of Liberty" to boycott English products, and of calls for an intercolonial Stamp Congress, he had to quickly shift his position and thinking. The uproar far away over the ocean was rather disconcerting, and was luckily offset by two fortunate occurrences closer at hand. He was the recipient of quite a substantial land grant in Nova Scotia, and the man who had no special fondness for money by itself, no doubt saw, through land speculation which could be highly profitable, a way to greater security, which he truly cherished.

Also, on September 25, 1765, a new commission was issued to Franklin and Foxcroft. This renewed his grasp upon a position that now yielded a nice addition to his income, but on which he seemed to have a more tenuous hold as the years moved by. By this newer arrangement he and his partner retained control of the area from Canada to Virginia, while a separate new district including the Carolinas, Georgia, East and West Florida, and the Bahamas was organized.

Although the gathering at Albany eleven years previously had been intercolonial, the meeting of nine colonies at New York in October was the first session in which concerted resistance to parliamentary rule found expression. A new era in British-American relations began, and the memorials and declarations which flowed from this Stamp Act Congress gave firm support to the increasing belief in England that the colonies would one day seek independence. The group action there taken made a profound impression upon the House of Lords, where the Stamp Act vote had been unanimous, and in Commons as well, where it had been supported five to one. Face saving was now in order at Westminster.

The hearings on Pennsylvania's petition for a change to a royal colony status, postponed through the summer, finally opened before the Privy Council in November, right in the midst of all this unanticipated tumult. The air being surcharged with politics, a political response was almost to be expected. And seemingly it was contained in the contention made that the king was not equipped legally to intercede in the matter. But it was really the case of a larger issue having swallowed a smaller one, and Franklin was forced to forget the petition and concentrate on rescinding the Stamp Act. He worked effectively, but kept under cover as far as possible. He was becoming a marked man in ministerial circles, and his position as colonial agent was at stake in one direction, while the post office arrangement, now considered very much a sinecure, was vulnerable from another. Also he was developing plans through trustworthy friends for what turned out to be a real moment in the sun.

By January the opposition was mentioning this unpopular item of legislation by the previous government as an "unhappy act." Yet the king and his ministers were dead set against repeal, and a parliamentary struggle welled up rapidly. Early in February the Franklin letters written a dozen years before to Shirley were published in Strahan's *Chronicle* as evidence that the colonial position was neither new nor born of opposition to the recent legislation. Toward the end of that same month he fairly panted in a letter written to Deborah, "I am excessively hurried, being, every hour that I am awake, either abroad to speak with members of Parliament or taken up with people coming to me at home concerning our American affairs."

But in between had come a memorable opportunity to throw light on colonial matters in a manner that was certain to count heavily. Since the third day of this second month he had been on summons to attend all sessions of the Commons sitting as a committee of the whole to hear witnesses express opinions regarding America. On the thirteenth, and possibly the day before as well, the Pennsylvania Agent had been called to the bar of the House to answer questions. Some of them he seems to have shrewdly "planted" with friendly members, while there are others that were very evidently unrehearsed, for they were openly hostile. What ensued, though, was a most remarkable performance, and did much to assure the repeal of the Stamp Act the following month. Said one of his British acquaintances, "He stood unappalled, gave pleasure to his friends, and did honor to his country," while even the great parliamentarian, Edmund Burke, admitted the scene reminded him of "a master examined by schoolboys."

About four weeks before he had been swept past his sixtieth milestone. Now, a little belatedly perhaps, had come added acclaim for his demonstration of diplomatic skill as a sort of birthday remembrance.

From this point on he was veritably "Mr. America," spokesman for a group of colonies growing toward the proud day when restraints would be thrust aside. But Parliament was still very much possessed by the "mother complex." The Stamp Act was withdrawn, but just to keep the record straight as to who was parent, a Declaratory Act was pushed through, which affirmed that the Houses of Lords and Commons had power to bind the colonies in any legal manner which seemed to be in the common interest.

And his contention that he had been encumbered by much serving of causes was evidently well taken, especially during the early weeks that year, for he seems to have undergone a bombardment of letters. A wealthy acquaintance in Birmingham, Matthew Boulton, who had a partner, James Watt, whose name every school child knows, had shipped a model of a very, very new steam engine to Craven Street for his criticisms. But politics evidently exercised such a demand on him that he had little time for philosophical considerations. It was not until after repeal that he hurriedly shipped the device back, and it was a week later before he could scrape together a moment to acknowledge the fact of return. Strangely enough the merits of steam as a motive power do not appear to have impressed him, for years later he would refuse aid to John Fitch when that impetuous creature was doing his utmost to popularize his steamboat making regular runs on the Delaware River in the year of the writing of the Federal Constitution.

He had reason to be disturbed when General Conway, who had become secretary of state, issued an order in the name of the Crown permitting the opening, reading, and copying of letters of any and all colonial agents or other persons on a prescribed list. From then on he would be forced to write every letter with the realization that what he had said might later be used against him.

But in America at that moment he had become a very great hero. It is said that he was the first to bear the designation "Father of His Country," later transferred to Washington. And as word of the altered attitude reflected back to him in London, and the future seemed less uncertain, he perhaps began to think a little about a summer outing.

There was a brief space, however, when a small complication might have seemed to threaten. A Franklin cousin from well up in the Midlands came for a visit, bringing his thirteen-year-old daughter Sally. She soon found a chink in the Doctor's heart into which to crawl, and on his promise of putting her to school in the city, and Mrs. Stevenson's willingness to have charge of her, this child who was so "sensible and of a sweet obliging temper," became a regular member of the household. And he kept young Sally by him most willingly until her marriage seven years later.

At the moment of taking her in at Craven Street he had perhaps thought it was for a few months only, for he had applied to the Assembly for relief from his duties as Agent so he could return home. Thinking, too, that his request might be allowed, and a friend, Sir John Pringle, being of a mind to accompany him, the pair set off across the Channel for Germany on the fourteenth of June. In Hanover they met and perhaps heard at first hand some of the fabulous tales of the Baron Munchausen. At least this formidable person gave them letters to friends at the University of Göttingen. There Franklin became a member of another Royal Society, and one of its foreign correspondents.

By mid-August he was in London again, but little wiser, and without great addition to either friends or honors, but pleasantly rested and renewed by the change. His principal souvenir was a pulse-glass, a sealed container in which bubbles behaved freakishly, and the water seemed to boil from the heat of one's hands alone.

In London there was another small souvenir by way of a testimony of the Pennsylvania Assembly's continuing regard. He had been reappointed for another year at his present post. Also, there had been a change at the British post office, a Lord Le Despencer having been made the Postmaster General. This evidently required a courtesy call, which was quickly made, and he and this brilliant but rather bizarre nobleman soon were fast friends.

For the time being this provided an increased sense of security regarding postal affairs, and especially the income his co-deputy post produced. Money matters were bound to be on the Agent's mind, for in September the Franklin-Hall partnership would terminate, as had been agreed upon when it was entered into eighteen years previously. The income it had afforded would definitely be missed. So, too, would the effective political support the *Gazette* had for years afforded Franklin and his adherents, for, shortly after the Franklin name was dropped from the masthead, Davey Hall shifted his own and his paper's allegiance to the opposition, or proprietary, party.

This publicity void forced Joseph Galloway and Thomas Wharton the following year, 1767, to subsidize a Connecticut Yankee, William Goddard, who launched the *Pennsylvania Chronicle*. This quickly became the ablest journal in the province, and a strong advocate of the popular party, which Franklin represented in London.

In the fall of the present year two more young men from the Philadelphia area, Jonathan Potts and Benjamin Rush, arrived in England under rather harrowing circumstances, after a strenuous sea journey during which a companion had succumbed. They were headed for a medical education in Scotland, and, like many others to follow, called upon Franklin for letters of introduction and assistance of one sort or another. In England he was becoming something of an institution. There were times when in America he was considered too British, while in Britain, and particularly in governmental circles, he was felt to be far too

American. And then during the months ahead he would begin to cultivate a wide circle of acquaintances in still another nation, and to some his loyalties would then seem even more diluted and mixed.

While the Stamp Act was buried, and the whirlwind that followed its enactment had abated, the political skies were still lowering and even threatening in spots. The Quartering Acts that had hurriedly been passed dumped regiments of soldiery in the colonies, particularly New York, and called for their maintenance by local taxation, which greatly increased tension and resistance. Even despite the partiality he would naturally have for things American, such short-sighted British laws were diametrically opposed to the Franklin political philosophy. The intent evidently was to keep the colonies completely dependent upon the mother country, and exact from them the cost of their governance in such subservient state by one form of taxation or another. This was certainly no way to build an empire in which Britain and America were to be partners. If colonial loyalty and respect provided a dependable barometer, the rate at which they were falling was a distinct storm warning.

With political matters so definitely in the ascendency there had been little or no time for philosophical concerns. Now came a brief opportunity to mix politics with economics. The grain crop on the Continent in 1766 had been a dismal failure, while the yield in England had been almost bounteous, leaving a surplus for export, and at a good price. However, the ill-conceived Corn Laws forbade grain being shipped out of England, much to the detriment of the local farmers. Free trader that he was, Franklin readily reacted most unfavorably to this inequitable situation, and turned out a clever satire titled *On the Price of Corn, and the Management of the Poor*, aimed at just such narrow-guage, restrictive legislation. It was a growing conviction with him that sound wealth was based primarily on agriculture, and that farmers must have the opportunity to profit if all were to be benefited.

Another shot had been fired in his war of propaganda, and, with this small chore out of the way, the philosopher looked forward to a more leisurely period in which friends and interests too little cultivated of late might have deserved attention.

## XVI. America Becomes a Problem Child

### *1767–1769*

*I received your obliging letter of the 10th May, with the most acceptable present of your* Physiocratie, *which I have read with great pleasure, and received from it a great deal of instruction. There is such freedom from local and national prejudices and partialities, so much benevolence to mankind in general, so much goodness mixt with the wisdom, in the principles of your new philosophy that I am perfectly charmed with them, and wish I could have stayed in France for some time, to have studied in your school, that I might by conversing with its founders have made myself quite a master of that philosophy. . . . Since I had not that good fortune, the next best thing is the advantage you are so good to offer me of your correspondence, which I shall ever highly value, and endeavor to cultivate with all the diligence I am capable of. I am sorry to find that that which sees the welfare of the parts in the prosperity of the whole, seems yet not to be known in this country.*—Letter of July 28, 1768, to Pierre Samuel Du Pont de Nemours.

THE holidays were hardly past, and January of 1767 barely underway, when America was faced with a new threat. Charles Townshend, chancellor of the exchequer, had taken over the government, and began to boast that he would find a manner of extracting revenue from the reluctant colonists. To do so would help placate those at home who were having to bear heavier land taxes, and also curry the support of another segment much perturbed by the tendency to disobedience growing ever more pronounced in America.

As tension began to mount higher that spring, the gentleman who would be expected to lift his voice in defense of the rights and privileges of the nearly two million men, women, and children now living to the west across the Atlantic was again sitting for his portrait. The artist this time was the able Scot, David Martin. He pictured his subject as stocky, well-preserved, intelligent, and thoroughly self-possessed, reflective, educated, and benign, with the strength of his convictions, yet having abundant liberality and understanding, an escape valve of humor, and a hearty humanism. And the very best of these exceptional talents, and of such an effective personality, would be called into play continuously during the next seven critical years.

The spring packets brought in mildly disturbing letters from back home, but their theme was not political. Twenty-four-year-old Sally had set her cap for a young Yorkshire merchant, Richard Bache, who had lived not too long in America. Brother William was much opposed to the match and certain that the thirty-year-old Bache was merely a fortune hunter. But Deborah seemed satisfied, so the father imposed no objections. He did feel the occasion called for a few words of caution. His circumstances were comfortable, but definitely he was not wealthy. Circumstances demanded he maintain two households, and the times were uncertain. Sally should have ample clothes and house furnishings, but no sizable dowry. Also let his Debby, like her Pappy, keep an eye on family finances. He was not becoming parsimonious, but merely cautious, for "when people's incomes are lessened, if they cannot proportionably lessen their outgoings they must come to poverty. If we were young enough to begin business again it might be another matter; but I doubt we are past it; and business not well managed ruins one faster than no business."

The Agent had also stressed in his letter the frugality with which he lived on Craven Street, yet his life there was by no means somber. Benjamin West having established himself as an artist in London, the young aspirants in the art world, as well as the fledgling physicians, began to arrive, and seek aid of the good Doctor. Among the earlier of the painters to drop by was the small genius, Charles Willson Peale, with a breadth of talents much like those of Franklin.

In response to his knock, a maid admitted him, and, perhaps being busy at the moment, failed to announce him, merely motioning the Philadelphian up the stairs to the famous second floor suite. Peale, on his best behavior, silently mounted the flight of steps, and presented himself before the open door, only to freeze in his tracks, and find that his mouth had flown open until his chin rested firmly on his chest. Within sat the Doctor, a sweet young damsel perched upon his knees, and the pair engaged in a bantering conversation.

Charlie winced, and, as yet unseen, started a rapid retreat. Almost at the front door again, he recalled that it was most urgent he contact this famous man he had just surprised. So he retraced his steps, this time with sufficient clatter so that when he presented himself in the upstairs study, the Doctor was quite alone, and busy at his writing desk. His partiality for and interest in the opposite sex was looked upon by some as a weakness. Yet it was actually more in the nature of a strength, for it was born of an understanding and appreciation rather exceptional between the two sexes. Women adored him as a man, and he in turn adored many of them just for being women.

Soon there was a visit at Craven Street by another gifted young man. Tradition likes to picture him as a small boy sitting before a peat fire all intent upon his mother's teakettle on the hob, and fascinated by the possibilities of the energy going to waste as the escaping steam rattled the lid. His name was James Watt, and within the next two years he would be granted a patent upon his condenser engine. This young Scot perhaps brought to mind the fact that another trip to the northern kingdoms was long overdue, for there was a letter to Lord Kames at about this same time in which Franklin dallied with such an idea.

Yet the very same note bore evidence of the American's alarm at the prospects of an ever-widening breach between Britain and her colonies, and so he ably set forth his concept of what those relations should and could be. A better understanding of what was at stake was called for. The inhabited strip along the seaboard was still a young and rather raw land, but such "an immense territory, favoured by nature with all advantages of climate, soil, great navigable rivers, and lakes, etc., must become a great country, populous, and mighty; and will, in a less time than is generally conceived, be able to shake off shackles that may be

imposed on her and perhaps place them on the imposers. . . . If
*Force* is used . . . a total separation of interests will be the final
consequence."

These sounded like fighting words. At least they proved prophetic words, even if Lord Kames did not get to read them. For
the letter was never delivered, since the post office seems to have
exercised its rights of espionage. The Pennsylvania Agent was
quite evidently being watched, and his relations with certain of
his majesty's ministers began to take on a decided cloak-and-
dagger flavor.

By good fortune, though, the Earl of Shelburne, newly appointed secretary of state for colonies, was partial both to America
and especially to the emissary who more and more spoke for all
the lands across the sea. So Franklin had been profiting by this
younger man's frank and sincere regard as a means of advancing
a land scheme in which his son and a group of friends back home
had involved him.

One of the partners was George Croghan, the Indian trader he
had met at the Carlisle parley fourteen years previously. George
had recently sent to London some specimens of mastodon tusks
and teeth unearthed in the Ohio country, and the philosopher had
given him a few learned commentaries on these huge beasts that
Jefferson, thirty-seven years later, cautioned Lewis and Clark
to be wary of, lest they meet them alive, and on the hoof, out
beyond the broad Missouri.

These mementos of the great West had brought the land
project back into the forefront of Franklin's mind. So an opportunity was arranged to dine with Shelburne early in August, when
the matter was strongly pressed as a certain means of strengthen-
ing the western frontier. Then, since Parliament, which had
passed the unpopular Townshend Acts in May, was now out of
session, and one could perhaps be away from London for a few
weeks without jeopardy, the Envoy made a move which was
eventually to have rather profound consequences. He and Dr.
Pringle set off together, but this time they headed for France.

This would be the first of three visits, the last of which would
extend for nearly nine years. He would come to love the French,
and they him, saying of him that he possessed a "French mind,"

which, by their standards, expressed the ultimate in compliments.

It was August 28 when he arrived in Paris, and he was soon welcomed among the philosophically minded. He was able to feel the political pulse, too, for the French were eager to learn the reaction of the colonies to the onerous burdens of the Townshend enactments. It was but four years since a treaty in their own capital had torn their American empire from them, and as the Envoy explained to his son, now a royal governor, these people south of the Channel would be quite delighted to dip into colonial affairs and "blow up the coals between Britain and her colonies." Being still loyal to Britain and to the Empire, he added, "I hope we shall give them no opportunity."

Of particular moment during his six weeks' stay was his intimate contact with the economic group known as the Physiocrats, believers in the doctrine that wealth stems most certainly from the land. This aggregation had been for ten years solidifying its beliefs, and six months previously had started a monthly magazine. Early in the next year a great apostle of his faith, Du Pont de Nemours, began to edit this periodical of which Franklin came to be a subscriber and ardent reader. Thus his letter quoted at the head of this chapter was quite sincere. He not only became a correspondent of Du Pont, but began to reason according to physiocratic tenets, and his earlier theories, which he had acquired as a callow youth from Sir William Petty, went into the discard.

British mercantilism, based on the belief that money alone was wealth, rasped on Franklin's strong leanings toward free trade. The resulting restrictions which flowed from the overdose of mercantilism in British politics was, he felt, ruining America. Thus his fondness for France and the French began to increase at the ultimate expense of Britain and things British.

On a Sunday, September 9, a former Philadelphia printing craftsman and "military person" made his bow before a king, having been presented at Versailles to Louis XV. Among the royal family on that day was Louis' thirteen-year-old grandson, the Dauphin, who would ascend the throne in 1774, and to whose court, two years later, would come this same American as an envoy. Yet the visit throughout was philosophical far more than political, and it was the fame and acceptance he soon had among the Physiocrats which provided the foundation and conditioned his acceptance as a politician nine years later.

It was the eighth of October before he and Sir John were back in London, having been stalled for a full week in Calais by contrary winds. At about this same time, but three thousand odd miles away to the west, a handsome young woman was plighting her troth before the altar in Christ Church in Philadelphia. And the many ships at dockside or anchored in the river were decked out with flags. Their captains and crews wished the young lady well, no doubt, but the gesture was a subtle toast to her father, the city's beloved Ben Franklin.

Among other benefits, the trip just completed had permitted a better perspective on the differences towering up between Britain and America—between mother and daughter. Now that these disparities had been emphasized, the breach between seemed both wider and somehow deeper. Also the French interlude that had strengthened his faith in the daughter, America, had lessened his regard for the mother, Britain.

Soon he was back in harness again, doing his utmost in his calm but purposeful manner in behalf of this daughter. Tired of hearing her condemned for *stealing*, he wrote out a pointed rebuttal to such unfounded charges, titled *Smuggling*, and sent it off to the newspapers. And almost by coincidence there came very shortly from his sister, Jane Mecom in Boston, a request which he finally found time to acknowledge on Christmas Eve of the year 1767. Although his letter does not disclose that fact, the spirit of the season—peace among men of good will—may have been upon him, for he wrote, "You desired me to send you all the political Pieces I have been the Author of. I have never kept them. They were most of them written occasionally for transient Purposes, and having done their Business, they die and are forgotten. I could as easily make a Collection for you of all the past Parings of my Nails."

Little Georgia, youngest of the colonies, appointed him her representative in January 1768; and on the seventh day of this new year he had Strahan publish in his *London Chronicle* a piece which may have been "written for transient purposes" but managed to become rather celebrated, his *Causes of the American Discontents before 1768*. It had been more fiery than was Franklin's usual wont, and the editor had thought it prudent to tone it down a bit at quite a number of points before it appeared in type. Its main thesis was expressed in the form of an adage, "The waves never rise but when the wind blows." The implication was that America's discontents stemmed from Britain's ill-considered acts. Considering its tenor, his friends were convinced he was secretly planning to return home.

But all his thinking was not political, for in February he wrote to Dr. Cadwallader Evans on a subject which had had his attention since his own days of setting type, lead poisoning. And his comments were such that physicians today could well approve of them.

Political considerations continued to loom large, nevertheless, and in March he was writing to son William, and taking a rather advanced stand privately on taxation and British relations. He advocated rejection of Parliament's right to legislate for America, and contended that the king alone, since he was the tangible expression of empire, was the bridge between mother-country and colonies. Westward over the Atlantic at the same time the Massachusetts legislature was issuing an appeal to the other colonies to band together in resisting what were adjudged to be predatory acts by the British government. Family ties were most certainly fraying out.

Riot and lawlessness horrified Franklin, whether they occurred in Boston, where the levying of custom duties was being resisted and had instigated the above appeal, or in London, where the king's attempt to keep John Wilkes out of Parliament had the British capital in an uproar. He was concerned, too, by another shift at the head of the postal department. The Earl of Sandwich had taken over, and Franklin soon began to feel the hot breath of the opposition on the back of his neck. There were trumped-up charges of inefficiency in the American system, yet an indication that nothing was wrong there that could not be immediately adjusted if the Pennsylvania Agent would quit England and hurry back to America.

Since the resolute Philadelphian did not frighten easily, and gave
every indication of his intention to hold on until formally dismissed, guarded attempts were made to shift him over into the
government's camp. Would he not like to resign the unimportant
post of co-deputy to accept a far better governmental assignment? Rumor had it he might be made an undersecretary of state
for colonies. But this gentleman had long since cut his political
teeth, and decided to let the opposition make the first move. Then
the gossip had it he was to be summarily dismissed, but he merely
stood pat, and waited. The consequence was that such uncertainty prevailed for another four years, and there would be subtle
attempts to buy him off almost to the moment of his final farewell as a colonial agent. He could be supple, and he could be
adamant, as necessity dictated.

As a relief from politics, which seemed more and more tainted,
he started a series of experiments on the operation of canal boats.
Through a barrage of letters he tried to stimulate interest back
home in silk cultivation, so that advantage might be taken of
bounties provided for its encouragement in a recent act of Parliament. Also he helped to choose suitable astronomical instruments
for shipment to the colonies in anticipation of the much talked
about transit of Venus to take place the following year. Before
the summer was over he would even have a go at spelling reform;
for he thought it more prudent to remain in London lest an un-
toward movement against him be launched in his absence.

Also it may have been in this year that another child came
to join the household of "Dr. Doubleface, the Judas of Craven
Street," as his enemies now preferred to call him. It was about
this time that little William Temple began to appear out of the
fog of obscurity. Just when the grandparent was first conscious
of a son's indiscretions eight years before is not certain. Neither
is the exact time of the youngster's advent in the Stevenson home.
But he was not there long before he had an everlasting clutch on
the old Doctor's heart. The few knowing friends were happy
when the boy's name was amplified to William Temple *Franklin*,
and it was not long before he was entered in a school in Ken-
sington kept by Strahan's brother-in-law.

The city was warm that July, and soon the Doctor was ex-

plaining the relief and other benefits received from his fresh air
baths to the young Frenchman, Barbeu Dubourg, who was to
edit the Franklin works in French. For his day and age the man
could have been taken for a nudist, although he confined his
nakedness to his own boudoir, where he sat in the buff at his
writing desk with windows open wide. Long an advocate of
physical exercise, his sedentary life had begun to tell on him, and
he sought to compensate for his lack of activity by work with a
pair of dumbbells. Tension and confinement, however, were
building up in him a noticeable uneasiness.

In August seventy-four-year-old Peter Collinson, great friend
of Franklin's and of things American, passed away, and Ben felt
the loss acutely. In fact the unhappy event seemed to give a new
impetus to his wish to head back to America.

But the fall season promised to require the utmost of his persuasive powers, for there were unmistakable signs of further
coercion being prepared for the colonies. New York had been
threatened the previous year, and now it was Boston's turn for a
far sterner reprimand. In October a fleet of warships appeared
in its harbor and discharged several battalions of red coats to
maintain order and assure collection of custom duties.

It was perhaps a unique experience at that same time to dine
with and discover that his philosophical activities were well-
known to the dissolute young King Christian VII of Denmark.
But his thoughts were chiefly on the rapidly decaying British-
American relations. By the year's end there would be loud demands in Parliament that leaders of the colonial defiance be
dragged to England and tried for treason, and as the year 1769
opened up active rebellion seemed too close for comfort.

In January he received two appointments. New Jersey made
him London Agent, and the American Philosophical Society
elected him its president, and would repeat the honor each remaining year of his life. He was not only dean of colonial diplomacy, but the dean also of American learning.

In March there was a call at Craven Street by a sister of Dick
Bache, the son-in-law he had never seen. He reported to Deborah
she seemed a sensible young woman, and he very likely assured

this visitor that if he was ever again in the vicinity of Preston, in the north of England, he would call on her mother and sisters. Would the worsening state of affairs ever permit him to keep this promise? At that moment it might have seemed dubious.

He found time toward the end of the same month to inspect some philosophical apparatus being dispatched to the college later known as Princeton. Then, as spring advanced, he began to brace himself against the unsettling news seeping through to him in London. The colonies definitely had their backs up. There could be no question of that, for when two such independent entities as Massachusetts and Virginia began to join hands for common action, it was ample evidence that a long advance had been made down the road toward *union*. And it was not a union which promised to be as beneficial to Britain as the one he had advocated at Albany fifteen years before.

Samuel Wharton, active member in the western land scheme, had come over from Philadelphia to lobby for a substantial grant in the Ohio Valley. Since he realized he was somewhat "obnoxious" to members of the ministry, Franklin thought it best to keep in the background, yet he gave much time to the guidance of Wharton's every word and move, whose efforts, with such competent piloting, promised much. However, the Wharton success seems to have focused the animosity of a young Virginian on Franklin. He was a Dr. Arthur Lee, a law student, carrying on lobbying efforts of his own for a similar project centering in his home colony. This enmity would flare up the following year, smolder for nearly ten years, and then burst into flame threateningly toward the end of the Revolution, when both were American agents in Paris.

By July the Doctor was determined to have a change of scene and atmosphere. While he had been buying and reading travel books as far afield as China and West Africa, he and Pringle set off for Paris again, very likely in search of French cordiality as an antidote for the growing hostility back across the Channel. Without thought of gross disloyalty, he may also have wished to again measure the interest of France in the colonies. In any event he reported it to American friends as being very considerable. Once more his stay was a period of intense adulation, with his time so pleasantly well filled otherwise that there was little left for correspondence.

He was back in Craven Street before August had run out, and soon attending the evening sessions at St. Paul's coffeehouse of the "Club of Honest Whigs," to which he belonged. Its members, while political liberals, discussed religion, philosophy, and the humanities as well as politics, and did so "sometimes sensibly, and sometimes furiously," as James Boswell recorded.

Soon word came from back home of the arrival of a grandchild. This first legitimate representative of a third generation was christened Benjamin Franklin Bache. He was quickly the darling of his grandmother, and later on would stake out and mine a substantial claim in his grandfather's affections. One of the finest characteristics of the Franklin heart was its especial warmth for children.

Polly Stevenson was just then deeply involved in a romance with a young physician, and discussed her affair with her adopted parent via correspondence with a fullness and frankness that she very likely might not have employed with an own father.

Beyond these sentimental matters there were philosophical concerns in some variety. He was still doing his utmost to stimulate silkworm culture in the colonies. As an increasing property owner back there he had a keen interest in fireproofing, having studied the subject, as far as time permitted, on his visit to France. Also, as a colonial postmaster, and with consequent interest in rapid transmittal of letters across the ocean to the colonies, he wrote in detail about the Gulf Stream to Anthony Todd, operating head of the British Post Office. With this communication he sent a large chart, engraved apparently from Franklin data by one James Poupard.

While whalers and other sailors were conscious of this huge Atlantic current, Franklin seems to have been the first to approach it from a scientific standpoint. He had had reports on it from his Folger kin in Nantucket, who had harpooned whales along the edges of this ocean river. But arrogant postal authorities and British shipmasters paid little heed to advice by which the latter might often have saved from two to four weeks in their crossings.

As the year closed the proposed colony to be based on a grant of western lands began to show signs of fruition. Wharton had found that his chances were much brighter if London politicians were cut in on the enterprise. In June the first petition was handed in, and when Lord Hillsborough had passed it on higher up, he suggested that the request be increased sharply from two-and-a-half to twenty million acres. Again Franklin seems to have busied himself effectively, but chiefly behind the scenes.

In December the company was completely overhauled and a goodly number of politically potent Britishers taken in. Access to operating funds was found through sale of shares. The lands at interest lay in a huge tract ceded by the Indians to the Crown at Fort Stanwix in the New York Colony in 1768. So, since the Crown must give both lands and its consent to this colonization scheme, the Crown would have to be taken care of. To this end the cost of effecting this Indian treaty was paid over as reimbursement, and a liberal arrangement made to pay quit rents. Thus, as the year closed, the prospects of approval seemed bright, and the Doctor may have felt his financial future was soon to be better secured. Also he may have felt that the "manifest destiny" which he had so long sought to envision for the American colonies was about to be implemented.

## XVII.  The Storm Clouds Gather

### 1770–1771

*Before leaving Ireland I must mention, that, being desirous of seeing the principal Patriots there, I staid till the Opening of their Parliament. I found them dispos'd to be friends of America, in which I endeavoured to confirm them, with the Expectation that our growing Weight might in time be thrown into their Scale, and, by joining our Interest with theirs might be obtained for them as well as for us, a more equitable Treatment from this Nation. There are many brave Spirits among them. The Gentry are very sensible, polite, friendly and handsome People. Their Parliament makes a most respectable Figure, with a number of good Speakers in both Parties, and able Men of business.*—Letter of January 13, 1772, to Thomas Cushing.

IN THE lean and rather emaciated *London Directory* of 1770 is the entry, "Franklin, Benjamin, Esq., agent for Philadelphia, Craven Street, Strand." The compiler's knowledge of America, like that of many of his contemporaries, was faulty and incomplete. And no one was more conscious of that fact than the Envoy from Pennsylvania. There were many times when, considering the responsibilities involved, the ministers and members of Parliament seemed woefully ignorant with respect to ever more important colonial matters.

It was not that the Agent had neglected to educate them as often as he was able. Now, along with his informative offerings, he was beginning to have to issue warnings as well. Also he had become so considerable an irritant in certain quarters that it was more effective when his name of identity was not too clearly associated with his contributions. The man had become so skillful in

argument that many of his opponents found it especially necessary to be on guard against his persuasive ways.

It seemed to him most fitting to open the year 1770 with a
cautious admonition. Thus in the January 2 issue of the *Public
Advertiser* there were three short, Aesop-like, unsigned fables,
which were nonetheless Franklin productions. Any one of them
will indicate their type and their common warning. The man
who some years later protested at the use of the eagle as the
American symbol employed it then as a token of the British
government. He had written, "An eagle, king of birds, sailing
on his wings aloft over a farmer's yard, saw a cat there basking
in the sun, mistook it for a rabbit, stooped, seized it, and carried
it up into the air, intending to prey on it. The cat, turning, set
her claws into the eagle's breast; who, finding his mistake, opened
his talons and would have let her drop, but Puss, unwilling to fall
so far, held faster; and the eagle, to get rid of this inconvenience,
found it necessary to set her down where he took her up."

Read in connection with the current relations between Britain
and her colonies, this barbed dart served notice that it would be
far better if the ministry and Parliament made no more blunders
with respect to America. The accompanying story about the
mastiff and the lion whelp, and another about cows and the
farmer, were similarly pungent little parables. It was some years
before the Doctor disclosed the fact he had authorized them.

Slavery, not tolerated on the free soil of England, was expanding in America, and particularly in the southern colonies. While
the number of Negroes was such as to cause alarm in some
quarters, the trade was still brisk, and, although handled in British ships, began to be used by that government to oppose the
American demand for a larger measure of *liberty*. Franklin, who
was having to face up to charges then being tailored from the
cloth of this shameful human traffic, sought to bring the evil out
into the open for searching consideration. Thus it was but
shortly after his fables appeared that he anonymously published
the pamphlet *A Conversation between an Englishman, a Scotch-
man, and an American, on the Subject of Slavery*. It is only
within the last few years that this bit of propaganda has been
credited to his pen.

To pacify the colonists, growing ever more strident, Hillsborough had promised them in 1769 that no added taxes for revenue would be levied. Actually the tax yield was proving to be only an inconsequential fraction of the expense of collection, and there were some who would have terminated all duties exacted in America. But the parliamentary die-hards, backed by the king's henchmen, were determined to retain the right to tax, and on the fifth day of March Lord North introduced a compromise tax arrangement. By most unlucky coincidence on that very same day, but an ocean's breadth away, a group of colonists and a handful of redcoats clashed on the Bay City's streets, and this unhappy but somewhat minor incident was fanned into flame, and became the *Boston Massacre*.

In New York on that most fateful day the Sons of Liberty met and determined to examine the sales and purchases of every businessman in the province in an effort to cut down trade with Britain, and to do what they could to oppose British domination of American soil and peoples. Representatives from Boston were present, but of course not cognizant of what took place at home that evening. Yet their being on hand was indisputable evidence that the colonies were beginning to sense the need for co-operative action.

There was a minimum of a month, and often twice that period, before word of such happenings reached the Agent in London, and the time was now a little longer since the British secret service had taken to reading the Franklin mail. Actually this peace-loving American ambassador had become something of a stormy petrel. While his friends were as many and as close as ever, and the number of friends of America were considerable, he had also acquired opposition in London as rabidly outspoken and well organized as the anti-proprietary party had been in Philadelphia. However, it stemmed solely from politics.

There has long been the opinion that the American philosopher had some part in Adam Smith's production of his classical work *Wealth of Nations*. If this is true, it would be at about this time that he aided the Glasgow professor, who made occasional trips to London to contact his patron David Hume. As a consequence,

Smith may well have brought word from friends in Scotland, and stimulated the desire that recurred each spring for another visit to the north country.

But American affairs were far too threatening to permit consideration of any other enterprises. He had for some time been in most earnest correspondence with Samuel Cooper at Harvard, and had reported to him immediately after the visit in France the past year that "all Europe (except Britain) appears to be on our side of the question. But Europe has its Reasons. It fancies itself in some Danger from the Growth of British Power, and would be glad to see it divided against itself." Then, either because he was still hopeful of a partnership arrangement between Britain and America—a sort of *commonwealth*, or *dominion*, status—or maybe in view of the fact he had no inviolable diplomatic pouch for his letter that assured him immunity to espionage, he added this suggestion, "Our prudence will, I hope, long postpone the Satisfaction our Enemies expect from our Dissensions."

By mid-April of 1770 the fat was in the fire in Boston, and the word of it no doubt in Franklin's possession in the British capital. Once again he may have felt it prudent to damper his real feelings and seem to hope for the best, since he then wrote Cooper, "I own I have a Satisfaction in seeing, that our Part is taken Everywhere; because I am persuaded, that circumstances will not be without its Effect here in our favour." And again there was the hedge which very likely was principally born of the deep desire for a solidly built empire, in which he said, "At the same time the malignant Pleasure, which other Powers take in British Divisions, may convince us on both sides of the Necessity of our uniting."

There were cool and conciliatory words, and some of the already red-hot patriots in Massachusetts would look on them, and other Franklin comments, somewhat suspiciously as the year wore on.

Recently deprived because of distance of a father's part in bringing his own daughter's romance to final fruition, he now took a lively interest in that of his foster daughter, Polly Stevenson. In May young Dr. Hewson proposed and was promptly accepted, and within but a few weeks they were married, while in September they joined the household on Craven Street.

It was now seventeen years since Harvard had honored the Doctor with a degree, and he had done the school many kindnesses as the occasion presented. Astronomy was becoming a part of most formal educations, the chief practical applications being navigation and surveying, and in July he took charge of purchasing a suitable telescope for the college's observatory.

It was early in this same month that James Parker, long his partner in New York, New Jersey, and Connecticut, and the comptroller of the postal system, died. Then, three months later, another old acquaintance also passed on. He was the Rev. George Whitefield, herald of the "Great Awakening," and one of the many reverend gentlemen who prized the friendship of the mildly anti-clerical Franklin. Though his own approach to life was relatively timeless, these final exits by friends always gave him a most unpleasant twinge.

With Polly and her new husband to take over at Craven Street, Mrs. Stevenson took Sally Franklin and set off for an early fall holiday down the Thames at Rochester. Two purposes now had to be served: Polly had to come in for some affectionate banter as a housekeeper, while the vacationing pair had to be remembered. So for several days the heavy diplomatic schedule had to yield sufficient time so that he could compose a daily edition of *The Craven Street Gazette*. And apparently this bit of banter might have to substitute for a holiday. The demands upon him had become considerable, yet he was questioning friends about accommodations to Scotland by ship, and even then was promising himself an outing the following summer.

His duties were, however, materially increased that December when, despite the fact that some members of its Assembly considered him "a pussyfooter" and a tool of Lord Hillsborough, he was appointed to represent a fourth colony, Massachusetts. Dr. Arthur Lee, the Virginia physician turned lawyer, became his associate in this post. The budding barrister was much given to jealousy, later became the egotistic prince of marplots, and was in a short time a trouble-maker of the first order.

Among other unkindly and disturbing things that were bruited about Boston while Franklin's appointment was under consideration had been the report of his impending dismissal from the post office. This had brought dismay to his sister Jane, and she had written him regarding the circumstances. Said he in reply, "My rule, in which I have always found satisfaction is, never to turn aside in public affairs through view of private interest; but to go straight forward in doing what appears to me right at the time, leaving the consequences with Providence. What in my younger days enabled me more easily to walk upright, was, that I had a trade, and that I knew I could live upon little; and thence (never having had views of making a fortune) I was free from avarice, and contented with the plentiful supplies my business afforded me. And now it is still more easy for me to preserve my freedom and integrity, when I consider that I am almost at the end of my journey, and therefore need less to complete the expense of it."

Specifically regarding the post office, he added, "I have heard of some great men, whose rule it was, with regard to offices, never to ask for them, and never to refuse them; to which I have always added, in my own practice, never to resign them."

The winter of 1770–71 was a harsh and protracted one, for there was a fall of snow even in the latter part of April. Political harshness was in the air, too. Whether incidentally or by design is not clear, but the Envoy chose his sixty-fifth birthday on which to present his credentials as Massachusetts Agent to Hillsborough. Refused admittance at first, he was driving off when there was a call to return, and he soon stood before his lordship. Much to Franklin's amazement the peer claimed that there had been no legal authorization of the appointment. There was an extended and heated exchange, of which the Agent made and kept a transcript. His final rejoinder, as he bowed himself out of the infuriated nobleman's office, went as follows, "I beg your lordship's pardon for taking up so much of your time. It is, I believe, of no great importance whether the appointment is acknowledged or not, for I have not the least conception that an agent can *at present* be of any use to any of the colonies. I shall therefore give your lordship no further trouble."

The Hillsborough attitude could be accounted for in but one

way. From now on it was the intent of the government, if possible, to force the appointment only of men willing to truckle to the ministerial wishes. And from now on Benjamin Franklin became more and more anti-British.

For a time he was thoroughly dejected, for he had about convinced himself that eleven years of intense effort on his part had been very much a total loss. Although naturally on the taciturn side, he now withdrew until Strahan remarked in a letter to William Franklin early in April, "Besides his temper, he has grown so very reserved, which adds greatly to his natural inactivity, and there is no getting him to take part in anything." The Agent himself wrote in a letter to Du Pont de Nemours, "I propose returning to America in the ensuing summer *if our dispute should be adjusted.*" To while away time, now there was less demand for lobbying, he worked out a downdraft stove that consumed its own smoke. There was also an invitation from a type founder in Dublin to come over to Ireland for a look about.

But he had had his fill of London and could not wait to make extensive plans. Hardly were the roads dry in May before he was in the chaise heading for the Midlands. With him he took a nephew, Jonathan Williams, Jr., who for some months had been serving him as a clerk, the Dutch natural philosopher Jan Ingenhousz, long a friend and correspondent, and John Canton, one of the Honest Whigs and an authority on electricity. Obviously it was an intended escape from politics, and so it proved to be. After a pleasant swing through Birmingham, Sheffield, Leeds, and Manchester, the party was back in the capital on June 2.

He was in time to be godfather for Polly Hewson's baby. He also found his accumulated mail had been trifled with, and so warned his regular correspondent Thomas Cushing in Boston. No doubt his letter written the previous month to the Massachusetts Committee of Safety, in which he had forecast rebellion and separation of the colonies, had also been copied and circulated in the ministry. In fact he trusted that it had. If it would only help open the eyes of some of these obstinate, short-sighted office holders.

Still restless, he made the two-day chaise trip south to the home of his dear friend Bishop Shipley at Twyford by the

Pilgrims Way near Winchester. Here he spent a week, then hurried back to the city with promises of a prompt return. But it was near the end of July before he was again at the stately old Tudor home, where, with the placid river Itchen flowing restfully by the foot of the broad lawn, he began work on one of the most widely read books in the English language, his *Autobiography*. Intended as a record, and a guide, for his posterity, he managed during a week or a little more in these blissful surroundings to carry forward the account from his birth to the year 1731. This was fully half of all the text he finally completed.

Taking eleven-year-old Kitty Shipley with him in the chaise, so she might return to school in London, this apparently ill-assorted pair had two lovely days of conversation on a host of topics along the way. It was late on the afternoon of August 14 before he was back on Craven Street. He would have been a day earlier except that Mrs. Shipley had insisted he remain and celebrate with the family the second birthday of tiny Benny Bache, who was now being referred to in his grandmother's letters as the "King Bird."

This second Twyford visit, just terminated, had perhaps been to fill in a waiting period, for a large-scale project was in the making. He may have wished to take his final leave of William Samuel Johnson, the Connecticut Agent, just now returning home. More likely he was awaiting the arrival of Henry Marchant, attorney general of Rhode Island, coming over to press certain of that colony's claims. At least he did remain in town until this latter gentleman arrived, and then spent six days in earnest conferences with him, while another Franklin acquaintance, old "Omniscience" Jackson, champed impatiently on the bit. It seems the two were about to set forth for Ireland.

And on the twenty-fifth of August they were on their way, going first to Birmingham. Then pushing to the northwest through Shrewsbury, they crossed Wales to Holyhead. After sixty-five miles over the Irish Sea, they were ashore at Dunleary, and then by carriage again the four miles into Dublin, where they arrived on the fifth of September. There Franklin spent nearly six weeks, and most pleasantly, too, for he was at the Irish capital longer than he had expected to be absent in all from London.

He was admitted to the floor of the Irish Parliament, an extreme mark of courtesy, and he also re-encountered Lord Hillsborough. This Irish nobleman was most friendly in contrast to their last meeting nine months before; and, finding that Franklin was heading north for Scotland, made it next to impossible for the American to refuse to stop at palatial Hillsborough House, which he did on his way to the tiny port of Donaghadee on Belfast Lough.

Just where he parted company with Jackson is uncertain, but he does not seem to have gone aboard ship for the twenty-mile crossing of evil repute to the wee, rock-walled harbor of Port Patrick, on the outer edge of The Rhinns in Wigtownshire. The Doctor made it during the brief tranquil period between two interminable storms, and twelve days after leaving Dublin was once again in Edinburgh. There, by prearrangement, he met Marchant, and they spent ten spirited days. Some few changes had appeared in a dozen years, but a surprising number of the old friends were on hand to welcome and entertain him and his companion.

Then the American tourists swung northwest to spend a few days with Lord Kames at his huge estate at Blair Drummond. Next they were three days in Glasgow, and on November 15 inspected the facilities at the huge Carron Iron Works at Falkirk. After four more days in the northern capital, they left Edinburgh on the twenty-first, cut back toward Carlisle on the west coast, and passed on down to Preston. Here he would be able to keep his promise of calling upon the mother and sisters of his son-in-law, Dick Bache. But fancy his astonishment and pleasure when he arrived at their home to find his own daughter's husband there on an unexpected visit. With detailed words of his family in Pennsylvania, this surprise meeting was the high spot of a memorable journey. He did manage during his two days in the little city to drop by the hair-dyeing shop of one Richard Arkwright, on the threshold of great things with his inventions in power spinning. Somewhat more to the point perhaps was his meeting with debonair Johnny Burgoyne, whose timely surrender six years later at Saratoga gave Franklin his first real break in negotiations that brought France into the Revolution on the side of the Americans.

Feeling that he must be back in London, he loaded Dick, who had suffered some minor leg injury on the trip over, into the chaise and set out with all possible speed to the south. The several days of travel gave him an excellent opportunity to come to know this young man, and also to reorient him with regard to the thinking that had primarily brought him to Britain—a place in the American post office.

Actually what was his own status in the post office as of that moment? Rumors were still bobbing about at the time he had quitted the capital that he was on the verge of dismissal. Had the ministry screwed up their courage and turned him out during his absence? There had been no intimation of it along the way, but one could never be certain. The government seemed to grow more decadent by the month. And what about the whole complex of American-British relations? The storm clouds had indeed been gathering during the early months of that year, and there had been nothing to indicate a change in the political weather. After his most friendly visits in Ireland, in Scotland, and in Preston, the trip back to London was very much a journey into uncertainty.

And with young Dick Bache by his side he was very keenly aware that it was now more than seven years since he had left his home and friends in America for what was fast becoming a most thankless post.

# xviii.   Crisis Ahead

## *1772–1774*

*At the Time of making up the Mail for the August Packet I was down at Lord Le Despencer's, and wrote the above letter to you from thence, frank'd by his Lordship. A week after the Packet had sail'd my letter was returned to me, having been, by a Blunder at the Office, sent to Burlington, in Yorkshire. I have now open'd it to add this. . . . You say my Presence is wished for at the Congress, but no Person besides in America has given me the least Intimation of such a Desire; and it is thought by the great Friends of the Colonies here, that I ought to stay till the Result of the Congress arrives, when my Presence here may be of Use. In my Opinion all depends on the Americans themselves. If they make, & keep firm Resolutions not to consume British Manufactures till their Grievances are redress'd and their Rights acknowledged, this Ministry must fall, and the aggrieving Laws be repeal'd. This is the opinion of all wise men here. . . . But you, who are a thorough Courtier, see everything with Government Eyes.*—Letter of September 7, 1774, to Governor William Franklin.

THE Doctor was well into January of 1772 catching up on the accumulation of correspondence received during his extensive travels in England, Ireland, and Scotland. Several of his letters emphasized the somber impression the appalling and widespread poverty of the working classes had left with him. Said he to Mr. Joshua Babcock of Rhode Island, "I assure you that, in the Possession & Enjoyment of the various Comforts of Life, compar'd to these People every Indian is a Gentleman." Yet the bulk of this particular letter was given to one of his favorite topics, agriculture. The merits of oxen over draft horses were discussed, as well as protection against frost damage to crops, stump-pulling machines, and a French suggestion for "a machine for raising chickens from eggs without the aid of hens."

The western land scheme was being pressed, and seemed to have good prospects, eventually. In March came an unusual incident. A Boston sculptress, Patience Wright, sought him out at Craven Street bearing a letter from his sister Jane Mecom. She had with her some wax figures which the Envoy thought extraordinary." So he recommended her to his acquaintances, and soon she and her exhibitions were the rage in London.

In April he gathered with a few close friends, including David Garrick, the actor-manager, and an exceptional French priest, the Abbé André Morellet, at the country place of Lord Shelburne at Wycombe, about twenty-five miles out along the road to Oxford. While walking in its park, he professed to his companions that he had the power to still the waves on the small pond ahead of him. The response was, as he probably anticipated, a series of guffaws. Whereupon, he strode ahead of the others to the edge of the water, waved his bamboo walking stick several times as though it was a conjurer's wand, and finished with a broad sweep encompassing the entire surface. By the time the remainder of the party sauntering along had caught up with him the small waves had fallen, and the pond had hardly a ripple. It seems he had had a phial of oil concealed in his hollow cane, which he had scattered on the surface. Pliny and Plutarch had suggested this phenomenon, and the Doctor had seen evidences of it on two ocean crossings. A year and a half after this incident he and members of the Royal Society attempted to demonstrate the principle of oil on troubled waters on a far larger scale off Portsmouth, but without very conclusive results. His contacts with the French Abbé on this holiday would be renewed most pleasantly in France several years later.

It proved to be not too demanding a year, so in June he was off once again to the north of England, where he spent a month, going as far as Preston. Back in July, there is little record of his activities just then in London; although in Boston a lawyer named John Adams was bringing suit in Franklin's behalf against one Samuel Hall, a debtor under a loan. Little did either man realize by what circumstances the antagonistic Franklin and Adams temperaments would in a short while be grating on one another. August, too, was a fairly serene month, aided in that respect by Lord Dartmouth succeeding the obstructionist Hillsborough as secretary for America. There was also word to the Doctor of his having been made a *foreign member* of the Royal Academy in Paris, the last American to be so honored for a full century. For a time, too, he began to feel his correspondence was again free from prying eyes.

While the colonists, by and large, were serenely buying sufficient copies of the definitely non-political *The Vicar of Wakefield* to make the Oliver Goldsmith novel the first best-seller that had appeared in America in four years, the sense of alarm regarding Britain's intentions was still increasing, and those "agitators" we now think of as "patriots" were organizing their Committees of Correspondence to implement concerted action.

The fall moved along without the tension of past years, almost like the calm before a storm. It would have been easy to get involved in the commotion Benjamin Wilson, the electrician and erstwhile Franklin portraitist, was raising over the Doctor's recommendation of pointed rather than blunt lightning rods on government powder magazines. But he refrained. He did give, in a letter in September, his formula for *prudential algebra*, whereby you wrote out in opposing columns the *pros* and *cons* of any proposition, and then carefully weighed and balanced them out in arriving at a solution, rather than depending upon snap judgment. Also at the behest of Bishop Shipley's children, to whom he had presented an American squirrel now deceased, he drew up a suitable epitaph, which read:

> *Here Skugg*
> *Lies snug*
> *As a bug*
> *In a rug.*

In October he was again at Wycombe, but this time at the estate of the notorious, but intriguing, Francis Dashwood, Lord Le Despencer. The two complete deists spent much of their time during this visit on a somewhat dubious project, an *Abridgement of the Book of Common Prayer*.

His return to Craven Street was to a new house, yet close by the former one, which Mrs. Stevenson had turned over to her daughter and son-in-law and their burgeoning family. This gave him several relatively busy weeks restoring order to his papers and records. Still, he was not too busy but that he managed to devise the great machination that climaxed his years as a colonial agent, and finally took him back to America. This sly political move proved to have a far greater chain reaction than he had anticipated.

Thomas Hutchinson, then governor of Massachusetts, had formerly been its chief justice and lieutenant-governor, while he had in turn been succeeded by Andrew Oliver, who had served as provincial secretary. During a period of nearly three years this respected pair had written a series of letters to a Thomas Whately in England, for a time a member of Parliament. Previous to his death in 1772 this gentleman had circulated the correspondence among a limited number of friends in the government. Hutchinson and Oliver were both "American," yet they favored attitudes toward British-American relations which within a couple of years would be deemed "Tory," or "Loyalist." In some mysterious manner never divulged, these letters came into Franklin's possession.

He was then playing the waiting game, his philosophy in this respect stated very succinctly in a letter the following January to Thomas Cushing, in which he said, "Our great Security lies, I think, in our growing Strength, both in Number and in Wealth; that creates an increasing Ability to Assist this Nation with its Wars which will make us more respectable, our Friendship more valued, and our Enmity feared; thence it will soon be thought proper to treat us not with Justice only, but with Kindness, and thence we may expect in a few Years a total Change of Measures with regard to us."

Having gone over the Hutchinson-Oliver letters carefully, the Doctor felt that if they could be read dispassionately and at leisure by certain leaders in Massachusetts, opinion there might be calmed down somewhat, and a period of time gained sufficient to make worthwhile accomplishments. So on December 2 he had bundled them up and shipped them off, placing certain very distinct restrictions on the use to which they might be put. They were *not* to be made public, neither were they to be published. In the weeks ahead he perhaps visualized them being passed about guardedly, and studied dispassionately. It would be a full six months before the truth was known, and the explosion came.

That spring of 1773 he seemed to be thinking of home again, or at least professed to be, for he wrote sister Jane he might very likely be in Boston, he "having left it in 1723, and visited it in 1733, 43, 53, & 63." It did seem a shame to break this ten-year rhythm. His being there perhaps did not appear so certain when the Tea Act for relief of the East India Company passed in April. While it levied no new revenue, it tended to make more certain collection of the tax already borne by that popular beverage and being stoutly resisted. About the same time he talked with Dartmouth, and sensed far greater understanding on the part of this new minister, anxious at the moment to hold back protests until he could test the spirit of Parliament and find if that body was more tractable. Franklin wished to be co-operative.

But in the Massachusetts colony the fields were fairly afire. Sam Adams and John Hancock, together with others of the more radical group, had found much incendiary material in the letters forwarded. Then, to get the greatest possible benefit from them, they forgot the promises to Franklin, and on a sleazy pretext had them read to the Assembly, and then published. Promptly the legislative body petitioned the king to remove both Hutchinson and Oliver from office, sending their demands hurriedly across the ocean to the Agent to present. By July sparks from the blaze in New England were setting fires in Whitehall.

It was a tense month, but it opened Franklin's eyes to certain conditions, or at least brought him to a point of frankly admitting their existence. Chief among them was his altered attitude toward the king, for he remarked in a letter to son William, "The late measures have been, I suspect, very much the King's own." He had long doubted the Parliament, and now was dubious of the good intentions of the sovereign under whom he had believed empire could be achieved. Still he was not desperate, and was far from advocating a break, for he counseled America to bear with "the infirmities of her government, as we would with those of an aged parent." And as to being through with life, or even in search of an ivory tower in which to hide away, nothing was further from his mind.

In fact in the midst of these taut moments his works appeared in a French edition under the title *Œuvres de M. Franklin.* In them was published the letter in which he had expressed the desire to be embalmed in a cask of Madeira, and then brought back to life in a later age so he might witness the immense progress that he felt lay in the immediate future. But, since a few days away from London would no doubt have their customary tonic effect, and there were possible political returns to be had from the trip as well, he set off for Oxford to see Lord North installed as its chancellor. He was then for going home in September.

But his leaving was postponed at least until after the coming winter. Taking the long view, he may have been already contemplating possible armed strife, for he assured Josiah Quincy in a letter that, "There never was a good war or a bad peace." Polly Stevenson, too, was told that "all Wars are Follies, very expensive and very mischievous ones," and he claimed he would far rather see two contending parties roll the dice for a decision of their difficulties than to fight and destroy each other.

With a particularly sharp and almost venomous pen he ran off and got into the newspapers two of his most biting satires, *An Edict by the King of Prussia,* and *Rules by Which a Great Empire May Be Reduced to a Small One.* These appeared within eleven days of each other. In the first hoax he contended the Germans had as great a right to dictate laws for the British Isles as the English king had with respect to America. The more sober *Rules* emphasized ministerial pride and short-sightedness, and strongly reasoned that the bureaucrats cease and desist abusing his homeland before an irreparable break came.

Many in the ministerial clique were now determined to have Franklin's scalp, their reasoning being that the sooner he was silenced, no matter what the means, the better. Had not Hutchinson maintained, at the time the Massachusetts Assembly had asked his removal from office, that Franklin was the master mind, and the chief encouragement, of much of the mischief originating in

Massachusetts? Why this daring troublemaker now had the audacity to employ a cartoon of Britannia dismembered of her colonies on his stationery. Such actions were revolting, if not outright treasonable!

Once again he was at Le Despencer's for a stay in October, returning to the city the following month with his hopes elevated somewhat, although it may have been due to the fact that Parliament was still in recess. He was pleased to be admitted to membership in the exclusive Society of Antiquaries, and perhaps a bit apprehensive when he heard of stiff resistance which prevented the landing of a cargo of tea in his own Philadelphia. It was consoling to realize this episode had resulted in no disorder.

Since the king had asked that the petition for the dismissal of Hutchinson be laid before the Privy Council, it would very likely be coming up soon for some sort of attention. Consequently the Doctor may well have hoped that the controversy over the Hutchinson letters might die down a bit before there were any hearings. But instead the matter was being kept very much alive by a running argument carried on in the press between William Whately, brother and executor of the gentleman to whom the missives had been written, and John Temple, former American, now a British customs official and presumed acquaintance of Franklin's. This wrangle over how the letters came to be made public waxed hotter and hotter until it resulted in an indecisive duel between this pair in Hyde Park on December 11. Whately, though wounded, was mending, and since the affair was still alive, and the contest would probably be fought over again, Franklin decided to end this stupid wrangle by acknowledging his own responsibility. A statement to that effect appeared in the *Public Advertiser* on Christmas Day. At once the ministerial cohort speeded plans for the kill.

On January 10, 1774, he was informed that there would be a hearing the next day at the quarters where the Privy Council then customarily met, known as the "Cockpit." There Franklin went through a preliminary hearing by the vitriolic, vindictive Alexander Wedderburn, solicitor general, who appeared for Hutchinson and Oliver. The Colonial Agent demanded his right to have counsel, and also for three weeks in which to prepare his case. So a continuation of the hearings on January 29 was agreed to. However, Franklin's defense was badly weakened by his full admission of obtaining the letters and his utter refusal to divulge how the letters were put into his hands. Actually his opponents could hardly have planned a more advantageous dilemma, which must have seemed to them to have almost achieved perfection when, on the twenty-seventh, two days previous to the resumption of hearings, most astounding news broke. Five weeks before, on December 16, the refractory Bostonians had held a "tea party." Ministerial tempers flared up at this new evidence of colonial villainy, and they were all for dealing more drastically than ever with the Colonial Agent.

Probably no other hearing during Franklin's years in England received more intense billing. Virtually everyone of consequence in governmental affairs tried to crowd themselves, along with thirty-six of the privy councilors, into a cramped and limited chamber which, on this occasion, was misnamed. For what the Cockpit was about to witness was a very one-sided encounter, Wedderburn alone being permitted to use his spurs. Not only was the sixty-eight-year-old defendant prohibited from a single syllable in his own defense, but he was forced to stand for well above an hour while his opponent worked him over with a verbal flail. By dint of will power inspiring to see, Franklin is said not to have once altered the expression on his face during the whole of this vile excoriation.

It was contended he was a thief, and a base one at that, who would not refuse to purloin a man's most intimate private effects. He was an incendiary, an abettor of evil, the master of the insidious "Dr. Franklin's school of politics," and in the perverse and contemptible practices taught therein, he was a ready coach. He was a man on a horse, building a following, and biding his time, intending to set up a "great American Republic." As a flogging with words, Wedderburn's philippic was almost a classic, and his majesty's fawning privy councilors laughed uproariously at many of his malicious sallies and on occasions, according to Franklin, even applauded.

At long last his farcical "hearing" was over. It was not unanimously approved by those who heard the tirade, and even the

London press was about equally divided. But the clique in power were not through. The following day was the Sabbath, but so zealous were they that they refused to rest their case. That Sunday a letter was delivered at Craven Street bluntly informing Franklin he was dismissed from the postal service. Bright and early on Monday there was a demand that he make up and turn in his accounts, for his successor had already been appointed.

There were bound to be repercussions in the colonies, but they came totally without stimulation on Franklin's part. The colonists refused to employ the "royal post," and there was soon a demand for a substitute "constitutional" post. By the time the former co-deputy arrived home the following year the two parallel systems were in operation, with a second *independent* post office in virtually every town of size between Boston and Williamsburg. To Sister Jane he wrote, "I am depriv'd of my office . . . [but] don't let this give you any Uneasiness. You and I have almost finished the Journey of Life; we are now but a little way from home, and have enough in our Pockets to pay the Post Chaises . . . The displacing me is a Testimony of my being uncorrupted." What a pity it is that Deborah Franklin did not retain the letters her husband wrote to her with that same fine consistency his sister, Jane Mecom, did.

Regarding the Wedderburn affair, there was some division in the American press, but majority opinion was definitely on his side. The rift between patriots and loyalists was already apparent, however; and the Boston *Public Ledger* charged the man sometimes called the *First Civilized American* with being the brains of a huge plot to form a "Great American Commonwealth," of which "the Great and Learned Doctor was to be the Regulator and Dictator! The old dotard thought he saw himself as the founder of empires and the father of kings."

What were his own reactions? He believed he had done right, and was prepared to do the same thing over again if the circumstances so dictated. But his illusions with regard to the building of an empire in which the Colonies would have equal share in the partnership faded rapidly. The probability of eventual Independence began to gain ground. He had had but indifferent faith for some years in Parliament, and now his respect for king and ministers became similarly doubtful. In Philadelphia Dr. Kinnersley was preparing for his last season of electrical lectures, and in keeping with local indignation arranged effigies of Wedderburn and Hutchinson so they might be set afire electrically.

In London Dr. Franklin seemed quite content to let the matter die down, and found it more satisfying just then to employ his time looking into the subject of fireproofing. Also he was in hope of turning the agency affairs over to Arthur Lee, but that unstable young man selected this critical moment to disappear to the Continent on an extended tour. Ugly rumors now began to float about that the Agent was to have his effects seized and be himself hauled off to Newgate Prison.

To curb the expansionist hopes in the original colonies, the Quebec Act, incorporating areas in the Ohio and Mississippi Valleys into Canada, was passed in April. This seemed to put limitations upon the western land scheme, and, to remove whatever personal detraction with which he might be burdening the project, he promptly gave up his share in the matter. In May there was great worry, and suddenly then extreme sadness, on Craven Street. Three of the Hewsons contracted smallpox. The two children recovered, but the father died, leaving Polly a widow.

Across the seas Virginia was suggesting a Continental Congress to meet that fall in centrally located Philadelphia, while in June, the Boston Port Bill closed that port to commerce, and threatened it with starvation and decay. By July Paul Revere headed to Philadelphia in search of promises of assistance from the Pennsylvania province in resisting British ruthlessness.

In August the Doctor took the Oxford road to Le Despencer's for a visit, and also called upon other friends in that area, with the inclusion of a most fortunate chat with the former William Pitt, now the Earl of Chatham, who professed great friendship for and interest in America.

In September Ben wrote a letter of introduction for a man wishing to remove to America. While he seemed to have several well-developed abilities, it was perhaps his writing talents that the Doctor thought might find ready employment, especially in putting the American cause into words. His name was Thomas Paine, and Franklin asked his son-in-law, rather than his own son William, to do what he could for the newcomer.

There was a letter to William, however, at about this same time, a portion of which is reproduced at the head of this chapter. As the last sentence tends to indicate, a breach was opening in the relations between father and son, and strangely it was something of an inversion. In this case the younger man was the conservative standpatter, while the father was the incipient rebel. William had informed his parent that friends were wishing him home for the forthcoming session of Congress; but English acquaintances had assured the Doctor his presence in London should be helpful, especially since Parliament had been dissolved and an election might bring in members more favorable to the American cause.

He did have suggestions, however, for this Congress; and he also began to caution his American friends not to be too hopeful of a new Parliament, since the Court would in all probability dominate it again. He had current reason to know how heartily opposed to him George III had become. The question was again raised as to lightning rods, this time a set to be installed at Kew Palace. The monarch had ordered his physician, Sir John Pringle, a member of the commission, to side with him for knobbed rather than sharp points. But Franklin's old friend indicated his refusal by informing the autocratic king that he had no power to abrogate nature's laws. This attitude eventually deprived Pringle of the presidency of the Royal Society and his post as royal physician.

The Agent had not mistaken the sovereign, for the latter in addressing the incoming Parliament on November 29 informed its members that their predecessors had been dismissed because they had not been sufficiently incisive and severe in treating with the American malcontents. Such an attitude hardly seems to portend favorable reception for a petition received from the Continental Congress, which came to Franklin's hands on December 18, and was promptly lodged with Dartmouth. The latter gentleman, however, was quite optimistic, and thought it conceivable that a satisfactory adjustment of the whole American situation might be achieved.

The Agent's fortitude must have seemed rather remarkable to many of his ministerial opponents. They had rather expected to see him gather his tail between his legs, and hurry away to America. But here he was, as big as life, and twice as annoying, seemingly a rallying point for subversion, and an evident inspiration to rebellion. If he could not be driven off, could he be bought in? To jail him would have precipitated a crisis, and an unfortunate one, and no one knew it better than Franklin. But did he have a price? Was there any manner in which he could be taken over? Would a complete reversal of procedure soften him up, help to bring him around? It was worth a try, and suddenly the good Doctor found himself more popular in London than he had ever been before. Seemingly the word had gone out, and the ministers in concert were hoping to reach the American through his vanity.

Early in December some of Franklin's closest friends made arrangements for him to play chess, of which he was quite fond, with a mature spinster, a Miss Howe. She was a member of a celebrated family, several of her brothers even having had some experience in America. And, since she talked quite entertainingly, along with playing a challenging game, he paid her a number of visits.

Dropping by on Christmas Day, he soon found himself in earnest conversation with her brother, Admiral Lord Howe, who finally begged the Envoy to draw up a plan of reconciliation which he believed the colonies might conceivably agree to. The prospects were extensively explored in several meetings, and the matter gone over with his own close friends, even to handing some of them a draft of proposed *Hints for Conversation* with the proper parties to a settlement.

Then, unwittingly, Howe tipped his hand. A copy of these *Hints* seems to have found its way to him. The terms "hinted" at in the document were, he assured the Doctor, far too harsh. And that was a great pity, for much good might come from what was being attempted. He had no thought or wish to influence

the American against his better judgment. Still, if he would but
lower the demands he "might with reason expect any reward in
the power of government to bestow." Aha! This was the cul-
mination of the goodwill build-up. It was a bare-faced bribe! He
was being asked to compromise the American cause, the implication being that if he would but do so, he might expect to be elevated to the peerage. How rotten could politics get?

Suavely Franklin agreed to see what could be done. He did
draw up a "revision," and even sent it in Miss Howe's name, lest
the brother be placed in an embarrassing position. But it was an
unmistakable refusal, for the demands contained were not one
whit less harsh than the original compilation.

And when Parliament came back into session after the holidays,
there was ample evidence that the American Colonies, like their
principal spokesman in London, had no thought of being bought
off. There had been a few days of Indian summer. But now they
were quickly over, and a chill and depressing season was at hand.

## xix.  A Revolutionary, Aged Seventy

## 1775–1776

*When I consider the extreme Corruption prevalent among all*
*Orders of Men in this old rotten State, and the glorious publick*
*Virtue so predominant in our rising Country, I cannot but apprehend*
*more Mischief than Benefit from a closer Union. I fear they will drag*
*us after them in all the plundering Wars, which their desperate Cir-*
*cumstances, Injustice, and Rapacity, may prompt them to undertake;*
*and their wide-wasting Prodigality and Profusion is a Gulph that will*
*swallow up every Aid we may distress ourselves to afford them.*
*Here Numberless and needless Places, enormous Salaries, Pensions,*
*Perquisites, Bribes, groundless Quarrels, foolish Expeditions, false*
*Accounts or no Accounts, Contracts and Jobbs, devour all Revenue,*
*and produce continual necessity in the midst of natural Plenty. I*
*apprehend, therefore, that to unite us intimately will only be to cor-*
*rupt and poison us also.*—Letter to Joseph Galloway, February 25,
1775.

THE ministry, which had so badly misjudged American hopes,
aspirations, and reactions, was also similarly in error as respects
the American Agent's intents and purposes. It had been assumed
that he was a crafty old double-dealer, empowered to bind the
colonies to any program, and motivated merely by the extent of
his personal benefit in any deal concluded. His standing pat on
the demands he had first offered was interpreted as his determination to drive a hard bargain now that the government had expressed willingness to make some redress of past excesses. Did
this man Franklin actually speak for America? Were his professions the professions of a majority of the colonists?

When Parliament came again into session on January 19, 1775,

210

Lord North laid before that body a mass of data which included many letters, pamphlets, handbills, and other documentary evidence gathered from all colonies from New Hampshire to Georgia. The tenor of this material was unmistakable. Massachusetts might be a sort of bellwether in the matter of resistance and reparation, but there was a remarkable unanimity in attitude and determination in all thirteen colonies. No doubt about it, the Americans, or a fair share of them, had their dander up. Since the unfortunate, but hardly unprovoked, incident they insisted on calling the Boston *Massacre*, there was a growing disposition to resort to armed conflict, if need be, to gain the stringent demands they now resolutely considered their just due. Parliament, still activated to some extent by the age-old preference for rule by despotism, began to bristle at this unmistakable evidence of insubordination.

On the nineteenth Howe had told Franklin he was sorry the Envoy could not see his way to being more reasonable, and the Doctor had demanded to know what promises the ministry would make. His lordship seemed unprepared to answer, and their contact pretty much ceased.

The following morning there was an invitation for the still much-cultivated Agent to be in the lobby of the House of Lords at two that afternoon. Thereupon Lord Chatham had Dr. Franklin admitted to the House. The purpose was to have him present during a proposal and debate on America. It did warm his heart a trifle to hear British peers praise Americans for seeking to emphasize and protect their basic liberties. Yet the day's efforts in behalf of withdrawing the troops from Boston went for naught, being voted down nearly four to one.

The small contingent of noble lords favorable to America was still determined, and, on the peer's insistence, Franklin met Chatham at his country place, "Hayes," the following Friday the twenty-seventh. There they went over the plan this Whig leader had prepared. On the following Sunday my lord paid Franklin a very considerable compliment by calling on him in Craven Street. Since his carriage stood before the door for a full two hours, the visit became gossip throughout the city.

It was on February 1 that Chatham championed the American

cause, being aided by the remarks of several other peers who strongly favored his proposals for reconciliation. Greatly to Franklin's consternation Parliament treated this important plea "with as much contempt as they could have shown to a ballad offered by a drunken porter." When, on the following day, the majority readily backed a motion by the opposition to send a small army to the colonies to suppress the *rebellion* there, the Colonial Agent was disgusted. A break now appeared to be inevitable.

Matters dragged along during February, and merely tended to crystalize the attitude to which Franklin gave expression near the end of that month in the letter above to Joseph Galloway. There was to be a meeting with Howe on the twenty-eighth, but the post that arrived from America on that or the previous day brought further disturbing news, which strengthened the feeling of futility.

Deborah Franklin, his wife of nearly forty-five years, and whom he had not seen in more than ten, had had a stroke on December 14, and died five days later. Regarding England, there was now a feeling of surfeit. He was through! And at once he began preparations for leaving, convinced he had done his best, and similarly certain the governing class in Britain were incapable of seeing the light.

Reserved, even beyond his wont, and also a trifle embittered, he bade hurried good-bys, and there was cold civility in leave-taking. The ministry, not wanting the charge of persecution laid upon it, made no attempt to detain him. So by mid-March the Doctor and fifteen-year-old William Temple Franklin were on their way to Portsmouth. And by the end of that month they were aboard a packet, and heading west through the Channel, homeward bound.

For the first three weeks the ex-envoy was busy compiling his notes on the happenings of the past four rather hectic months. But this highway home was paved with water. He had once wished to be a sailor upon it, and may have had some salty traces of it still in his veins. So the latter half of the pleasant six weeks' voyage went pretty much into a study of the Gulf Stream.

He and his grandson landed in Philadelphia on May 5, the good news of his safe arrival far overshadowed by other news received that same morning of a grave incident in Massachusetts sixteen days previously. There, on Lexington Common, certain "Minute Men" had been in an armed clash with British regulars, and before the day was over the latter had taken severe drubbing. It had been one of the *continental* post riders, a chap he had never met, named Paul Revere, that had "spread the alarm through every Middlesex village and farm, for the country folk to be up and arm."

Once ashore Franklin was taken to a home nearly ten years old, yet completely new to him, where he found his beloved Sally, and Dick Bache, her husband, ensconced. Benny Bache, the first grandchild, now almost six, was sharing honors with a more recent arrival, William, familiarly spoken of as the "Infant Hercules." Within a few days young William Temple Franklin left for Amboy to live with his father the governor.

While Philadelphia might afford a change, it promised little in the way of rest. Before he was hardly through his first breakfast in America the Assembly had selected him as one of its deputies to the forthcoming second session of the Continental Congress. He would be its oldest member, and of sufficient age to have been the father of at least half, or more, of its delegates. These latter were arriving in town on the ninth and tenth, and meetings began on the tenth.

Within a short time Franklin was a member of ten of its committees. But next to Congress the provincial Committee of Safety was perhaps the most important body in Philadelphia, and he was soon unanimously elected its chairman, which office laid a heavy demand upon his time. Some of its two dozen members were a trifle uneasy over the readiness with which their chairman dared think and speak of independence from the English Crown. This was particularly so of the grave, moderate John Dickinson, who seemed willing to undertake rebellion, but lacked the outlook and fortitude to move aggressively into outright revolution. Distance from London still left an aura of enchantment in the minds of some of the colonials; but in Franklin's case the last few years had washed it quite away.

To take advantage of daylight, candle grease being scarce, the committee meetings throughout the summer session of Congress began promptly at six in the morning, and terminated earlier on some days, but customarily by four in the afternoon, so that the members might give attention to other committees of lesser import. The cares of this major body were manifold and heavy, for they dealt with the military problems of all the colonies, and with a very considerable extent of territory. It was something of a coincidence that, while its chairman had but recently returned from many years residence abroad, he was still, with his travels as Deputy Postmaster General to draw upon, probably more familiar with a greater extent of the colonial domain than any other delegate.

On May 29 he was the very logical choice as a member of a committee charged with forming a permanent postal system. Deliberations carried on for more than a month, and in July he was appointed the first Postmaster General under the Continental Congress. His salary in this post he promptly assigned to a fund for the aid of wounded soldiers.

In late June a famous meeting took place which, due no doubt to the press of affairs, was perhaps rather casual, and the details do not seem to have been recorded. A tall, redheaded, freckled-faced Virginian had arrived to take his place as a delegate. His name was Thomas Jefferson, and it is a great pity that no one has left us a word picture of the occasion when these two foremost American philosophers bowed to each other. While the elder of the pair was more than twice the age of the younger, then but thirty-two, Franklin and Jefferson were to join hands in several very worthy enterprises in this country, one of which, about a year later, was due for immortality. Later they would be together for nearly a year in France.

Before the month was out, in fact, they were both members of a committee to draw up *A Declaration by the Representatives of the United Colonies of North America, now met in Congress at Philadelphia, setting forth the causes and necessity of taking up arms.* Franklin, able propagandist, was too heavily involved for much writing beyond letters to his wide circle of British acquaintances, and so a new and most able pen was furnished by Jefferson. His Declaration on Taking Up Arms was in the nature of a warm-up for a far more potent Declaration yet to come.

Franklin meanwhile was heavily involved in a wide array of matters as diversified as procuring saltpeter and gunpowder, designing huge *chevaux de frise* to keep British ships from ascending the Delaware, petitioning the king, and printing an issue of paper money, to name but a few. He had decided in his own mind for Independence, as letters to English acquaintances that July indicated. Of a different nature was one penned to perhaps the oldest of London friends, which rather pathetically read: "Mr. Strahan. You are a Member of Parliament, and one of that Majority which has doomed my Country to Destruction.—You have begun to burn our Towns, and murder our People.—Look upon your hands.—They are stained with the Blood of your Relations! —You and I were long Friends:—You are now my Enemy,—and I am Yours, B. Franklin." Most happily it was never sent.

On July 21 the Congress sitting as a committee of the whole, listened while its oldest member, who had so valiantly championed Union at Albany twenty-one years before, now read his proposed *Articles of Confederation and Perpetual Union*. But that body, yet to be chastened by adversity, and still zealous of individual colony prerogatives, was not ready for such a move. Although the Congress recessed on August 1, the provincial Committee of Safety kept daily about its tasks. There was no Scotland, no Ireland, no France to entice its chairman away, and too many concerns having to do with salt, trade, Indians, conscientious objectors, and other matters, to think of protracted absence.

There was a matter involving two people rather close to his heart that had plagued him not a little. Since his return William had ridden down from New Jersey to pay his respects. Joseph Galloway, long his loyal lieutenant in the Assembly, had joined them in the evening, and over their Madeira they had talked far into the night on the current state of affairs, and particularly about independence. Astounded, and no doubt a little hurt, the Doctor had found the younger men strongly opposed to his views. William was still the "thorough courtier," while Galloway was demonstrating his attitude by refusing to sit in the

Congress, to which he had been elected. Such cleavage between *patriotism* and *loyalty* would now begin to tear friends and families asunder.

The situation was much in the older man's mind through the long, hot, busy summer days. Unlike London, where an extensive social life had been a part of his stock in trade, he had become something of a social recluse since his return. Too much concentration upon the somber affairs of rebellion, together with too little activity, and by the end of August he felt himself growing stale. A change of scene might help, so he set off for Perth Amboy to talk further with William. But it proved to be love's labor lost. The very same diversities that were widening the breach between Mother England and her American daughter were operating just as certainly in the Franklin family between father and son. Thus they parted, agreeing only to disagree.

Congress reconvened on September 13, and one of its first acts was to grant permission to the former Envoy to bring ashore papers, records, and other goods that had followed by a later ship. The boycott was very definitely in force, and making Tory sympathizers of some of the affected merchants. Late in the month Ben conducted his first meeting of the American Philosophical Society, although he had been president for better than six years. Then came an outing on which he had not planned.

The fourth day of October he, Benjamin Harrison of Virginia, Thomas Lynch of South Carolina, and their three grooms, set off for Cambridge to make arrangements with Washington and the New England authorities for the raising and support of an army. There were four rather inconclusive days of conferences in which colonial *union* was more apparent than evident, but some progress—and much more in the way of promises—was accomplished.

From the Massachusetts Assembly he managed to collect the balance owing him for services in Britain, and he also chanced to meet a spirited lady whom he would see again under unanticipated circumstances some years later. She was Abigail Adams, who intrusted a letter to him to be delivered to husband John, now at the Congress in Philadelphia.

At Cambridge he had met a young blacksmith turned soldier

much to the dismay of his Quaker family and friends. His name was Nathanael Greene, a nephew by marriage of Catherine Ray Greene, and in command of the Rhode Island militia. From him he had recent news of his friends in the little colony on Narragansett Bay. And, since Jane Franklin Mecom had taken refuge in Warwick when the British seized Boston, it was but natural that the Doctor would so route his return journey that he might stop in this smallest of the colonies among friends who insisted he was "the most famous man in the world."

After a very pleasant visit, he set off home, taking along with him Catherine's ten-year-old son, whom he placed in school and played foster parent to in Philadelphia. It was November 15 before he was back again, and much of his time for the first few days was given to the Pennsylvania Assembly, of which he was again a member. He was again a member of Congress, and reappointed to the Committee of Safety, and the days were filled almost beyond endurance.

On the next to the last day of November he met with four other members of a new Committee of Correspondence. Its immediate purpose was to contact by letter the friends of America abroad. It thus began to deal in foreign affairs, and was the early forerunner of our present Department of State. Within a day or two, and almost as though by prearrangement, a secret agent of France arrived. Here was a new diplomatic task for Franklin, and the beginning of one of his greatest contributions to American Heritage. In December he would cast his vote in favor of building thirteen armed frigates, which signaled the birth of the United States Navy.

The city to which the Doctor had returned the previous year had grown and altered tremendously, not only in the half century since his first arrival there, but even in the decade of his last absence. Its 40,000 population made it second only to London in the empire, and nearly five hundred of its more than six thousand homes had been built in 1774 alone. But at the beginning of the critical year 1776 only about one in fifty of these inhabitants owned sufficient property to qualify them as voters. An aristocracy of wealth and privilege had established itself, in comparison with which the well-to-do Franklin was definitely middle-class.

Along with the New Year a new flag also appeared. While Washington had selected the colors, the design seems to have been borrowed from the ensign of the East India Company, and was made up of thirteen alternate red and white stripes, with the combined crosses of Sts. George and Andrew on a blue corner field. The "stars and stripes" emblem was still eighteen months in the future. And very shortly after the new year and the new flag came a pamphlet which Franklin had suggested its author produce. Its title was *Common Sense*, its writer Thomas Paine, its success was immediate, and its influence virtually a bombshell. Its twenty-two thousand words made it a smash hit, and no less than one hundred fifty thousand copies had been distributed before the year's end.

Far less auspicious was the Franklin seventieth birthday on January 17. Yet this three score and ten milestone was for him not a goal, but the beginning of new and vital contributions. To very few men in all history has the opportunity come to double an already enviable reputation after achieving age seventy.

So considerable was his prestige in fact that the Congress employed it prodigally. It was most essential that Canada, if possible, be encouraged to make common cause with the thirteen rebellious colonies to the south. The Committee of Correspondence, in a report written in Franklin's hand, having made such a suggestion, it was perhaps not strange that he should have been chosen on February 15, along with Samuel Chase of Maryland, to gain Canadian support. With them they arranged to take the wealthy young Charles Carroll of Carrollton, a little later elected to the Congress, and his cousin John, a Jesuit priest.

It was the end of March before the roads were at all suitable for travel, and the mission was on its way. The party went overland to New York, and then started a boat trip to Albany that turned out to be a small nightmare. It was pleasant to enjoy General Philip Schuyler's fine hospitality and rest a bit at this up-river town before plunging on to the north through April snow that bogged them down for a week at Saratoga.

The party finally reached Montreal. It had been a real trial to
the three younger men, only one of whom had achieved forty.
But the hardships had all but finished Franklin. Indifferent diet
had touched off a rash of huge boils, and his legs swelled so that
he was positive he had an advanced case of dropsy. Also their
efforts had been completely wasted, while on top of that the
arrival of additional British troops made their further stay in
Quebec highly hazardous.

Finally on May 11 the ailing man was forced to set out for
home. Despite many kindnesses along the way, it is quite probable he would not have completed the journey had it not been
for the devoted ministrations of young Father Carroll. Franklin
had the good fortune to repay him in part several years later,
when he aided in smoothing the path so the able Jesuit was
consecrated first Roman Catholic Bishop in the United States.

It was early June before he was back in the Philadelphia area
again, yet so exhausted he could not think of being at home,
which, since it was but a couple of blocks from the State House,
would have exposed him to an endless procession of callers. So
he accepted the hospitality of his good friend and the town's
leading watch and clock maker, Edward Duffield. In his comfortable country home, well out on the Bristol Road, the semi-in-
valid had a better chance of rapid recovery.

Such seclusion, however, did not cut him off from news of
what was happening in Philadelphia, and elsewhere. In Congress,
Richard Henry Lee, on instructions from Williamsburg, was
offering his famous resolution that "these United Colonies are,
and of right out to be, free and independent states." Across the
river in New Jersey the Assembly was placing Governor William Franklin under house arrest, while about three weeks later
the Continental Congress banished this loyalist to Litchfield in
Connecticut for safe keeping. The action, and the need for it,
must have pained the father severely, yet it seemed to be inevitable.

On June 10 he had been chosen one of a five-man committee
to draw up a suitable declaration addressed to the whole world
of the colonies' intention to assume an independent status. While
Ben was still at the Duffield home, it is conceivable the other four

saddled their horses and rode out there for an organizational session. But the actual drafting fell to the lot of Tom Jefferson who, with tongue in cheek and a twinkle in the eye, maintained that Congress had not trusted good old Dr. Franklin, fearing he might draw up the document with a huge joke or hoax in the very midst of it. Yet the elder statesman seems to have checked over the far younger Virginian's text before the committee approved his efforts. Jefferson, whose stable charges for his several horses exceeded the cost of his own keep while in Philadelphia, may have jogged out the Bristol Road for one or more conferences of his own while the drafting was in progress.

But Franklin was back in Congress, and comforting the author, when that body began to debate the great manifesto. Also he and Jefferson served rather fruitlessly on another committee that tried to arrange a seal for these new *United States*. They may very well have stood together at an open window on July 8 while Col. John Nixon made the first public reading of the Declaration from a platform in the yard directly behind the State House.

Once more restored to health, the Doctor was soon back in harness again, dividing his time between Congress and added duties as president of the convention framing a new government for the *State* of Pennsylvania. He did receive and read to the Congress a letter from his friend and pupil in France, Dr. Barbeu Dubourg, who assured him that the French foreign minister, Comte de Vergennes, was most partial to the Americans. At once Congress decided to enlist French aid, although Franklin sought to dissuade the body from hurrying into this business of "suitoring for alliances."

While the Declaration was approved on July 4, it was not actually signed until August 2, on which date Franklin is supposed to have made the sally about the signers "hanging together" or risking the chance of "hanging separately." By this time, too, he was perhaps toying with another of his humorous exploits. As the Postmaster General his mail was carried without payment of postage, since he was privileged to frank it by writing beside the address *"Free*, B. Franklin." Sometime after the independent post office was set up, and especially now that

Independence had been declared, it amused him to alter this franking endorsement to read *"B. Free* Franklin."

Some of his recent correspondence had been with Admiral Lord Howe. His lordship, who had long wished to act as a peace commissioner to America, was finally so appointed by Parliament, together with his younger brother, Sir William, the general. Between the sailors and ships of one and the soldiers of the other, New York was firmly in their hands. As the result of an exchange of letters, Franklin, John Adams, and Edward Rutledge met with his lordship on September 11 in a house on Staten Island across the mouth of Arthur Kill from Perth Amboy. But the commissioners sensed that Howe's powers to parley were limited, and the conference came to nought.

At home he found William and Catherine Greene from Rhode Island, who had brought Jane Mecom along with them. The Greenes could stay but a week after he was back, and saw very little of him unfortunately because of the continued demands upon his time. Sister Jane, however, stayed on, since Philadelphia then seemed far safer than Boston. She was consequently there when her brother, together with Jefferson, lately returned to Virginia, and Silas Deane, already in Paris, were chosen as commissioners to represent the United States at the Court of France. Franklin was greatly disappointed when Jefferson asked to be excused because of the precarious health of his wife, and even more so when he was replaced with the highly unstable Arthur Lee, presently in London.

There were hurried preparations, although once again his being away was of course expected to be only a matter of a few months. Dick Bache was installed as Postmaster General, and young Bennie Bache made ready to accompany his grandfather to enjoy a spot of schooling abroad. Also a hurried call was sent off to Amboy to the daughter-in-law who had remained behind when her husband had been sent away to Connecticut. If William Temple Franklin could be spared by the foster mother, something much to his advantage was promised through the grandparent. Young William was soon in Philadelphia.

Although Joseph Galloway still stood aloof from the American cause, Franklin found it convenient to entrust to him for safekeeping certain papers which it seemed well not to leave in the home in Philadelphia. So these were taken out to the Galloway country place at Trevose. The remaining preliminaries at last out of the way, Commissioner Franklin and his two grandsons went quietly aboard the American sloop, the *Reprisal*, commanded by Captain Wickes. On October 26 it was on its way down the Delaware River.

As the stream widened all sail was set, and the little ship made Quiberon Bay, above the mouth of the Loire, in but thirty-three days. But they had been jam-packed with exciting chases and brushes with the enemy. Just off the French coast the stout little *Reprisal* had captured two British vessels, and the prize money they brought pretty much offset the expenses of the trip.

On December 7 they were in Nantes, where a carriage was had, and the three travelers pushed up the Loire Valley and on to Paris. Their journey was completed four days before Christmas. And a week later the commissioners were received by the Comte de Vergennes, news of which fact was promptly hurried across the Channel to Whitehall by the British secret service.

Back in Philadelphia the Bache family and Jane Mecom, together with hundreds of others, had been seized with panic, and fled to places of safety. On December 15 Jane wrote to her brother from Goshenville, a Quaker village thirty odd miles west of the city. Had the Doctor not gone to France, he would at the moment probably have been in Baltimore, where Congress had taken refuge as Lord Howe threatened Philadelphia. Yet it would be nearly a year before this threat was made good.

But in France the atmosphere was quite different. There he was known and loved, and accepted as one of the world's greats. Soon, as he walked along the streets, men were pleased to tip their hats to *Bonhomme Richard*.

## xx.   In Search of an Ally

### *1777–1778*

*I received your favour by Mr. Austin, with your most agreeable Congratulations on the Success of the American Arms in the Northern Department [Burgoyne's surrender]. In Return give me leave to congratulate you on the Success of our Negotiations here, in the completion of the two Treaties with his Most Christian Majesty; the one of Amity and Commerce, on the Plan of that Projected in Congress, with some good additions; the Other of Alliance for Mutual Defense, in which the most Christian King agrees to make a Common Cause with the United States, if England attempts to Obstruct the Commerce of his Subjects with them; and guarantees to the United States their Liberties, Sovereignty, and Independence, absolute and unlimited, with the Possessions they now have, or may have, at the Conclusion of the War. . . . The great Principle in both Treaties is a perfect Equality and reciprocity; no Advantages being demanded by France, or Privileges in Commerce, which the States may not grant to any and every other Nation.*—Letter to Thomas Cushing, February 27, 1778.

BEING the best-known foreigner in France had some small disadvantages, yet its benefits were manifold, and Franklin soon began to capitalize on the situation. He did his best to play to the interests of the masses as well as those of the nobility, confident that if he could influence enough people to favor the American cause, the Court could not long withhold its aid. That such aid could be built up to effective volume seemed certain, but it would take careful, diplomatic handling.

While Vergennes received him privately in December 1776, together with Deane and Lee, the foreign minister was already looking aside as cannon and other munitions were removed from arsenals and loaded aboard ships headed for unusual destinations. Some months before France and Spain had each furnished the playwright-adventurer, Caron de Beaumarchais, with one million *livres* (francs), and in July he had set up the fictitious Roderigue Hortalez and Company for the purpose of "trading" to America. Thus it would seem that the French looked upon the colonists as revolutionaries seeking independence as early as those same colonists made a declaration of their intentions.

Wickes put out to sea in the *Reprisal,* and was back shortly with five more British prizes. The ministry that had been so conscious of Franklin's presence in London were soon unpleasantly aware that the American was now representing his country in Paris. More and more British secret-service men began to appear to keep an eye on the envoys and to try to learn the intentions of American armed vessels now stealing in and out of French ports. Also they did their best to shut off the Envoy's correspondence; and between spies and British men-of-war it would be into the spring of the next year before any word was exchanged between these Paris representatives and the Congress at home.

In early March the Doctor moved out to Passy, a half-hour's drive from Paris, and more convenient to the Court. He took a house on the estate of Le Ray de Chaumont, known as the "Hotel de Valentinois," and would be first his guest, and then a tenant, during the next eight years. There he soon set up a small printing office, partly for convenience in connection with his duties, partly for his amusement, and also perhaps with the thought of stimulating the interest of one or the other of the grandsons. In the village he found a school into which to put the younger of the two, Benny Bache. Temple, now seventeen, was old enough to serve as his clerk and aide. Jonathan Williams, who had worked for his Great-uncle Benjamin on Craven Street, was also with him, traveling about in connection with American shipments.

The war had not progressed into its bitterer stages, and in April in England, Wedgwood was still casting and selling Franklin medallions. Archrebel to some, no doubt, the American would retain many friends in the British Isles throughout the prolonged hostilities. Some of Britain's diplomats in France, however, were not exactly friendly. The Viscount Stormont, wishing to embarrass both the American cause and its chief local advocate, manufactured some fantastic tales. Promptly a very popular *bon mot* was coined by Franklin, the name Stormount becoming a synonym for *lie,* or *falsehood.*

Already Arthur Lee was showing his true colors by flaring up in anger and bitterness, but the older envoy was too busy to carry on the other side of a feud. There was a procession of French adventurers to Passy, seeking out the Doctor, and demanding places in the American army. Some arrived with political backing which it might have been unfortunate to take too lightly or to overlook, and such applicants became a burden. Others were self-recommending only. Soon Franklin's wit came to his rescue, and he drafted a form letter which subtly indicated his contempt for the whole procedure. It read:

"The bearer of this, who is going to America, presses me to give him a letter of recommendation, though I know nothing of him, not even his name. This may seem extraordinary, but I assure you it is not uncommon here. Sometimes, indeed, one unknown person brings another, equally unknown, to recommend him; and sometimes they recommend one another. As to this gentleman, I must refer you to himself for his character and merits, with which he is certainly better acquainted than I can possibly be. I recommend him, however, to those civilities which every stranger of whom one knows no harm has a right to; and I request you will do him all the good offices and show him all the favour, that on further acquaintance you shall find him to deserve."

Franklin did, however, recommend and also enhance the reputation of that most remarkable Prussian drillmaster, Baron von Steuben. Also he was able to give sincere commendation to Washington in behalf of the youthful Marquis de Lafayette, whom he had never met.

Much time was spent in the drudgery of accounting, letter writing, and other routine and detail. There were enough of these activities with which he had very little patience so that pamphleteering was a pleasant relief. There can be but little doubt that the anonymous satire *The Sale of the Hessians* was his, and produced about this time, while the *Comparison of Great Britain and the United States in Regard to the Basis of Credit in the Two Countries* was unquestionably from his pen.

This latter dates presumably from the spring of 1777. By then Franklin must have realized he had a role in a huge and involved melodrama, which called for great tact and an abundance of patience. The French were in no mood to openly support the American colonists and hazard a war with England until there was certainty as to its beneficial outcome. Vergennes, cordial in private, was aloof in public, seeking to appease the British. The truly disturbing situation, however, was the complete lack of harmony among the American commissioners, which condition might have seriously crippled the American call upon French aid had the Doctor been a less well balanced person.

The summer seems to have been pretty much a continuation of the monotonous routine of earlier months, and the pace forced the Doctor to steer clear of scientific controversy, for which he had no available time. War activity was mostly on land, and thus chiefly in America, and made bad news as it filtered in through the British spy ring, leaving little upon which to trade. When a request for recognition of the Independence declared more than a year before was filed with the French, it received but little consideration. Among the American news items was word of the death in July of Elizabeth Downes Franklin, wife of the imprisoned Governor William. It was comforting to realize that Temple was right here in Passy. But far from comforting was the word of a battle in the Brandywine Valley in September, and then of another a few days later at Germantown, and the fall of Philadelphia to Lord Howe. The threat of the year before had this time been made real. What had happened to Franklin's family, to his home? It would be months later before he learned the Baches were safe far to the west of Philadelphia in Manheim, with Congress at York, and the house on Oriana Street full of British officers.

With the termination by the Congress of the commission of the reasonable, likable Silas Deane, the late fall became almost a period of despair. It was especially apparent on a Sunday afternoon, December 4, 1777, when the group of Americans gathered for dinner at Franklin's could do little but sit and eat in silence. A carriage ground to a stop in the courtyard, yet no one sensed one of the most dramatic moments of the war and made the effort to see who it might be. Finally a servant entered and announced a Mr. Jonathan Austin of Massachusetts. Ah! Here was someone from beyond the ocean, and a bearer of late news. The host and several others made their way to the out-of-doors expectantly questioning the stranger, "Is Philadelphia *indeed* taken?"

"Indeed it is," admitted the young courier from the Bay State, "But I have other much later news. Burgoyne has been beaten, and his whole army taken prisoner." This was perhaps the most poignant moment in all the Envoy's years in France. Here was a valuable coin in trading for alliance and aid. Before the rapidly wasting year had run out, satisfactory treaties were pretty well assured, and the prospects of France as an ally far, far brighter. "Gentleman Johnny" Burgoyne, whom Franklin had met at Preston, England, six years before, could not possibly have done a more acceptable favor for the two commissioners still at the French Court.

Less than a full week after the turn into the new year, 1778, Britain had its top secret-service man in France working on Franklin. And the gentleman, observing as he was, did not seem to realize the elderly diplomat was in turn working upon him. The Doctor would be seventy-two now in a few days, and his mind was still keen and on the hair trigger. Less than a week later he cleared the way for the treaties, for the king had given his word, and they were finally signed early in February. Among the first benefits to accrue from the Treaty of Alliance was the availability of naval forces under Comte d'Estaing, made up of eleven ships of the line and six frigates, together with a considerable body of land forces. With this added strength on the American side, communication between the Congress and its envoys might be established again.

It was in February, too, that he met the famous Voltaire, who had returned to Paris to spend the few remaining weeks of his life. The Frenchman had been a wizard with words, while the

American had tamed the lightning. But if the rumors then flying about London could be believed, the latter was something of a wizard, too. It was soberly believed he had thought up a horrendous machine "the size of a toothpick case and materials that would reduce St. Paul's to a handful of ashes." Horace Walpole found it necessary to rise in Parliament and scotch this fantastic report. Not that the ministry believed such propaganda items, but they were still under necessity of silencing him and bringing him to heel. Thus the king's minions were once again approaching him with conciliatory offers, and also trying to buy off other key figures, such as Washington and the Adamses, in what was still looked upon as merely a rebellion.

In March there was another last-ditch offer by Britain, offset by a further French loan, and an audience with Louis XVI. Things seemed to be looking up in the American embassy, and then came a bad schism, with cleavage right in the top strata between the two commissioners. At a most arduous moment, the reckless, conceited Lee started rocking the boat. Actually this was far more than a clash of personalities, which would have been quite enough in this case. As in most congresses, or in most common causes, there were two opposing party groups. In the American revolutionary movement there was an intense but rather impractical *liberative* group, largely centering about a compact between two families—the Lees and the Adamses. Long on zeal, they were correspondingly short on practicality, especially as it involved diplomacy, administration, and military affairs. Sometimes it seemed that they stood before a looking glass, rather than before a clear window.

In the other *constructive* party were Washington, Franklin, Morris, Jay, Livingston, and others who had been less active in lighting the fires of conflict, yet who "showed themselves far better qualified for conducting it from a spasmodic rebellion into a successful revolution."

At Passy, Lee's chief difficulty was, as it had been earlier at London, that an older, sounder, far abler man stood in the way of his ambitions. To him, Franklin was "the meanest of men, the most corrupt of all corrupt men." Aiding and abetting Arthur Lee in his determination to take over single-handed the representation at Versailles was his brother William, appointed to Berlin, and the vain, excitable Ralph Izard, Jr., of South Carolina, appointed to Tuscany. Since neither country cared to commit itself by receiving an American minister, these amateur diplomats remained in Paris, and employed much time in aiding Arthur muddle affairs. Franklin was highly conscious of the opposition of this Lee-Adams junto back home. It was combating and probably trying to oust him in France, while in war-ridden America the very same group was doing its utmost to get rid of Washington.

And then, on April 8, came no less an opponent than John Adams to take the place of Silas Deane. The Braintree lawyer was a good politician, but never did develop much diplomatic know-how. Certain that he was irresistible while Franklin was rather lightweight and something of an old fogy, he began butting his head into stone walls the more astute gentleman had sense enough to walk around. But the Doctor's sagacity had been mistaken for guile, and even for fraud, by others, and Adams soon was highly suspicious. On his own part the gentleman from Philadelphia felt that Adams "means well for his country, is always an honest man, often a wise one, but sometimes, and in some things, absolutely out of his senses." Young John Quincy Adams, still only ten, was with his parent, and was put into the same school with Benny Bache, while his father settled down as best he could to being an American envoy.

The British still persisted in offering terms of reconciliation, and had come by now to promising all that had been asked of Howe three years before. There were not only patents of nobility for a list of leading Americans but also liberal pensions for life. The attempts were still to *buy*, rather than to *make*, peace. There was a picturesque attempt in June in a document tucked in through the grated doorway at Passy, signed with a pseudonym "Charles de Weissenstein," which Franklin had reason to believe originated with the king. But nothing came of it except a difference of opinion as to its purport and handling between him and Adams.

Of far greater import to the Doctor were the promises made by the French of outfitting John Paul Jones, who had plundered and burned along the English and Scottish coasts during the spring. Such plans were disclosed only to Franklin, since he alone of the American representatives was trusted by Vergennes, and all official dealings were limited to him when possible.

The celebration on July 4 went off most pleasantly, and there was some comfort in more frequent letters from America. Jane Mecom, dislodged first from her own home in Boston and then from her brother's home in Philadelphia, was once again in Rhode Island with a granddaughter. Joseph Galloway's estate at Trevose outside the Quaker City had been "attainted" after he had been declared a Tory, and was bought in at an auction by young James Wilkinson, destined to play a shady role in American post-Revolutionary history. Somewhere along the line in this Galloway affair a chest of Franklin records disappeared, and are still missing, unfortunately, to this day.

But the British found it advisable to evacuate Philadelphia, and on July 14, 1778, Richard Bache wrote once again from the home on Oriana Street, reporting among other items of news that there had been some plundering by the British, and that "a Captain André also took with him the picture of you which hung in the dining room." This was the officer who as Major John André was captured and executed in connection with the sorry Benedict Arnold affair. He was either an aide or rather close to Major General Sir Charles ("No-flint") Grey, into whose hands the Franklin portrait, painted by Wilson in 1759, eventually passed. It went home with him as a sort of trophy of his campaigning in America, and hung in the Grey estate, Howick House, Northumberland, until 1906. It was then returned to this country, to hang permanently in the White House.

John Adams's inherent honesty soon showed him the true lay of the land in France. While he could not see eye to eye with Franklin, he was forced to the conclusion that no other American possessed either his general prestige or his ready acceptance in government circles. In what the Doctor would have judged to be one of Adams's wiser moments, the Massachusetts patriot had recommended to Congress that there be but a single minister at the French Court. In September this suggestion was adopted, and the task became solely Franklin's. Yet it would be February of the following year before his new commission arrived, delivered by none other than the Marquis de Lafayette, home on leave.

What would his duties be as plenipotentiary? While his most important function would still be to act as ambassador to France, he would divide his time among such chores as banker, consul, merchant, naval director, judge of admirality, and intermediary on prisoners. In view of today's involved and cumbersome bureaucracies, it might seem strange to realize that John Paul Jones and other American commanders operating in European waters were then under Dr. Franklin's direction.

One most ticklish duty was to act as a Court of Admiralty in connection with the many prize ships taken by American vessels. There was frequent friction between officers and men over the prize money involved; and there were cargoes to sell, or to ship to America, and vessels to be repaired, refitted, and manned, not to speak of men to be paid. These naval obligations became so heavy that later on he had to request being freed of them.

Then for several years there was much time given to arrangements for exchange of prisoners—the trading of captured Britishers for seized Americans. Many demands in connection with individuals were made upon him, and the days might seem to have been bewilderingly full. And so they were.

Yet in all this turmoil he found some moments of relief while he composed *The Ephemera*, the first of his sparkling bagatelles. This one preserved something of the spirit of a holiday with friends at a country home on an island in the Seine. Despite his burdens, he found time, too, for the social contacts he had missed in Philadelphia. He had become a member of the noted Masonic Lodge of the Nine Sisters, as well as of the Royal Medical Society. And he had already made the acquaintance of two ladies with whom his name would be much linked, even to the point of scandal in certain puritanic American minds—Madame Brillon, and Madame Helvétius.

The great sculptor Houdon had immortalized his features in marble, and Turgot, in a Latin epigram, had pointed up his foremost accomplishments—"He snatched the lightning from the sky and the sceptre from tyrants." So considerable was his renown that the French people willingly began to build a Franklin legend, and the wily old man, knowing a good thing diplomatically when he saw it, gladly played along with them. Two symbols in particular that represented America were, first, the *Noble Savage* and the virility of the frontier, signified by the fur hat. The other was the *Good Quaker*, typified by plain dress and manners. The obliging Franklin donned both, and again his fame began to spread. His Poor Richard philosophy, now assembled as the *Way to Wealth*, had, during the past year, taken the new title in its numerous French editions of *La Science du Bonhomme Richard*. And in popular esteem he was indeed the Good Man Richard, the prudential, earthy, rustic philosopher, yet having most civilized tastes.

# xxi. Bonhomme Richard

## *1779–1780*

*I have received but lately the Letter your Excellency did me the honour of writing to me in Recommendation of the Marquis de la Fayette. His modesty detained it long in his own Hands. . . . Should peace arrive after another Campaign or two, and afford us a little Leisure, I should be happy to see your Excellency in Europe, and to accompany you, if my Age and Strength would permit, in visiting some of its ancient and most famous Kingdoms. You would, on this side of the Sea, enjoy the great Reputation you have acquir'd, pure and free from those little Shades that the Jealousy and Envy of a Man's Countrymen and Contemporaries are ever endeavoring to cast over living Merit. Here you would know, and enjoy, what Posterity will say of Washington. For 1000 Leagues have nearly the same effect as 1000 Years. . . . I must soon quit the Scene, but you may live to see our Country flourish, as it will amazingly and rapidly after the War is over.*—Letter to George Washington, March 5, 1780.

So GREAT had the Franklin popularity become in France that everyone possessed of a few sous wished to own some likeness of the good man. Thus, in a letter in the year 1779, he wrote to his sister Jane, "Perhaps few Strangers in France have had the good Fortune to be so universally Popular. . . . This Popularity has occasioned so many Paintings, Busto's, Medals & Prints to be made of me, and distributed throughout the Kingdom, that my Face is now almost as well known as that of the Moon." Actually the king himself seems to have had some concern over this wide acclaim. One of the monarch's courtesans suddenly began to show considerable interest in the American philosopher, many years her senior, when she was a bit dismayed to receive from his majesty a very handsome *vase du nuit*, or chamber pot, adorned with the Franklin likeness.

Such acclaim nettled the vulpine Arthur Lee also, and when Lafayette brought the new Franklin commission in February, and since Lee's own recall was imminent, he went into a tantrum. He refused to turn over more than merely *copies* of the papers held by him applying to the joint commission, saying the originals would be needed for his "vindication." The Doctor generously, but with just the faintest trace of sarcasm perhaps, offered copies of anything in his own files, if they could be made to serve in so essential a purpose. He had occasion to warn friends in Philadelphia to beware of the two Lees and of Izard. He was conscious of their conniving against him at a distance, and he realized they would put out even greater efforts when back in direct contact with their backers in Congress. But somehow he felt no need of "vindication" for his own actions.

A bad siege of gout had him housebound for a time. Perhaps it was then that he decided Benny might do better at school at Geneva, and sent the youngster there. It was actually late in March before his legs were equal to a bow at Court as the new minister. In the meanwhile he had made a typical Franklin gesture. Captain Cook, whom he had known in London, had been on a long cruise of exploration in the Pacific, and was supposed then to be returning home. This Englishman being a servitor of science and trade rather than a merchant of death, the American minister issued a "passport" in his name, and distributed it to every United States naval vessel he could reach. Cook and his ship were not to be harmed or detained, but aided if need be in reaching an English port. Unhappily the explorer then lay dead in the Sandwich [Hawaiian] Islands. Yet the Franklin thoughtfulness was not lost.

He exchanged a few formal words with Louis XVI and Marie Antoinette at Court on March 23, and several days later was attempting to advance a suggestion first made by Lafayette for a naval attack on the west coast of England and Scotland. At about the same time he was in correspondence with a young student,

Jean Paul Marat, on the nature of fire and flame, little realizing
what a fiery revolutionary this young Frenchman would become
within a few short years.

Now that the internecine strife had been removed from the
United States embassy, he was getting more enjoyment out of
life, and informing his friend Josiah Quincy that he found the
French "a most enviable people to live with." Also he was writing "Dear Master Johnny" Adams, who had affectionately addressed a letter to him from the port where he and his father
awaited transportation home to Boston. He could write with
equal facility to an old friend, an interesting youngster, or
an imprudent Congress. And in May he did the latter, warning
the Committee on Foreign Affairs that drafts against loans were
pouring in so fast that the public credit of the new United States
might be ruined.

News of the peace between Austria and Prussia, which came
in May, was encouraging, for the Continental countries, now
less afraid of involvement in that quarrel, were more susceptible
to French enticement toward joining in curbing Britain. The
following month Spain openly declared war on England. Still,
despite all his political and martial involvements, there was some
time for the Doctor to engage in more pleasant activities. In the
closing months of the previous year, he had written a paper on
the *Aurora Borealis*, which had just been read during the spring
before the Academy of Sciences. During the summer he wrote
another of his bagatelles on the *Morals of Chess*, a game which
he was employing extensively as a diversion from care and
routine.

The Fourth of July fell upon Sunday that year, and the third
anniversary of the acceptance of the Declaration was celebrated
on the following day, and invitations printed on the press at
Passy were sent to friends of America. There was, however,
rather disturbing news, which may have furnished some of the
conversation at this affair. John Paul Jones had left L'Orient on
June 19 aboard the *Bonhomme Richard*, named for Franklin, and
in command of a small squadron made up of French vessels.
Jones's objective had been another blow at the English coast to
follow up his success at Whitehaven the previous year. But there

had been a collision at sea, the ships were back in port again for repairs, and there were awkward rumors of insubordination on the part of some of the French officers. Franklin was concerned until the second sailing in mid-August, and then somewhat impatiently awaited news.

It was well into October before Jones returned safely. The *Bonhomme Richard* was at the bottom of the sea by Flamborough Head, well up the English east coast, but an American command had won a major naval battle, and the intrepid sailor had forged a name for himself, and given a boost to Franklin's hopes. Said the latter in a letter to Jane:

"The Enemy have been very near you indeed. When only at the Distance of a Mile you must have been much alarm'd. We have given them a little Taste of this Disturbance upon their own Coast this Summer; And tho' we have burnt none of their Towns, we have occasioned a good deal of Terror & Bustle in many of them, as they imagined our Commodore Jones had 4000 Troops with him for Descent. He has, however, taken and destroyed upwards of twenty Sail of their Merchantmen or Colliers, with two Men of War, and is arrived safe in Holland with 400 Prisoners. Had not contrary Winds and Accidents prevented it, the intended Invasion of England with the combined Fleet and a great Army might have taken Place, and have made the English feel a little more of the kind of Distress they have so wantonly caused in America."

Back in Philadelphia things were in a pretty mess that October. James Wilson, a signer of the Declaration, was attacked by a mob in his home for having acted as counsel for two Tories who had no one else to defend them. Rioting spread through the city and out to Germantown, for distress and tension were rather general. The paper currency issued by Congress was "not worth a Continental." Butter that had sold for $7 to $10 a pound in June required $12 to $18 in this depreciated scrip a month later. A pair of shoes, or an iron-hooped barrel cost $120, while lump sugar brought $20 a pound, and tea on the open market was worth four times that amount. These inflated prices, together with conditions in the other colonies, make it easier to realize why Congress at times seemed brusque and very much lacking in understanding in dealing with its minister in Paris. Under such circumstances it is easier, too, to appreciate why some at home misunderstood the playfulness that cropped up in some Franklin letters. A typical instance was one written that same October of 1779 to a stepniece in Boston, in which he says:

"Somebody, it seems, gave it out that I loved ladies; and then everybody presented me their ladies (or the ladies presented themselves) to be embraced; that is, have their necks kissed. For as to the kissing of lips or cheeks it is not the mode here; the first is reckoned rude, and the other may rub off the paint. The French ladies have, however, a thousand other ways of rendering themselves agreeable; by their various attentions and civilities and their sensible conversation."

In November of 1778 Madame Brillon, wife of a government official many years her senior, yet perhaps not quite as old as Franklin, had written the Doctor a billet-doux, saying in part, "Never call me anything but 'my daughter.' Yesterday you called me 'Madame,' and my heart shrank." Twice a week he and Temple spent the evening at her villa during the months she and her husband and daughters resided at Passy. His calls were less frequent, but their exchange of notes quite regular, in the winter months when she resided in Paris or Nice. In November of 1779, soon after she had left for the city, the Ambassador sent her the bagatelle entitled *The Whistle*, the adaptation of an instance of his childish extravagance to certain phases of their own relations. She was a handsome, brilliant woman, an object of marital neglect and unhappiness, and there was a mutual attraction that yielded a wealth of satisfaction from their exchange of spirited gallantry and lively femininity.

However, she had no exclusive claims upon this rather mature Lothario. One of the grande dames of the French intellectuals was Madame Helvétius, sixtyish, and the widow of but a few years of the wealthy farmer-general, or government tax contractor, who had been one of the leading Gallic philosophers. Her friends spoke of her as "Our Lady of Auteuil," in which Paris suburb, not too far from Passy, she had her home, which embraced cats, dogs, pigeons, and a priest, her personal confessor. By contrast, her more indifferent acquaintances and critics knew the once beautiful matron as "the ruins of Palmyra." Abigail Adams, who was later to encounter this forceful, uninhibited woman, considered her loud, dowdy, and *possibly* something of a strumpet.

But Franklin, who had known her since soon after his arrival in France three years before, held her in warm and sincere admiration. His bagatelle *A Madame Helvétius*, completed about January 1780, was easily his most winsome and his best. What is more, it was surely a sincere proposal of marriage, rather than being solely a bit of pleasant mockery. He dined with her, or she with him, at least once a week, and as much oftener as could be arranged. Several years later, when these two mesdames, as well as other French ladies, were heartbroken at the old gentleman's leaving to spend his last few years in his homeland, Madame Brillon berated Madame Helvétius for having been the cause of his loss to them. The implication was that the latter, a widow, might have held him in France through marriage.

Dalliance, though, was somewhat remote from his principal business of diplomacy. Also there were birthdays that came along, and counseled a glance in the mirror, and then demanded the taking of an inventory. His response to his latest milestone varied. In a sprightly note to an old friend, Dr. Thomas Bond, with whom he had helped launch the hospital, he remarked, "Being arrived at seventy, and considering that by travelling further in the same road I should probably be led to the grave, I stopped short, turned about, and walked back again; which having done these four years, you may now call me sixty-six." At least it was a pleasant deception.

By contrast there was no illusion with respect to his decadence in his letter to the sober-sided Washington quoted at the head of this chapter. And in another missive at the same time to Priestley there was a trace of concern that the light might be blown out and darkness come too soon. Said he, "The rapid progress *true* Science now makes, occasions my regretting sometimes that I was born so soon. It is impossible to imagine the Height to which may be carried, in a thousand years, the Power of Man over Matter. We may perhaps learn to deprive large Masses of their Gravity, and give them absolute Levity, for the sake of easy Transport. Agriculture may diminish its Labour and double its Produce; all Disease may by sure means be prevented or cured, not accepting that of Old Age, and our Lives lengthened at pleasure even beyond the antidiluvian Standard."

How this clear-eyed prophet would thrill over the world of today—all but in one respect. And that point of delinquency was equally apparent to him in his own time, for he added in this letter, "O that moral Science were in fair way of Improvement, that Men would cease to be Wolves to one another, and that human Beings would at length learn what they now improperly call Humanity."

Then early in February there came a very considerable surprise. John Adams was back again. It seems that Vergennes, unbeknown to Franklin, and operating through the French minister at Philadelphia, Conrad Gérard, had asked Congress to send over a peace commission. The Adams-Lee junta had seized the opportunity, still hoping to by-pass or dispose of the present minister, and hurried their delegate-at-large over to take control in Europe. Franklin treated him most civilly, and left him completely alone. But the foreign minister and the overly ambitious peace commissioner soon developed an antipathy to each other, got exactly nowhere in concert, and in midsummer, Adams, blaming Franklin for his failure, went on to Holland seeking aid there.

At the end of 1778 the British forces in America had sought for a foothold in the southern states, had found one in Georgia, and reduced that state to submission by October of the next year. Then, in May of 1780, Charleston was captured, and by August a rather decisive battle won at Camden apparently gave Britain firm possession of the South. This news dampened Dutch ardor, and the restless Adams could make little progress with his fund-raising in Holland. A former president of Congress, Henry Laurens, who had set out for the Netherlands seeking American aid, had been taken prisoner at sea, and was now lodged in the Tower of London.

American credit was strained, and, with the military situation taking so decisive a turn for the worse, the crisis which had developed in March, when the Congress had as much as repudiated the paper currency it had issued, had grown still worse. Also the fact that Spain was demanding the Mississippi Valley weighed substantially on the debit side. As a letter from Washington, some of whose troops were mutinying, assured Franklin, the choice lay between peace with Britain, or money from France.

The minister at Paris went to work. By the time of the arrival the following year of a commission hurriedly sent over by Congress to "demand" a huge loan of twenty-five million livres, he already had a promise of six million, and more would be forthcoming. This much is clearly evident. Had our receipt of French aid been solely dependent upon the diplomatic skill of Deane, Lee, Adams, Izard, or even John Jay, still to appear on the scene, the United States might well have reverted to thirteen British colonies in North America. Franklin's *diplomacy of friendliness* may have appeared to be of questionable merit to certain gentlemen with flint-sharp legal minds—but with the French it worked.

There was another tremendous session with the painful and immobilizing gout that fall. This called forth one witty bagatelle, the *Dialogue between Franklin and the Gout*, and also very likely a second similar composition, *The Handsome and Deformed Leg*. There was rousing news in the early winter of a glorious victory by the coonskin-hatted boys from the Smokies and the Blue Ridge Mountains over the redcoats, fought on top of King's Mountain in October. But unhappily it was offset by other word of the battle for balance of power still raging in and handicapping the Congress. Bloodshed and strife, five years and more of wasteful, senseless war—of man's inhumanity to man— weighed heavily upon Franklin, the man of peace.

To Richard Price in Massachusetts, he wrote, "We daily make great improvements in *natural*—there is one I wish to see in *moral*—philosophy; the discovery of a plan that would induce and oblige nations to settle their disputes without first cutting one another's throats. When will human reason be sufficiently improved to see the advantage of this?"

Benjamin Franklin knew there must be some substitute for war, and hoped, labored, and prayed that it might be found. An avid internationalist in an era when nationalism was strangling some of men's better impulses, his great desire was that "not only the love of liberty, but a thorough knowledge of the rights of man, may pervade all the nations of the earth, so that a philosopher may set his foot anywhere on its surface, and say, 'This is my country.' "

## XXII.   Let There Be Peace
### *1781–1782*

*I thank you for your Information relating to the Batteries opened against me in America. I since hear that a Motion has been made in Congress by a Caroline Member for recalling me; but without Success; and that A. Lee has printed a Pamphlet against me. If my Enemies would have a little Patience they may soon see me remov'd without their giving themselves any Trouble, as I am now 75. . . . As I read Spanish a little, I wish you would send me the* Gazette of Madrid *by the Court Couriers, and any new Pamphlets that are curious. There is also a Book that I desire to have, but it being in two volumes Folio, you cannot easily find an Opportunity of sending it; It is the* Bibliotheca Hispana Nicolai Antoni.—To William Carmichael, January 27, 1781.*

A S HE admitted in the letter above, he was indeed seventy-five. It was an age which should put one above rancor and animosity, yet it need not dull an eager mind or take away the relish for life. And this was fortunate, for he would need his sagacity, and particularly his zest for living, since the next several years would be exacting ones.

And for a time he was a little uncertain as to whether he felt obligated to make the effort, especially in the face of the opposition in Congress. If his launching of the Library Company be taken as its beginning, he had been giving more and more of his life during a full half century to public affairs. Had he not completely discharged his obligations? There were rumors that peace must be had soon on the best terms possible. He also wanted some semblance of peace personally. So to his report to the Congress on current conditions he appended his resignation.

Then, since young Captain John Laurens, along with Thomas Paine and others, would soon be on hand stomping their feet and very likely alienating the French in their demands for money, the elderly diplomat went earnestly to work on the project himself. By the time this Congressional committee arrived in March funds were beginning to flow. There was news of another American victory at Cowpens in the foothills of northwestern South Carolina. Had the war truly swung in favor of American arms during the previous fall? The extreme tenseness of recent months lessened a bit, and Franklin began to find a little time for matters scientific and social.

He was much interested in the report that workmen in a quarry near his home in Passy had found live toads imprisoned in solid rock. He visited the pit, saw such inconclusive evidence as was available, speculated on possibilities in this connection, and moved on to other and quite unlike affairs. Eager matchmaker that he always had been, he was presently attempting a union between Temple, whom the Brillons called "Franklinet," and one of their daughters. But it ultimately came to naught, due to religious and other differences. While his score in such enterprises ran low, he was certainly well entitled to an "A" for effort. His next involvement, however, proved a huge success.

The Comtesse d'Houdetot, whose salon was perhaps the most famous in Paris, wishing to honor Dr. Franklin, made him the hero of a *fête champêtre* given at her country home at Sannois in April. She and a party met his carriage some distance away, and welcomed him with verses of her own composition. There was further poetic accompaniment to each round of wine at dinner. After the meal the party led the Ambassador to the gardens, where he planted a Virginia locust tree, while further poetry was recited, which sometime later was engraved on a stone pillar erected nearby. At his parting he was escorted to his carriage by the whole body of guests, and the hostess paid a final compliment to the man who as a legislator had brought benefits to one world, and as a scientist to still another. Could Congress afford to dispense with the services of one so popular and deserving of adulation? Obviously not. And in August came a refusal of his plea to be relieved from further service.

The departing commission led by Captain Laurens had left a broad trail of illwill behind it in the French ministry, and he was busy tidying up after this hardly necessary visitation. But the political load was not too stringent that summer, and he found time for a little science. The smoke-consuming stove, planned some years before, had now to be described in detail to French friends. Also there was additional time in which to get well involved in the linguistics of the American Indians.

In September of 1781 Franklin was at last appointed to the peace commission. The French ministry had preferred not to deal with John Adams alone, so four more members had been added. They were John Jay, Thomas Jefferson, Henry Laurens, and, after quite a struggle, Benjamin Franklin. While the Congressional contest had been going on, the French minister had implied somewhat pointedly that it would be better if the Doctor were a part of this body, and the Lee-Adams faction had little choice but to back down.

Yet the Envoy was still in hope he might get home once more. In September he wrote to Francis Hopkinson, son of an associate in the electrical experiments years before, asking, "Let me know if you are in possession of my Gimcrack Instruments, and if you have made any new Experiments. I lent, many years ago, a large Glass Globe, mounted, to Mr. Coombe, and an electric Battery of Bottles, which I remember; perhaps there were some other things. He may have had them so long as to think them his own. Pray ask him for them, and keep them for me, together with the rest." Someday there might be leisure for such matters again.

On October 19, in far away Virginia, British musicians were playing *The World Turned Upside Down* as Lord Cornwallis surrendered to Washington. Ten days later the word had been speeded as far as Boston, and Jane Mecom seized her pen to tell her brother over the sea that "the Glorious News we have now recd from the Southard makes us Flater our selves you may Return to us soon."

It did seem a bit more probable now, except that while the fighting was over in America, embers of the conflict still smoldered in Europe. The news of Yorktown, which had come into the French ministry toward midnight on the nineteenth of November, had been quickly relayed to Franklin. He then busied himself through the remainder of the night running off a sort of bulletin on a copying machine he had invented, so that copies might be distributed to his acquaintances at the crack of dawn the following morning. There was naturally much revelry, yet the American Envoy was still somewhat dubious that Britain had been conclusively taught a lesson, and would be willing to call it a day. There did seem to be rather definite feelers out for peace, but immediately he was not too hopeful.

It was perhaps a good omen, however, when a haggard, shabby man stumbled in upon him one day toward the end of that year, and handed him a manuscript. His name was Pierre-André Gargaz. He had communicated with Franklin about two years before, as he was completing his twenty-year stretch as a galley-slave, describing his proposals for universal and everlasting peace. Now that his term had been served out, he had come to Paris, seeking a patron who would help promote his project. Having been turned away from the doors of the wealthy and the powerful, he had hastened out to Passy.

A fervent disciple of peace himself, it was perhaps much easier for the good Doctor to be charitably inclined toward this man who had suffered so long and brutal a servitude. Having read Gargaz's draft of the plan, he believed it should be printed. So it was run off on the private press, and soon after the beginning of 1782 this peace advocate was provided with an abundance of copies for whatever good they might do.

Franklin himself was somewhat disillusioned in the matter, for he had written to Edmund Burke in England just shortly before, claiming that "the foolish part of mankind will make wars from time to time with each other, not having sense enough otherwise to settle their differences." When the letter was read to the Commons, Franklin was once again back on the prescribed list of the ministry. But by the time the king had virtually informed Parliament in January that the war must go on, it seemed as though the Doctor's pessimism was justified. Yet there was much opposition to his majesty's stand, and rumors that Britain faced bankruptcy. War was certainly a scandalous waste of money, as

Franklin was well aware when demands for payment against new French loans poured in upon him. Still another loan of six million livres was being floated, and he felt constrained to tell Congress in mid-February that he was sick of his "Gideonite office: that of drawing water for the whole congregation of Israel."

Things took a very different direction toward the end of March when North's Tory ministry in England fell, and was replaced by the Whigs. This presaged peace, and almost at once Richard Oswald, emissary for the secretary of state for colonies in the new ministry, was knocking at the embassy door in Passy to begin informal peace talks. A little later the matter would be further complicated by the British secretary of state for foreign affairs sending his own representative. There was also the agreement on the part of Congress the previous year that no arrangements would be completed separately of France. Still it would do no harm to make a reconnaissance of the lay of the land; but where was the peace commission?

Once again Jefferson had asked to be excused from foreign commitments at that time. Henry Laurens was still busily engaged in pouring out a flood of propaganda although a prisoner in the Tower of London. Adams was bogged down with affairs in Holland, and John Jay was for the moment detained in Madrid. He would be the first to arrive at the end of June. So, beginning in April, Franklin carried on for a time alone. In the twelve months ahead there would be a minimum of dearly bought time for the ladies, none for science, but a rather sickening surfeit of matters political.

Not long after he and Oswald began their exploratory talks, the British Admiral Rodney won a huge victory over the French fleet under De Grasse. This triumph helped to plump out the rather lean British position, and for a day or two Franklin fully expected it to so renew British hopes that the war would be resumed.

But it began to develop that the new ministry was as anxious for peace as anyone involved, and as April wore on Franklin and Oswald began to get down to cases. The former had his demands drawn up, but refused to disclose all of them, since he

was dubious as to how far he should proceed alone. He did call
for the ceding of Canada to the States. Also he began to dispense
propaganda, and he put in a call for Adams to hurry over from
Holland.

It was perhaps during Oswald's absence in England to report
late in April that he read a book of Cowper's poems that had
been sent to him. It was long since poetry had had much place in
his mental diet, but this volume of poesy struck him as being
very good, and he said so to a friend across the Channel. The
word reached the poet that he was being read and praised by the
great American philosopher, and it threw him into ecstasy. Outside government circles the Franklin prestige still ran high in
England.

A breach of diplomatic protocol at about this same time must
have amused the informal American, to whom such sterile procedure had ever seemed vapid and affected. The Comte du Nord,
later Czar Paul I of Russia, was in Paris, and, as was the custom,
had his card left, by the hand of a lackey, at the home or office
of all the ministers to the French court. Franklin, playing the
game because it was part of his present role, stopped at the Russian embassy, and caused his name to be entered in the visitors'
register. The very next day a Russian equerry appeared at Passy,
with vision of banishment to Siberia engraved on his face. An
unpardonable blunder had been made. Since Russia did not as
yet recognize the United States as an independent nation, his
majesty's card should not have been left, for there could be no
official exchange between him and the American Envoy. What
was to be done? Franklin assured the harried man that if the
name in the register were erased, he in turn would agree to burn
the card, and no international incident would be precipitated.

In May, Thomas Grenville arrived to represent the British
foreign office in treating for peace with France "and her allies."
While it later developed that the powers granted him did not
include dealing with these allies, which embraced the United
States, he was very frank with the American Envoy, and on
June 1 disclosed the gratifying news that "he was instructed to
acknowledge the independence of America previous to the commencement of the treaty." Independence! The Doctor had had

some part in the declaring of it. Now he was the first American to have British assurance that America's separate status was accepted by the mother country as an established fact.

It was a glowing moment, but it may well have called up the question, "Why have we had to go through nearly eight years of strife, turmoil and wretchedness to arrive at it?" A week and a half later he was writing to Priestley, "I should rejoice much, if I could once more recover the Leisure to search with you into the Works of Nature; I mean the inanimate, not the animate or moral part of them, the more I discover'd the former, the more I admir'd them; the more I know of the latter, the more I am disgusted with them. Men I find to be a Sort of Beings very badly constructed, as they are generally more easily provok'd than reconcil'd, more dispos'd to do Mischief to each other than to make Reparation, much more easily deceiv'd than undeceiv'd, and having more Pride and even Pleasure in killing than in begetting one another."

Finally Jay had found transportation, and had arrived from Madrid on June 23. He and Franklin had several days of conferences, and then unfortunately influenza, epidemic locally, laid him low. Once more the older man went back to the lists alone in the joust for peace. There seems to have been agreement between the two Americans on what the demands would be. There were eight in all, four of which were "musts," and four more that were "sensible" to a lasting peace. The former included complete independence, and withdrawal of military forces, adjustment of boundaries, and the revision of the Canadian border to what it had been previous to 1774, together with fishing rights on the Grand Banks of Newfoundland. The latter embraced an agreement to certain reparations for damages occasioned by the war, acknowledgement of "war guilt" by Britain, trading privileges, and finally the cession of all Canada.

A political upheaval in London on July 1 left Oswald as sole British contact, and he and Franklin worked over the above points through that month. Then, in early August, Jay was sufficiently recovered to take part in the mediations. A somewhat longer residence in France would have benefited his understanding of that country and have made the months ahead perhaps more harmonious and easy. But Franklin, beginning to ail himself, welcomed his being available. He would like the aid of Laurens, too, and sent off letters in the hope he might be exchanged for General Cornwallis, and come on to Passy.

And then a violent bladder-stone attack put Franklin out of the running during the first week in August, and left Jay as sole negotiator. Age, which the Doctor had always treated rather lightly, and even with a note of disdain, was serving notice that he had exceeded the limits of reason during the past six years. There seemed to be nothing to do at the moment but beat an orderly retreat, so the old gentleman took to his bed and remained there for more than three months. Naturally he was no recluse, yet his participation from now on was not nearly as active as it would otherwise have been. Handsome Elkanah Watson, the American merchant who had stopped at Passy with dispatches, had sometime before remarked of the Envoy that he had "seen the populace attending his carriage in the manner they follow the king's." Such demonstrations were temporarily done with, but there was a constant procession of visitors to the sage in his sickroom.

It may have been during the illness, too, that "Elk" Watson played a subtle trick. He had had Patience Wright, the sculptress, turn out a life-size colored wax head of the envoy, which he set up in one of the Doctor's well-stuffed costumes, to give the appearance of his being up and about again. This greatly delighted the hangers-on at Court. Probably no one, though, got more amusement out of this bit of horseplay than Franklin himself.

Adams had arrived from Holland toward the end of October, and by the fifth of the following month there had been an agreement on terms, which were promptly transmitted to London. Heading the list was the understanding that independence was absolute and incontestable. Next the boundaries of the new nation were defined, and it was further provided that navigation of the Mississippi was to be unrestricted from its source to its mouth. These points incurred little friction. But the provisions regarding debts, commercial fishing on the Newfoundland banks and in the Gulf of St. Lawrence, and the treatment to be accorded "loyalists" would engender considerable conflict and dispute.

Laurens did not arrive until November 29, and so was in time for only the final day of deliberations. It had thus been Jay who had carried most of the burden in the closing negotiations. Franklin had started the procedure, and then lent such aid as he could from his sickbed. Yet Jay's obduracy at certain points had stalled proceedings by two months. By mid-November the ailing man had summoned his strength, was once more up and about, and on hand at Oswald's lodgings in Paris on the morning of November 30 to sign the provisional treaty. Then the signers repaired to the embassy at Passy for dinner.

The terms were not to become final until a peace had been concluded between Great Britain and France. Also, the treaty had been signed in violation of an agreement between the French Court and Congress, the commissioners taking the responsibility of so doing upon themselves. Adams and Jay had felt but little compunction in the matter, being certain they would be sustained by the Congress, to whom they alone felt any accountability. Franklin felt at least a moral responsibility to Vergennes, with whom an agreement, even if only in the interests of uniformity, had been made of no prior arrangements with the late foe. Also it was he that must soon contact Vergennes for another American loan. As a consequence, and somewhat to the amazement of his colleagues, he had immediately conveyed the word to the French foreign minister of their intention to sign. Then he had sent along to him a copy of the treaty the following afternoon after signatures had been affixed.

On his regular day for calling at the ministry early the following week, he contacted the comte in person. It was good to find that his conduct had been such that the relations of the two for a number of years encouraged Vergennes to trust him. Explanations were accepted, and the American position and action was seemingly understood. There had been a technical slight to the French king—that seemed to be all. So Franklin began to press at once for another badly needed loan.

It is possible the other commissioners might have argued their position with equal tact, and have received as ready a reception and agreement to their plea. Yet Adams had been thoroughly mistrusted by Vergennes, and Jay was willing to contend that "the French are not a moral people." Laurens, so lately arrived, had little time for participation, which is perhaps as well, for his imprisonment in England had made him most bitter to everything European. Thus impartial consideration seems to point conclusively to the fact that without the Franklin prestige, reliability, and friendly comprehension, the peace treaties which terminated what we call the *Revolution*—and which the British might well have termed the *War of the Lesson in Imperial Statesmanship*—might have dragged on for a far longer period before being signed.

## XXIII. "I Wish to Die in My Own Country"

### *1783–1784*

*I am glad, that the little Books are pleasing to you and your Children, and that the Children improve by them. I send you here some more of them. My grandson Bache has been four Years at School in Geneva, and is but lately come home to me here. I find Reason to be satisfied with the Improvement he has made in his Learning. He translates common Latin readily into French, but his English has suffer'd for want of Use. . . . You were once so kind as to offer to take him under your Care; would that be still convenient to you? He is docile and of gentle Manners, ready to receive and follow good Advice, and will set no bad Example to your other Children. He gains every day upon my Affections. I long much to see you and yours, and my other Friends in England, but I have not yet determined on the Journey. Our definite Treaty of Peace being now sign'd, I have indeed less to confine me here, and might make a short Excursion without much Inconvenience; but short Days and Winter are coming on, and I think I can hardly undertake such an Expedition before Spring of next Year.*—Letter to Mary (Polly Stevenson) Hewson, September 7, 1783.

It CAN well be that Franklin put his signature to the preliminary treaty with England with some mental reservations. Not only had the demands he had originally made been pared down materially during his illness, but he may also have felt that, since the commissioners had exceeded their authority, Congress would refuse to approve what had actually been accomplished. However, the skies brightened markedly during January 1783, when preliminary agreements between Britain and France, and Britain and Spain, were signed at Versailles. Vergennes was most careful to have Franklin and Adams on hand

so they might know what was agreed upon with respect to
America. The chances of the British-United States arrangements
being sustained were now virtually guaranteed. Even a shift in
the government in London in February, while it delayed the
final settlement, did not jeopardize the current armistice, or the
ultimate peace.

It is said that Pierre Samuel Du Pont de Nemours, the well-
known political economist whom Franklin had wished among
other French friends to take to America to help found a "little
happy society," had drafted that portion of his nation's treaty
with the former British colonies that recognized American Independence. His own publishing business and fortune would be
wiped out in but a few years during the French Revolution, but
his sons would emigrate to America, and in its atmosphere of
freedom found a mighty industrial dynasty.

That the United States of America, which later would receive
them, was in 1783 a free and independent nation was evidenced
early in the year. The Swedish ambassador approached Dr.
Franklin, and explained to him that because of the personal estimation in which he was held by the Swedish king, that sovereign
wished his land to be the first to enter into a treaty of amity and
commerce. Such an agreement was promptly completed in
March. While he was accredited only to the French Court, the
renowned gentleman from Philadelphia was for all practical
purposes ambassador-at-large to all of Europe.

There was at about this time another testimony of the great
personal regard in which the scientist-philosopher-diplomat was
held, and which paid dividends to the cause of the struggling
young nation beyond the Atlantic, adding indirectly to our
heritage. He was made Venerable (Worshipful Master) of the
Lodge of the Nine Sisters, whose members comprised many of
the most important men of the kingdom. Masonry in France,
especially this principal lodge, was strongly political in character,
and Franklin used his associations within the order to very great
benefit in waging the peace.

In April, Oswald, the British ministerial contact, was replaced
by David Hartley, an old friend whose home in Putney the
Doctor had visited nine years before to see the experiments in

fireproofing. The Envoy would have been glad no doubt to have visited others among his many friends—some of whom he had been in contact with for upward of a half century—had he been free to do so. In May he was writing to Bishop Shipley about the somewhat utopian ideas he had in connection with the holding of public office, and which, four years later, he did his best to have incorporated in the United States Constitution.

It was so pleasant to relax after the long strain, first of London politics, and then the war years. All tenseness is missing from his letter quoted above to his adopted daughter, the widowed Polly Hewson, written in the early fall. Benny Bache had returned from school in Geneva in July. The former "King Bird" was now fourteen, and it was time he was apprenticed to life. Having been christened "Benjamin Franklin," it was quite fitting that he be made a printer. So he soon had his leather apron, and, with a stick in hand, was setting type and operating the press there at Passy under the grandfather's solicitous eyes. As the youngster began to acquire the feel of the craft, the older man may have wished that he had also taught his trade to Temple, now quite a Beau Brummell, experienced in politics, but dependent upon its capricious employments.

Beside printing, in which he had managed to dabble to some extent almost since he had moved to Passy five years before, the Doctor returned briefly to another vocation which had afforded him extreme satisfaction. Anthony Todd, long secretary of the British post office, was in contact with him with regard to reestablishing mail packet service across the Atlantic. Soon, too, he was working on similar matters with the French postal officers, and in 1785 regular transoceanic mail service was restored.

Then in August came a thrilling experience that continued much in his thoughts during the months ahead, and surely must have made him wish he might lop fifty or more years from his age. In June an intrepid pair of Frenchmen, the Montgolfier brothers, had sent a warm-air balloon aloft in the Rhone Valley in southern France. Then in midsummer another flight was made under the direction of J. A. C. Charles with a varnished silk craft inflated with slowly produced hydrogen. Franklin drove into Paris to see the ascension scheduled for late afternoon on the twenty-seventh. Unfortunately it was a rainy day, and the old gentleman, no doubt fairly itching to examine the facilities for generating the hydrogen and witness the final preparations, had to be content to remain in his carriage at a distance. There were fifty thousand people, he estimated, on hand at the Champ-de-Mars to witness this historic event.

But the ascent of this free balloon, surprisingly enough, went off about on schedule, and the scientist watched the brightly painted envelope rise rapidly until it disappeared in the clouds. Then he hurried back to Passy to get off a report to Sir Joseph Banks of the Royal Society, and assure him that a whole new field in natural philosophy was about to be opened to examination. He seemed to sense that life had very positively taken on a third dimension and man need no longer be earth-bound.

Also his tendency to find some practical application for every bit of new phenomena quickly came to the surface in connection with this recently perfected plaything. While he probably manufactured it, he claimed to have been asked the question, "What good is a balloon?" Almost overnight his classic retort, "What good is a new-born baby?" became famous across the breadth of Europe. The implication was merely to be patient, either this new creation would provoke a few suggestions shortly, or, if these balls that floated so entrancingly through the air did no prompting on their own, he was certain he might conjure up some ideas to offer.

The high spot of his nine years in France surely came on September 3, the day on which the definitive treaties were signed. David Hartley, probably on orders from London, refused to permit the American document to be signed at Versailles. So Franklin, Adams, and Jay drove to Hartley's apartment in the Hotel de York in Paris, where the signatures were affixed in the morning. Seemingly the British envoy had permitted attendance by a French observer, for it was not until word had been conveyed of the actual signing to the waiting Vergennes at Versailles that the French foreign minister went forward with the British-French final treaty.

During the drawn-out conferences that had preceded the good works now consummated, the Spanish ambassador had written rather prophetically of the United States in a letter addressed to the French king, saying, "This federal republic is born a pigmy, but the day will come when it will be a giant to be reckoned with." As the ink of his signature was drying, Franklin can well have wished that he might exchange places with Temple, or even young Benny Bache, so that he might have another lifetime before him in which to watch this stripling nation develop into ever greater power in the Western World.

And as he drove back to Passy for a bit of deserved celebration, he may have recalled the final paragraph of a long diplomatic report he had sent to Robert Livingston at the beginning of the previous December, when he had said, "I am now entering upon my seventy-eighth year; public business has engrossed fifty of them; I wish now to be, for the little time I have left, my own master. If I live to see this peace concluded, I shall beg leave to remind the Congress of their promises to dismiss me. I shall be happy to sing with old Simeon, Now lettest thou thy servant depart in peace, for my eyes have seen thy salvation." The Lord had indeed delivered America from what many felt was becoming a form of servitude. That land had certainly been favored above either France or England in the treaties recently signed, and the aging Franklin, who had served his native land long and well, wished to return there while he still had the strength to do so.

Being a man of peace, he may have welcomed the fact that his relations with the rather venomous John Adams were now about to taper off. During the summer they had come close to the breaking point, as indicated by a sentence from the letter of this customarily placid man written to Robert Morris shortly after the signing of the peace. He had said, "I hope the ravings of a certain mischievous madman here against France and its ministers, which I hear every day, will not be regarded in America, so as to diminish in the least the happy union that has hitherto subsisted between the two nations."

While he had been known to protest over the hours squandered sitting for artists and sculptors, he did give some time to Joseph-Sifrède Duplessis during this stirring year. The able French artist had already painted several other portraits of the envoy, but still another had been commissioned by one of Franklin's neighbors and close Masonic friends, Louis Le Veillard. Long the property of the New York Public Library, it is by far the best known picture of the philosopher, especially in his later years.

Now that there was peace again, and he was the ambassador of an accredited nation, honors began to flow to him. He was made a member of the Royal Society of Edinburgh; and there was an Italian edition of his works published in Padua. Also there had been a publishing project undertaken right in his home in Passy earlier that year. Congress had caused the constitutions of the various states to be put in printed form, and a copy had come into the Ambassador's hands. He had mentioned the document in two of his diplomatic dispatches, saying, "The extravagant Misrepresentations of our Political State in foreign Countries, made it appear necessary to give them better Information, which I thought could not be more effectually and authentically done, than by publishing a Translation into French, now the most general Language in Europe, of the *Book of Constitutions*, which had been printed by Order of Congress. . . . They are much admired by the Politicians here, and it is thought will induce considerable Emigration of substantial People from different Parts of Europe to America." And they did perhaps encourage emigration, but they also had a very considerable effect upon the revolutionary enterprises that began to spring up in this older world, and especially in France.

In this latter connection there was a communication received at the embassy in October from a young lawyer in Arras, named Robespierre, who sent the scientist a plea which he had just made against the prohibition of lightning rods in a neighboring town. Little did Franklin realize that this man, and also the student Marat, who had appealed to him for aid four years previously, bore names which would make men cringe during a revolution destined soon to convulse the France he so greatly loved.

Almost as though in anticipation of his important mission there ten years hence, John Jay went on a visit to England, leaving his wife and two-months-old daughter in Franklin's care while a separate home for the Jays was being located. Thomas

Barclay had arrived to take over the consular affairs, bringing his wife with him, and the American colony at Passy was growing. With relief from more and more time-consuming detail, Franklin had an opportunity to begin some projects which must have for some time been slowly shaping up in his mind.

Whether one attributes it to religious or philosophic impulses, he had, nonetheless, arrived at a conviction common among Christians today but which very few ministers of his own day would have dared advocate from their pulpits. Not only was he unalterably committed to the belief that war and Christianity were incompatible, but also that war and carnage were the complete antithesis of Christ's teachings. In this respect he was years in advance of authoritative religion. Men in general still had a long way to go before coming to a hearty condemnation of armed strife.

But Franklin felt very strongly on the matter, and since his friend David Hartley, who also deplored the madness of war, had many humanitarian suggestions to make during the peace proposals, the envoy thought it might be fortunate to get certain of his ideas into the hands of the British ministry. So it was that he put them into a shrewd, witty letter to Hartley, which was in reality a proposal for a tripartite body involving England, France, and America in an alliance that might be considered a forerunner of the League of Nations, or the United Nations. This decided internationalist sincerely wished that some mechanism could be found whereby differences between nations might be resolved by arbitration rather than by slaughter.

The summer months of 1783 were especially foggy, and the philosopher is supposed to have predicted a cold winter because of the sun's rays having been shut off so much from the earth's surface. In any event it did prove to be a rugged season, and perhaps even colder than the snowy winter of 1770–71, so that by early December he had even begged off from his weekly attendance on the ministry at Versailles, excusing himself because of the depth of the snow. This gave him time for further writing, and it was perhaps then that he somewhat playfully drafted specimens of a proposed modernization of Bible text. Choosing the first chapter of the Book of Job, he replaced the Elizabethan

with contemporary English, and set the scene as though the
Lord were holding a levee, with Satan in attendance. The slightly
bantering style may have been for the purpose of pointing up
the shallow pretense of court etiquette and methods. The *Lord's
Prayer* also was somewhat revised. Far more practical, however,
were the efforts that went into a pamphlet titled *Information to
Those Who Would Remove to America,* which was rolling off
the Passy press and into distribution the following February.

The balloon, too, was very much in his mind at the year's end.
While soldiers dropped from the skies would not make their
appearance for a century and a half, Franklin did come forward
with a plan for paratroops. Also he became the recipient of one
of the very first airmail letters. Regarding the former scheme,
he had suggested that, "Five thousand balloons, capable of raising two men each, could not cost more than five ships of the
line; and where is the prince who can so afford to cover his
country with troops for its defense that ten thousand men descending from the clouds might not in many places do an infinite
deal of mischief before a force could be brought together to
repel them?" Here, too, was the beginning of the perennial
argument over the respective merits of sea and air power.

Jane Mecom had had as a neighbor in Boston a David J. Jeffries,
whose physician son, John, had been often in London in the
1760s. He had turned Tory, however, and served as a surgeon
in the British army. But he had managed to make rapprochement
with a recent enemy, Jean-Pierre Blanchard, the French aero-
naut, and the two made the first over-water flight across the
English Channel. Coming on to Passy, Jeffries called upon
Franklin, and delivered a letter to him from a friend in England,
which was as he later maintained "the first through the air."

The previous year in May a meeting had been held in the Ver-
planck house near Fishkill on the Hudson of officers of the
Continental army then making their last encampment. A patriotic
society had been proposed and was there being organized. Since
Lucius Quinctius Cincinnatus of old had forged his plow into a
sword, and then back into a plowshare after his sixteen days as
dictator of Rome, his name had been appropriated for this
hereditary organization which, in the minds of some, threatened

to saddle America with a perpetual military caste. The divergence of opinion in regard to the Society between two Virginia gentlemen, Washington and Jefferson, was somewhat prophetic of the political differences that would one day develop between them.

Franklin, who had lived for many years of his adult life in a Europe heavily laced with privilege and prerogative, and who heartily opposed favor and license, as well as domination and sloth built upon them, was dead set against saddling upon youthful America any such undemocratic organization. And, having added leisure because of the confining winter weather, he composed a very long letter in opposition to this military society, which he addressed, rather surprisingly, to his daughter. It was in this document that he made his classic remark about a proud American symbol and token, saying, "For my own part, I wish the Bald Eagle had not been chosen as the Representation of our Country; he is a Bird of bad moral Character; he does not get his living honestly; you may have seen him perch'd on some dead Tree, near the River where, too lazy to fish for himself, he watches the Labour of the Fishing-Hawk; and, when that diligent Bird has at length taken a Fish, and is bearing it to his Nest for the support of his Mate and young ones, the Bald Eagle pursues him, and takes it from him."

Another letter a few weeks later paid off an obligation seventy or more years old. It was written to Samuel, the son of Dr. Cotton Mather whom the printer's apprentice had irritated with his Silence Dogood articles. Said the old philosopher, "When I was a boy I met with a book entitled *Essay to do Good*, which, I think was written by your father. It had been so little regarded by a former possessor, that several leaves of it were torn out; but the remainder gave me such a turn of thinking, as to have influence on my conduct through life; for I have always set a greater value on the character of a *doer of good*, than on any other kind of reputation."

The winter weather was indeed confining, and lack of activity always tended to make the Envoy a bit crotchety. It showed up somewhat in a piece titled *An Economical Project*, which he apparently turned out sometime in March of 1784, and in which he expressed great surprise that so clever and thrifty a people as the French should choose to live so much by the smoky, unwholesome, and highly expensive light of candles, rather than by the light of the sun. For this stand he has been called the "Father of Daylight Saving."

But beyond the continuing unseasonable weather there was another cause for his petulance. It, and some of the things foremost in his mind, came out in a letter of March 12 to his erstwhile companion on the peace commission, Henry Laurens, now back in England again. Said Franklin, "I write this in great pain from the Gout in both Feet; by my young friend, your son, having informed me that he sets out for London to-morrow, I could not slip the opportunity, as perhaps it is the only safe one that may occur before your departure for America. I wish mine was that near. I think I have reason to complain, that I am so long without an answer from Congress on my request of Recall. I wish rather to die in my own Country than here; and though the upper part of the Building appears yet tolerably firm, yet, being undermin'd by the Stone and Gout united, its Fall cannot be far distant. You are so good as to offer me your friendly Services. You cannot do me one more acceptable at present, than that of forwarding my Dismission."

But prolonged as the winter had been, spring finally arrived. Its milder weather helped to take the sting from the departure of Mr. and Mrs. Jay and their daughters, with all of whom he had developed the greatest friendliness. The gout was easier, and also there was another project afoot which promised to be extremely interesting. Something approaching a national scandal was building up in France, and the philosopher-scientist had been appointed a member of an investigating body.

Although previously rejected in Berlin and Vienna, Friedrich Anton Mesmer had spent six profitable years in France preying upon the incredulous, selling them the supposed healing powers of his scheme of *animal magnetism*. While he had been denied permission to practice medicine, he had operated through a licensed practitioner, and, despite this subterfuge, had acquired as supporters some of the ranking nobility, including Lafayette. A stock company was being formed to establish a hospital for treatment, and even an academy-clinic for instruction in this new "science."

There was resistance, too, as well as all this support, and in March the king felt constrained to order an investigation of Mesmer's partner and collaborator, Charles Deslon. A commission was appointed, consisting of four physicians, including one Joseph-Ignace Guillotin, who managed to lend his name to a certain infamous device. There were also five members of the Academy of Sciences, including Franklin. Because of his objectivity, and his ability to insulate himself from fraud and trickery, the choice of the American was fortunate. And there was much trick and device in Mesmer's ministrations, principally hypnotic, despite the man's sincere belief in his methods.

The case dragged along through the spring and summer, and it was Franklin who was principally responsible for Mesmer's ultimate exposure. An *Information* was provided the king in August, while in September an *Exposé* was read to the Academy. The old gentleman drew up a report of his own that is still worth reading as evidence of the prevalence of quackery. Said he in the interest of continual vigilance, "Some think it will put an end to Mesmerism. But there is a wonderful deal of Credulity in the World, and deceptions as absurd have supported themselves for Ages."

He would have loved to have gotten in some travel that summer, perhaps to Switzerland, since that land was looking forward to 1791 when it would be celebrating five hundred years as a republic. But the gout still made walking next to impossible, and the stone rendered riding a test of endurance, so he did not move far from Passy. The previous year he had, as the letter at the outset of this chapter indicates, contemplated a trip to England, but that, too, was quite out of the question. The next best thing was to have the beloved Polly and her family in France, and as the summer moved along he wrote to her making such a suggestion.

In July there came an opportunity to discharge another obligation, which went back to the late spring of 1776, when a previous siege of the gout had forced him to make an excruciatingly painful retreat from the mission to Canada. Father John Carroll had tended him with deep concern, and had found an abiding place in his affections. The long journey had also afforded sufficient time in which to impress upon Franklin certain distinct needs of the Catholic Church in America. High upon this list had been the want of an American bishop, who could perform the sacrament of confirmation. Deeply indebted for the care at the hands of this young Jesuit, and convinced of his competence, the Envoy had gone to work in his behalf.

On July 1, 1784, "the Pope's Nuncio called, and acquainted me the Pope had . . . on my Recommendation, appointed Mr. John Carroll, Superior of the Catholic Clergy in America, with many of the Powers of a Bishop; and that probably he would be made a Bishop *in partibus* before the End of the Year. He asked me which would be most convenient for him, to come to France, or go to St. Domingo, for Ordination by another Bishop, which was necessary. I mentioned Quebec as more convenient than either. He asked whether, as that was an English Province, our Government might not take Offense at his going there? I thought not, unless the Ordination by that Bishop should give him some Authority over our Bishop. He said, not in the least; that when our Bishop was once ordained, he would be independent of the others, and even the Pope; which I did not clearly understand." Shortly afterward Father Carroll became the Vicar-Apostolic, but it would be six years before he was at long last consecrated a bishop.

Actually, religious rather than political matters seemed to hold a more prominent place during July of 1784. It was then that he received an inquiry from two young Virginians, Mason Locke Weems and Edward Gant, seeking Franklin's aid. They had prepared at home in America for the ministry, but in the Anglican faith there was no resident bishop at whose hands they might be ordained for the priesthood. Worse still, they had presented themselves in England, only to be told by the Archbishop of Canterbury that the laws of the church prohibited him from ordaining them unless they swore an oath of allegiance to the king. Could they, their letter asked, find a bishop in France who might undertake their consecration?

"No," advised the Envoy, "they could not be ordained in France." But why not in Ireland, there being quite a different group of bishops there? Or, continued his reply to them, why not "arise, go to the Altar, and receive your Office at the hand of God," as the first bishop of Scotland was supposed to have done, setting the miter upon his own head? "If the British Isles were sunk in the sea (and the surface of this globe has suffered greater changes) you would probably take some such method as this. . . . An hundred years hence, when people are more enlightened, it will be wondered at that men in America, qualified by their learning and piety to pray for and instruct their neighbours, should not be permitted to do it till they had made a voyage of six thousand miles out and home, to ask leave of a cross old gentleman at Canterbury."

In passing it is perhaps interesting to note that the first of these two prospective ministers became the celebrated "Parson" Weems, whose rather saccharine treatment of the life of Washington contained the debatable incident of the cherry tree. He was for many years a very effective itinerant book peddler, distributing the literary wares of a successful young Irishman, named Mathew Carey. At about the same moment Weems was writing Franklin, Carey was stealing into Philadelphia disguised as a woman. As a young rebel he had, some years previously, fled his native land for France, where he found work at the American Envoy's press at Passy. Returning to Ireland, it was no time at all before he was in hot water again, and on his second flight he steered his course over the ocean to America. Franklin, knowing his ability, aided him in finding a start in this new land, where he quickly became a leading publisher.

Religion and morality being far to the fore in the Doctor's mind that summer, he found time also to write a burning condemnation of dueling. These silly contests were supposed to settle differences by the will of "Providence," which was bound to favor Truth and Right with victory—and without error or exception. But the American who, like Solomon of old, believed that "a soft answer turneth away wrath," was equally confident that a duel decided nothing. It was such an affair that had precipitated the blistering "hearing" to which he had been subjected ten years since at the Cockpit, and he wanted no further part of them.

Temple had been sent to England on a visit with his father, who had fled there following the close of the war and his release. This may have stimulated a letter from the latter making advances for a reconciliation. In reply, Franklin assured his son, "I ought not to blame you for differing in Sentiment with me in Public Affairs. We are Men, all subject to Errors. Our Opinions are not in our own Power; they are form'd and govern'd much by Circumstances, that are often as inexplicable as they are irresistible. . . . I will be glad to see you when convenient, but would not have you come here at present." It is doubtful if deep in his heart he could ever forgive and bridge the gap now between them. But the civilities would be respected, and Temple given a reasonably free choice in the matter of adherence.

As he was getting accustomed to the bifocal glasses which he had perfected, there were a number of arrivals at Passy. Most welcome was that of Jefferson. Franklin's first assumption had been that he had come to replace him as minister to France, and that return to America could be made before winter weather set in. But it developed there would be a slight delay on that score.

Most gratifying, too, was his receipt from the British government of a copy of the posthumously published account of Captain Cook's *Voyage to the Pacific Ocean*, together with a commemorative medal struck in honor of the deceased explorer by the Royal Society. His gesture toward a safe conduct for his old acquaintance during the war had been pleasantly remembered.

Somewhat more mixed no doubt were his feelings with regard to the arrival of Abigail Adams, who had come to join her husband, who would have a hand in a series of treaties to be negotiated with European and North African sovereigns. This Puritan minister's daughter had begun to look down her nose at the man she had once thought great and whom she had viewed with silent admiration for a whole evening years since on one of his visits to Boston. She would soon be virtually outraged by Madame Helvétius' free and easy manners, and have some rather acrid remarks about the United States' envoy and his relations with the formidable dowager to relay to the gossips back home.

But of all arrivals at Passy by far the happiest was the descent upon him of Polly Hewson and her brood now rapidly growing up. It hardly seemed possible that he had known her for more than twenty-five years. During that long period he had seemed to her very much like a father, and it was fortunate she could now be with him and afford him so much comfort during several of the very few years that still remained to him.

Benny was doing exceptionally well learning his trade, and in the fall of 1784 a type founder was brought out to Passy so he might acquire knowledge of that essential phase of the business. The grandfather was happy, too, at about this time when Temple returned from two months in London, for he had missed the twenty-four-year-old grandson keenly.

John Adams, now back from his labors in Holland, together with Jefferson and Franklin began work on the treaty negotiations. The former had taken a house at Auteuil, about a mile from Passy, and drove over almost daily for the next ten months while their labors were constant, if not too arduous. It did prove rather a demanding period, however, for long confinement wearied Franklin spiritually perhaps more than physically, and between age, his ailments, and the demands upon his time, there was little opportunity for a change of scene.

Also there was a growing feeling of apprehension, some indication of which had crept into the closing lines of his letter to son William in August, when he had remarked, "I did intend returning this year; but the Congress, instead of giving me leave to do so, have sent me another Commission, which will keep me here at least a Year longer; and perhaps I may then be too old and feeble to bear the Voyage. I am here among a people that love and respect me, a most amiable Nation to live with; and perhaps I may conclude to die among them; for my Friends in America are dying off, one after another, and I have been so long abroad, that I should now be almost a Stranger in my own Country."

This uncertainty gave him deep concern. But return he would, in the coming year, after there had been a further call upon his abilities, and still more honors had been paid this world figure.

## xxiv. The President of Pennsylvania

### 1785-1786

*The inclos'd Paper will inform you of what has pass'd here between Scotosh, a Chief of the Wyondot Nation, and this Government, on his Way to Congress: He is recommended as having been always very friendly to our People, and the Council have defray'd the Expence of him and his Company here and to New York, where, as Col. Harmar informs, he is to visit Congress. He expresses a strong Desire of going to France; but as it must cost something considerable to support him thither, there, and back again, we have given him no Expectation that the Congress will approve of it: But if it could be well afforded, I should conceive it might be of Use to our Affairs in that Part of the Country, if, after viewing the Court and Troops and Population of France, he should return impress'd with a high Idea of the Greatness and Power of our Ally, and thence be able to influence the Western Indians with Opinions proper to defeat the Insinuations of the English who are posted on those Frontiers.—Letter to John Jay, July 6, 1786.*

THE winter of 1784–85 was, all in all, an exceptionally happy one, for with Polly Hewson and her children on hand to round out the household, the envoy was, as Jefferson observed, the village patriarch. He was generally loved and almost universally respected, and it seems a bit ironic that he should have been forced to spend so many years in the political arena, where acrimony and controversy are so prevalent. He had a very great talent for friendliness, and again it was Jefferson who attested that, "It was one of the rules which, above all others, made Dr. Franklin the most amiable of men in society, never to contradict anybody."

The chief discordant note in this otherwise most gratifying

period was his dissatisfaction with Congress. That body would neither permit him to return home, nor would it make a place in government service, as he had requested, for Temple Franklin.

Benny Bache was put to work in the Didot printing plant in Paris to finish his apprenticeship, and the time that had been given to coaching and overseeing the grandson could now be given again to writing. In March he was deep in the subject of criminal law, a fortunate prelude to the unexpected, but nonetheless actual, revision of a penal code the next year. As the spring opened up and planting in the neighboring fields was underway, he did his last bit of formal writing in France, titled *Observations on Mayz, or Indian Corn,* describing this peculiarly American grain and its advantages as food for both man and beast.

Then May 2 proved to be very much a red-letter day. The post brought permission from Congress to return home—to be his own master—and he fell to wondering if he did indeed have the strength of soul and of body to pull up the roots that in nine years had sunk so deep in the mellow loam of his French friendships. Would the bladder stone, that made every jolt or rigorous movement a torture, render a long sea voyage unendurable? Could he even stand the trip by carriage to the coast?

At once, too, he was under a barrage of appeals from his host of friends not to desert them. There were several who would most willingly have provided him a home for the remainder of his life. Soon after he had arrived in France the previous year, Jefferson, now to succeed him as minister, had noted that "more respect and veneration attached to the character of Dr. Franklin in France than to that of any other person, foreign or native." Now he had evidence of the complete sincerity of this attachment.

But the Doctor craved his native land, and would risk a test of his ability to get to the coast, and there measure his tolerance for the ocean voyage by a trip across the Channel to say farewell to a few friends in England. He also hoped he might persuade Polly, who had returned home, to join him with her family at an English port to accompany him to America.

In the nine years the ménage at Passy had grown to quite an establishment. Now it had to be broken up. The disposition of the printing plant alone was no small task. The house had been ample, and its furnishings had to be disposed of. Some items were distributed as remembrances among close friends, while a host of others had to be boxed and crated for a long voyage home. These crates and boxes finally ran well above one hundred, thirty of them being large chests of books. Provision even had to be made for a household pet, an Angora cat. Puss made the trip successfully, and was much admired as a very great curiosity, but unfortunately died in the following year. Her remains were turned over to Charles Willson Peale, who sought to stuff her pelt for exhibition in his museum. His taxidermy, which was later an exceptional talent, was still imperfect, and this novel feline never made the exhibit cases.

The Doctor's leaving hinged upon the completion of the treaty with Prussia. Although it was signed ultimately in the four separate European capitals involved, the signatures of Adams, Jefferson, and Franklin were affixed at Paris on July 9. Three days later the American-bound party were scheduled to set forth. There were diplomatic niceties to be cared for, and Vergennes and the former American minister parted with regret, for they had worked together for years with remarkable harmony. Widespread French admiration found expression in the king's own souvenir, his portrait in miniature in a frame set off with four hundred and eight diamonds, a princely remembrance indeed. Also one of the mule-borne litters used by the queen was made available to carry him to Harve, since it would be far easier than riding in the unsprung carriages of that day.

There were hundreds of good-bys to be said, a thousand and one details to be cared for, and it was late afternoon of July 12 before the ambassadorial party could get away. A host of friends, neighbors, and well-wishers had filled the courtyard during the day, and pressed in about the litter into which the Doctor was helped, and around the carriage into which mounted Temple and Benny.

As the two vehicles moved out of the courtyard this throng kept along with them, and accompanied the travelers down the road to Paris, through the city, and to its northern gate. Here there was a mass leave-taking, although a few close friends continued for some distance along the road to Havre, while M. Le Veillard went all the way to England. The royal mules, litter, and groom were somewhat symbolic, for this journey took on something of the nature of a "royal progress." There were deputations at virtually every village and cross-roads bearing expressions of regret at the sad parting, gifts, and wishes of *bon voyage*. The Cardinal at Rouen sent word ahead that if they would not consent to spend at least one night at his villa, he would exercise his authority and have them brought in from the highroad so he might enjoy their company. At last, after six days on the way, they came to Havre. Here they were joined by Jean-Antoine Houdon, the famous sculptor on his way to Virginia to do his celebrated bust of Washington.

The gentle motion of Marie Antoinette's litter had been most considerate of the Franklin ailment. Travel and change of scene had again roused his spirits, and he claimed to feel much better than when he had left Passy. But there was another and quite crucial test ahead, the Channel crossing to Southampton. In this instance it consumed two days of the roughest sort of sailing, but he came through with flying colors, being the only member of his small party not seasick. There was no occasion now to turn back—he was truly on his way home!

William was at the English port, but the meeting of the father and son was coolly civil rather than one of mutual regard and forgiveness. Its principal benefit was to complete the purchase of land owned in New Jersey by its former governor, which was deeded to Temple.

A far happier meeting was that with Bishop and Mrs. Shipley, who had driven down from Twyford, where, at their lovely home, he had begun the *Autobiography* fourteen years before. With them they had brought the once talkative Kitty, now a very handsome young woman, and to whom her given name of Catherine seemed more appropriate. There were three glorious days with these dear friends, and his happiness would have been complete had Polly, her children, and their baggage arrived. But in this latter he was to be disappointed.

Had his leaving Passy been delayed by a few more days, he would have had a communication there from the French minister of marine offering to put a royal frigate at his disposal for the trip to America. But as it was a trim American craft, the *London Packet*, on its maiden voyage, put into Cowes, on the Isle of Wight. Passage could be had aboard her, and she would sail in a day or two.

There had been other friends who had hurried down from London, and a farewell dinner was eaten in the afternoon of July 27. Then Franklin, together with Temple, Benny, Houdon, and the Shipleys went aboard a small sloop, dropped down the Solent to Cowes, and went aboard the larger vessel. Since the Doctor had engaged the "whole cabin that I might not be intruded upon by any accidental disagreeable company," there was ample room, and Captain Truxtun, after entertaining at supper, suggested the guests might care to stay for the night. Franklin, pleasantly tired after a strenuous day, was early to bed and to sleep. But favorable wind seems to have sprung up, for when he awoke the following morning, as the journal he had begun to keep records, he found "the company gone and the ship under sail."

In a letter to Jane Mecom, written the day after leaving Passy, he had said, "I did my last public Act in this Country just before I set out, which was signing a Treaty of Commerce and Amity with Prussia. I have continued to work till late in the Day; tis time I should go home, and go to Bed." He was hardly as disconsolate as this pleasantry might indicate, yet he went to work aboard ship with a resolution which might make it appear that he felt indeed that time was short. The seven weeks of the voyage were the apogee of his scientific writing, for these forty odd days showed greater production than any other like period. The Gulf Stream was given further study, which set off a still more comprehensive enterprise finally titled *Maritime Observations*. And before they swept up the Delaware on a flood tide on September 14, he had completed a dissertation *On the Causes and Cure of Smoky Chimneys*. Many friends had wished this leisure might have gone toward advancing the much neglected *Autobiography*, but his excuse was that he was without access to his manifold and much needed records. The papers he did complete were later published in the *Transactions* of the American Philosophical Society. This was necessitated, at least in part, by the fact that for the first time in several years he would have no immediate access to a printing plant, Benny Bache being hurried off to college to complete his general education.

Unequal this time to stealing surreptitiously into town, he received a rousing ovation, which he played down in the final entry in his *Journal.* How different indeed was this landing at the Market Street wharf than the first one he had made there sixty odd years before. Beyond cheering throngs, there was also a home and a loving daughter and her family awaiting this runaway printer lad who had become "the most famous private citizen in the world." Hardly was he inside the door of the house on Oriana Street than another procession of deputations began to arrive, these welcoming him home. So continuous was his stream of callers that it was almost a week before he could pen a letter of introduction and start Houdon on his way to Mt. Vernon.

There were several grandchildren he had never seen before, and with whom there was a mutual seeking of acquaintance. Another grandson, Temple, was sent off to New York to see if a personal appearance before Congress, now sitting there, would help procure him some opening in the government service. The grandparent would have liked very much to have accompanied him, and to have gone on to Boston, but, although he perhaps did not realize it, his traveling days were finally at an end.

Less than two weeks after his return he had a rather eccentric visitor, whose name was John Fitch. He claimed that he had been able to successfully adapt the steam engine of Watt and Boulton to the propulsion of boats, and had a working model right now out at Southhampton in Bucks County. But the old scientist, still trying to catch his breath, seems to have been little impressed by either the man or his scheme.

Deep in postwar adjustment, the new nation was in the midst of a most critical period. Pennsylvania, like her sister states, had many problems to face and solve. Here was a son by adoption who had shown his competence as a politician, proved a little later on his statesmanship, and was now at hand in the guise of a universally venerated sage. Why not reserve his talents to the Quaker State? Thus on October 11 he was elected to the Supreme Executive Council, and on the twenty-ninth he became *President* of Pennsylvania. The erstwhile speaker of the old proprietary Assembly had now become the ranking executive in the constitutional government he had guided into being soon after Independence was declared in 1776.

Honors flowed in that fall of 1785 from across the world. Even in the mountains of western North Carolina the settlers in the Holston River area decided to part company with the older commonwealth east of the mountains, and set up a new state, which they proudly named Franklin. The land-hungry were opening up the "West," and when he pressed his claim upon Georgia for unpaid fees as former agent for that state when it was a colony, the settlement was finally made by his acceptance of a deed to three thousand acres of newly opened land.

His possessions, which had followed from Europe on a later boat, finally arrived, and began to be unpacked. There seems to have been a distribution of momentos, for Charlie Peale records that in December the Doctor presented him with a lamp for exhibition in his museum. It was, "at very moderate calculation," brighter than the light of two hundred candles. More remarkable still, it consumed its own smoke. Just what eventually became of it is not clear.

Perhaps the persistent John Fitch had been conscious of a reference to "machine-propelled" ships in a paper of Franklin's read in early December before the Philosophical Society, for in January he was again knocking at the door of the Franklin home. This time he was selling stock, and highly incensed when, in place of a substantial investment, the President offered to give the man a few dollars to improve his seedy appearance. While he did subscribe a little later on to the support of efforts being made to achieve steam navigation by James Rumsey, this seems to have been principally because the man was sponsored by George Washington, rather than through any interest on Franklin's part in the future of steam as a source of power. The "applied scientist" completely failed to visualize the immense developments that would be made in this area in the years ahead. Actually the man who held the key to successful development of steamboats lived at this time but a couple of blocks from Franklin. The city directory, printed the year before the return from France, listed among the residents at Second and Walnut Streets the name of "Fulton, Robert, miniature painter."

On January 17 President Franklin would be eighty years old. And he was not above celebrating birthdays twice on small provocation. By the old reckoning he had been born on the sixth, and it always seemed as though that day deserved recognition, too. While his honors lay heavy upon him, he tried to keep his duties to a reasonable lightness. Also he was now inclined to pamper his age a trifle. Reaching books down from the higher library shelves had become a chore, so he designed a mechanical "long arm," very like such devices now frequently seen in food stores. In the warm months he sat in his chamber and read in the nude, blowing away hot air and flies with a fan actuated by a foot treadle. In the colder months he lounged in a sitz bath, the tub shaped like a huge copper shoe, with a seat in the heel, his legs and feet reaching out into the toe, and a rack for his book fitted on the instep.

While he may not have been in attendance at every session of the Council, he was fully aware of what was transpiring, and in February, 1786, told Bishop Shipley in a letter that, "We are, I think, in the right Road of Improvement, for we are making Experiments. I do not oppose all that seem wrong, for the Multitude are more effectually set right by Experience, than kept from going wrong by Reasoning with them." A month later, and in far lighter vein, he dispatched to the bishop's daughter, Catherine, a delightful bagatelle *The Art of Procuring Pleasant Dreams*. She had never forgotten some of the dream-hopes she had related to him fifteen years before during the two-day journey in the bouncy chaise from Twyford to London. Neither had the old philosopher.

The Adams-Lee combine was still functioning in the Congress, and Temple had returned from New York empty-handed, and ready to farm his acres on Rancocas Creek over in New Jersey. He had hoped it might be possible to get his grandfather there to look the land over, since the trip could be made by boat. But the old gentleman went nowhere now except where his own shambling steps, aided by his cane, could take him; or, if the distance was more than a block or two, he consented to be borne by the porters in his sedan chair. Still his interest in agriculture had not waned, and it was very likely this spring that he had an interesting demonstration made. On land harrowed and ready for planting, gypsum, or calcium sulphate, sometimes called "land plaster," was spread. But rather than being broadcast, it was this time carefully placed so that it spelled out "THIS FIELD HAS BEEN PLASTERED." When the grain came up, the deep coloring where the land had been "limed" still spelled out the legend.

From agricultural science he seems to have swung next into domestic science, for he went back to one of the very oldest of his interests, soap making, still a family tradition and source of pride. Much concerned because a supply sent him by sister Jane crumbled, he reworked the batch and found that a certain way of drying the cakes kept them from breaking down.

In early May he wrote Polly Hewson a long letter describing his manner of life and encouraging her to change her mind and come to America. He had hoped to build two new houses, but was held up by a boundary dispute, and so put the artisans to work erecting a substantial addition to his own home. It might be that she would come, and more room would be required. His own needs to entertain were considerable, and his social life appears to have been rather extensive. In fact, Dr. Benjamin Rush, often his guest although forty years younger, thought to make a compilation of Franklin's table talk, as Boswell had of Dr. Johnson's. And from the jottings in his diary, it is probable the enterprise might have been well worthwhile.

His contacts with these younger men tended to keep him young, and it would have been interesting to have seen him and the musically inclined Francis Hopkinson trying to fit a keyboard to the armonica. The Doctor also seems to have had a sort of marimba, or xylophone, which he called a stickado, or sticcado. It had apparently been built for him following a visit to Boston in 1763. Since he had been abroad the greater part of the time since, it is doubtful how much the instrument had been used. It was mentioned, however, in a letter of Jane Mecom's written in anticipation of the cold months of 1785–86. In it she asked permission to share the winter's wood provided her by her brother with a neighbor, Thomas Foote. He was the cabinetmaker who had constructed the stickado, and in his old age was incapacitated by having "had the misfortune to be Burst [ruptured]."

Early in July Franklin received the visit of the Indian chief, Scotosh, mentioned in his letter to Jay at the outset of this chapter. It must have recalled the time a half century before when the tepees of visiting red men frequently dotted the then open spaces beside the newly erected State House. Later in that same month he was much gratified to have the Philosophical Society add to its membership a substantial list of his foreign friends and correspondents.

The construction of two new houses and the addition to his own took considerable of his time, and most of the rest went to the sessions in which the state's penal code was being revised by the Council. All in all, that fall of 1786 seemed to be a busy one. Of the first of these concerns he said in a letter to Jane:

"I have ordered an Addition to the House I live in, it being too small for our growing Family. There are a good many Hands employ'd, and I hope to see it cover'd in before Winter. I propose to have in it a long Room for my Library and Instruments, with two good Bedchambers and two Garrets. . . . I hardly know how to justify building a Library at an age that will soon oblige me to quit it; but we are apt to forget that we are grown old, and Building is an Amusement." He was rather careful to build in the ideas on fireproofing which he had watched being developed, and his sole regret when the addition was completed seems to have been that his stairs had not been constructed of stone, the floors tiled, and the roof tiled or slated, as in France.

Once again he was an "expansionist," hoping to see a spread of population over the mountains to the west, and he was proposing that Spain be removed from North America "by a fair Purchase for some valuable Consideration." This would be far better "than to think of driving them out by Force, being almost sure it would be cheaper as well as honester." Such a treaty drawn at once seemed to him most advisable.

On November 4 he was re-elected President. But when it came to choosing delegates at the end of December to the Continental Congress, due to meet in the spring of the next year, his name does not seem to have been proposed. Perhaps it was felt the dual responsibilities would be too great a burden at his advancing age.

He contributed quite liberally to a college, which came into being several years later and was named for him. Also, as the cooler days arrived, he got back again to his writing. He drafted a paper on *A Description of a New Stove for Burning Pit Coal and Consuming all its Smoke*, most applicable in what was to become a great coal mining state, and a second on *A Slowly Sensible Hygrometer*. He had long been interested in measuring the degree of humidity. Also he found time to work again on the *Autobiography;* while in early December he reported to Jane, "My Buildings are now covered so as to fear no Damage from the Weather."

And evidently, too, the home on Oriana Street was full—Polly Hewson had changed her mind, and she and her children were now in Philadelphia.

As the year was closing he wrote to William Hunter, not his former co-deputy in the post office, but an old friend in England, and the following excerpts clearly show the mental stance, vitality, and outlook of a most remarkable man rounding out his eighty-first year:

"It rejoiced me much to learn by your kind letter . . . that you are still in the land of the living, and that you are still at Bath, the very place that I think gives you the best chance of passing the evening of life agreeably. I too am got into my *niche*, after being kept out of it 24 years by foreign employments. It is a very good house I built so long ago to retire into, without being able till now to enjoy it. I am again surrounded by my friends, with a fine family of grandchildren about my knees, and an affectionate good daughter and son-in-law to take care of me. And, after fifty years' of public service, I have the pleasure to find esteem of my country with regard to me undiminished; the late reelection of me to the presidentship, notwithstanding the different parties we are split up into, being unanimous. . . .

"Your newspapers, to please honest John Bull, paint our situation here in frightful colours, as if we were very miserable since we broke connexion with him. But I will give you some remarks by which you may form your own judgment. Our husbandmen . . . have plentiful crops. . . . Our working-people are all employed and get high wages, and we are well fed and well clad. Our estates in houses are trebled in value. . . . Buildings in Philadelphia increase amazingly. . . . Our wilderness lands are daily buying up by new settlers. . . . In short, all among us may be happy, who have happy dispositions; such being necessary to happiness even in Paradise."

## xxv. We the People

### 1787

*Sir, there are two Passions which have a powerful Influence in the Affairs of Men. These are* Ambition *and* Avarice; *the Love of Power and the Love of Money. Separately, each of these has great Force in prompting Men to Action; but when united in View of the same Object, they have in many Minds the most violent Effects. Place before the Eyes of such Men a Post of* Honour, *that shall at the same time be a Place of Profit, and they will move Heaven and Earth to obtain it. The vast Number of such Places it is that renders the British Government so tempestuous. The Struggles for them are the true Sources of all those factions which are perpetually dividing the Nation, distracting its Councils, hurrying it sometimes into fruitless and mischievous Wars, and often compelling a Submission to dishonourable Terms of Peace.—From Franklin's speech* On the Subject of Salaries *in the Constitutional Convention.*

THERE were a number of leading Americans, such as George Washington, who were convinced of the inherent impotence of the Articles of Confederation. They had served indifferently well under the stern compulsions of war, and they had held the new states in a tenuous union while the European nations were recuperating from the years of strife. But what of the future? As thirteen free and largely independent entities, without any vital, obligatory common loyalty, could they hope to be any more than so many ineffectual pawns in the international political game? Without a vivified unity they might, when a test came, as it most certainly would, find themselves back in Britain's clutches, or subservient to France or Spain.

An abortive attempt had been made in the summer of 1786 to hold a meeting at Annapolis where a stronger federal arrangement to bind the states together might be forged. While it had failed, there seemed to be promise of greater interest and better response to the call for another series of sessions to begin in May at the State House—the cradle of our liberties—in Philadelphia. Its purpose had been loudly proclaimed to be no more or less than the "revision" of the Articles of Confederation. Yet some of the more earnest patriots were whispering about that they had the very best intentions of forming a *new* and much stronger central government.

But the President of Pennsylvania did not show anything like personal alarm over American conditions as a whole. Since he had no firsthand knowledge of the situation in other states, the confident attitude taken in the letter closing the last chapter could apply only to Pennsylvania. Still, his pride in American competence was considerable, and he was in no sense a strong advocate of enlarged central powers. However, the fact that he had not been chosen a delegate to the convention called for early summer should not be attributed to this casual attitude, but solely to his age and physical condition, and his present heavy involvements.

He was conserving his health as much as he could, boasting to Benjamin Rush that he had never used tobacco in any form. He had also given up wine, but had returned to swinging dumbbells, and seemed to be keeping the painful bladder stone under reasonable control. Just as the American Philosophical Society had been launched years before to delve in affairs in the broad field of Nature, so now he was active in starting the Society for Political Enquiries, to investigate the area of politics and government.

This enterprise and its early meetings seem to have acted as something of an elixir. The confusion at home, due to the addition being built, plus two new houses hard by, was also tapering off, and local governmental activities shaping up in accordance with his preferences. Thus it promised to be a pleasant and profitable spring and summer, and he began to draw upon the hidden springs of vitality that had never failed him in the past when

demands were heavy. The need to call upon these reserves was
more apparent after the twenty-eighth of March, when he *was*
named a delegate to the forthcoming convention.

There was a considerable demand upon him by way of personal correspondence which lasted through much of April.
Among other letters were those introducing Thomas Paine to
friends in France, where the able penman was now headed in
search of backing to exploit an iron bridge he had invented. And
there he would stay to have a hand in a violent revolution which
Franklin did not seem to anticipate, despite the fact that he was
due to become this revolutionary upheaval's patron saint.

Toward the middle of May the delegates began to arrive in
Philadelphia. Washington rode into town on the thirteenth, and
at once paid his respects to his old friend, now President of the
state. He may well have been astounded to have seen in the yard
of the Oriana Street home a handsome new Connemara jaunting
car, just arrived from Galway, the present of an Irish admirer.
While he did not comment on this unusual vehicle, he did enter
in his diary, "Visited a Machine at Dr. Franklin's (called a
Mangle) for pressing, in place of ironing clothes from the wash,
which Machine from the facility with which it despatches business is well calculated for Table cloths & such articles as have not
pleats & irregular foldings and would be very useful in all large
families." The eighty-one-year-old Doctor was still active, still
being challenged by man's incomplete hold on the phenomena of
Nature.

While the sessions were to have begun on the fourteenth, there
were no more on hand by the late afternoon of the sixteenth than
could be accommodated at the table in Franklin's dining table,
where twenty-four might be comfortably served.

It was May 25 before there was a quorum on hand and the initial meeting could be called to order in the historic structure
that for nearly three quarters of a century more would continue
to be called the State House rather than Independence Hall.
Unluckily there was a drenching rain that first day which kept
the almost legendary Doctor Franklin housebound. It was to have
been his privilege to nominate General Washington as president
of the convention. But when regular sessions began on the fol-

lowing Monday, he was in attendance, and would be with remarkable regularity those sixteen hot summer weeks during which sessions were held.

Historians were fully justified in dubbing the thirty-six-year-old James Madison the "father" of the historic Constitution that finally resulted from these sessions. Still, the efforts expended might never have come to fruition except for the pacific influence brought to bear by the eighty-one-year-old Franklin, oldest delegate in this body, as he had also been fifteen years before in the Congress that voted Independence. Highly respected elder statesman, a sage, and a conciliator, his soothing tactics, his witty sallies at moments of extreme tension, and his well-built compromises at points of real emergency, saved this explosive assembly from blowing itself to pieces. He may have napped on occasion, especially when some of the silver-tongued members lost themselves in endless mazes of forensic twaddle. But he was fully awake to main issues, advocating his own preferences, yet willing and anxious to find common ground and agreements. He it was who stated the true purpose of such deliberate bodies when he maintained, "We are sent to consult not to contend with each other, and declarations of a fixed opinion, and of determined resolution never to change it, neither enlighten nor convince us. . . . Harmony and union are extremely necessary to give weight to our councils and render them effectual in promoting and securing the common good."

It was on June 2 that he spoke against a salary or emolument for the proposed chief executive, expressing the philosophy of a day then drawing to a close that those upon whom fortune had smiled were obligated to serve their fellow men. A very brief quote from his speech heads this chapter. Since standing for any length of time was agony, his speeches were written out, and read for him by others. Motions and short, pithy, and usually humorous comments that relieved stress and friction were by word of mouth.

Washington in the chair kept order and procedural direction; Franklin, working with him from the floor, helped guide the contending delegates around obstacles and away from fatal differences. Along with unpaid public service, he favored a plural exe-

cutive, and a single body legislature, ideas he had incorporated in
the state constitution, and which were unacceptable to the federal planners, and soon altered in Pennsylvania's state government.

Of one thing only was he at times forgetful. It had been
decreed that the affairs of this convention would be conducted
in complete secrecy. In private, the old gentleman did have a
tendency to be garrulous, as he admitted, and one of the younger
men usually was on hand to monitor his conversations.

A most critical moment arrived toward the close of June and
threatened a stalemate, if not a complete termination of proceedings. To the old seer it seemed to require an oblique attack, and
he arose to offer an unexpected motion. They should employ a
chaplain, and open each session with prayer. Very evidently
they needed heavenly guidance, and in his supporting remarks,
he said, "The longer I live, the more convincing proofs I see of
this truth, that God governs in the Affairs of men. And if a
sparrow cannot fall to the ground without his notice, is it probable that an empire can rise without his aid? . . . I believe that
without his concurring aid we shall succeed in this political
building no better than the builders of Babel." The motion was
not carried, but neither were their deliberations brought to a
premature close. He had saved the day.

There was in fact a most critical period stretching from the
last day in June to July 11. The big states were pitted against
the smaller ones over representation in a federal congress. It was
feared the larger states would dominate, especially if representation was on the basis of population rather than equal voting power
then accorded each under the Articles. Franklin, staunch advocate of a single body legislature, had to jettison his own preferences, and strongly advocated what Parton claims was the "happiest political expedient ever devised," an upper body, or Senate,
with equal representation, while the lower house would be made
up of delegates chosen on the basis of numbers of people. It
provided a bridge over a yawning chasm, and secured a constitution that might otherwise never have come into being.

Things were less taut beyond that point; and in July the phi-
losopher-politician had a visit from the able botanist Dr. Manas-

seh Cutler. He has left the only detailed description of the Franklin home on Oriana Street. He noted that the Doctor's "voice was low, but his countenance open, frank, and pleasing." The Bache grandchildren "seemed to be excessively fond of their grandpapa," but it was the library that caught the New Englander's eye. It occupied a room that was "a very large chamber and high-studded," filled with so great a collection of volumes that it must surely be "the largest and by far the best private library in America." There were many curios and pieces of apparatus other than just books. The Boston soap-boiler's youngest son had indeed come a very long way from his humble beginnings, and it is a pity this Franklin home could not have been preserved for posterity.

Cutler, a bit flippant ordinarily, was enthralled by the man's cordiality and simplicity as much as by his possessions. Said he, "I was highly delighted with the extensive knowledge he appeared to have of every subject, the brightness of his memory, and clearness and vivacity of all his mental faculties, notwithstanding his age. His manners are perfectly easy, and everything about him seems to diffuse an unrestrained freedom and happiness. He has an incessant vein of humor, accompanied with an uncommon vivacity, which seems as natural and involuntary as his breathing." It was ten o'clock in the evening before he could tear himself away from a rather long but fully rewarding call.

The tumult and the shouting were out of the way by September 15, and over the Sabbath a true copy of the Constitution was engrossed and made ready for the delegates' signatures. At eleven on Monday morning the final session was called to order, and the first item of business was the reading of the document which owed its wording in no small part to the competent pen of the extraordinary Gouverneur Morris. Then, after a speech, read for Franklin, and praying that "every member of the Convention who may still have objections to it would with me. . . . put his name to this instrument," he made a formal motion for its signature by the delegates.

There were some that demurred, and explained why, in good conscience, they could not add their signatures. But the overscrupulous were very much in the minority, and those who were disposed to do so began to sign by states in geographical order, from New Hampshire on the north to Georgia to the south. As this ceremony was drawing to a close the sage old man sought to leave a pleasant and promising thought in the minds of those who sat about him. Pointing to the sun at the horizon, portrayed on the high back of the chair which Washington had occupied behind his desk on the dais, he observed that painters had found it difficult to distinguish in their art a rising from a setting sun. "I have," said he, "often and often in the course of the session, and the vicissitudes of my hopes and fears as to its issue, looked at that behind the president without being able to tell whether it was rising or setting. But now at length I have the happiness to know it is a rising and not a setting sun." How true he was!

Another of the greater moments of his well-filled life had now become history, for he had added his signature to four documents of prime importance to our heritage. The first had been the Declaration which had proclaimed our Independence. The second was the Treaty of Alliance with France which so greatly helped to guarantee it. The third had been the Treaty of Peace with Britain which gave actuality to this Independence; while the fourth had been this Constitution, calculated to give it permanence. Of the founding fathers, Benjamin Franklin alone had this distinction.

He had been in England when the members of the first Continental Congress had moved in formal procession that fall afternoon in 1774 to the recently completed City Tavern, there to dine and become better acquainted before their opening sessions. This had been the first formal gesture ushering in the *Revolutionary Period*. How fitting then that the members of the Constitutional Convention should have repaired once again in a body to this fine old hostelry, and by dining together there inaugurate another and happier era, the *Federal Period*. The fires of contention and strife during these weeks of secret sessions had often flared to white heat, but a suitable flux had been introduced into their common affairs, and a shaky federation had been welded into an enduring nation.

One of Franklin's feminine friends had asked him, "Well,

Doctor, what have we, a republic, or a monarchy?" And the sagacious reply was, "A republic—if you can keep it!"

On September 18 the President and the other Pennsylvania delegates appeared before the State Assembly and presented the plan of federal government determined at the convention just closed. Franklin also recommended that a tract of land ten miles square within the limits of Pennsylvania be made available to the federal authorities for proposed use as a site for the national capital. Then, since a special convention within the state must be called together to consider ratification, he begged that his name be withheld from nomination. He was a little weary, did not think that in consideration of his position he should take part, and felt that affairs then before the Council demanded his special attention.

Also it was not certain that ratification would come too easily. He may have had this in mind when he wrote to a British friend, Alexander Small, a week or more after adjournment, saying, "To get the bad Customs of a Country chang'd, and the new ones, thought better, introduc'd, it is necessary first to remove the Prejudice of the People, enlighten their Ignorance, and convince them that their Interest will be promoted by the propos'd Changes; and this is not the Work of a Day." He had seen *union* turned down after the Albany Congress in 1754, and *confederation* laid aside when he had proposed that in 1776. He was hopeful—but not too sanguine.

Early October went toward getting an adjustment to the thorny Wyoming Valley mix-up, a contest over title to lands along the Susquehanna. The previous year he had even been forced to warn the governor of New York against the fire-eating patriot, Ethan Allen, who had threatened to head west from Vermont and start a rebellion among settlers in northern Pennsylvania threatened with eviction. It had been a grizzly business for a time, but now seemed to be resolved.

This pacific termination of local matters had brought the subject of more universal peace to the fore again and this man of many parts was envisioning a federal union for Europe, saying to America's banker in France, Ferdinand Grand, "I do not see why you might not in Europe carry the Project of good Henry the 4th into Execution, by forming a Federal Union and One Grand Republic of all its different States and Kingdoms, by means of a like Convention, for we had many Interests to reconcile." He had prefaced these remarks by the provision, "If it succeeds," and he was patiently awaiting reactions from his own and other state conventions considering possible ratification.

On October 31 he was once again re-elected as President. The following week he protested to his sister that he had refused unsuccessfully, for he had hoped to make the trip to Boston in the following spring. But this was very likely a gesture in Jane's behalf, for he went now almost entirely by sedan chair, and no longer dined out.

A hundred years before, as Philadelphia was being founded, the early Quaker settlers had spoken out in meeting in opposition to slavery, yet it was 1775 before there was an abolition society formed among them. This immature body was quiescent during the war, and, although Franklin had been a Dr. Bray Associate, had lived long on the free soil of England, and taken much interest in the James Somerset affair—the English Dred Scott case—he probably had no connection with this organization in the Quaker City during his eighteen months at home in the war years.

About 1785 the New York Quakers launched an aggressive attempt to abolish slavery, and by coincidence elected a Samuel Franklin, no kin of Benjamin, as president. But the latter had helped in the spring of 1787 to steer a new charter for the local group through the Assembly, and soon found himself its president, largely, no doubt, for the prestige of his name. This Pennsylvania Society for Promoting the Abolition of Slavery had petitioned the Constitutional Convention, but to little avail. He and his associate James Wilson were no doubt somewhat dismayed to find that, in the trading back and forth during the sessions, it had finally been agreed that the new Congress being set up was prohibited from legislating on this thorny question until the year 1808. He must, however, do something about this matter of slavery. The year wearing away had been a full one. Maybe the months ahead would be less demanding.

He was disturbed over the rioting between Federalist and Anti-Federalist groups as delegates to the convention to settle his own state's attitude toward the Constitution were being chosen. And he was much gratified when acceptance was finally assured on December 12 after three stormy weeks of sessions. On the following day he led the procession to the courthouse, where ratification was proclaimed. He had put forth effort in the twelve months just completed of which men half his years might justifiably have been proud.

He may well have remembered with deep satisfaction the passage in a letter received while the convention was still in its difficult early weeks. It had come from an English acquaintance, Dr. Erasmus Darwin, physician, scientist, botanist, poet, and grandparent of the better-known naturalist Charles Darwin. He had remarked, "While I am writing to the Philosopher & a friend, I cannot forget that I am also writing to the greatest Statesman of the present or perhaps any century, who spread the contagion of Liberty among his countrymen; & like the greatest man of all antiquity, the leader of the Jews, delivered them from the House of Bondage and the scourge of oppression."

The "American Moses," eh? Well, life was indeed worth living when your efforts were appreciated. But what a pity the hour was so late, and so much still remained to be done!

## xxvi. "I Ought to Have Been Abed and Asleep"

### 1788–1790

*I have subscribed for the* Encyclopaedia *now printing here, with the Intention of presenting it to the College. I shall probably depart before the Work is finished, but shall leave Directions for its Continuance to the End. . . . You desire to know something of my religion. . . . Here is my Creed. I believe in one God, Creator of the Universe. That he governs it by his Providence. That he ought to be Worshipped. That the most acceptable Service we render him is doing good to his other Children. That the Soul of Man is immortal, and will be treated with Justice in another Life respecting its Conduct in this. . . . Having experienced the Goodness of that Being in conducting me prosperously thro' a long life, I have no doubt of its Continuance in the next, though without the smallest Conceit of meriting such Goodness. My Sentiments on this Head you will see in the Copy of an old Letter enclosed, which I wrote in answer to one from a zealous Religionist, whom I had relieved in a paralytic case by electricity, and who, being afraid I should grow proud upon it, sent me his serious though rather impertinent Caution.*—Letter to Ezra Stiles, D.D., March 9, 1790.

WRITING to an English friend from Passy in 1784, Franklin had told him, "I look upon Death to be as necessary to our Constitution as Sleep. We shall rise refreshed in the Morning." To another sometime later he had facetiously remarked, "By living twelve years beyond David's period, I seem to have intruded myself into the company of posterity, when I ought to have been abed and asleep. Yet, had I gone at seventy, it would have cut off twelve of the most active years of my life, employed too in matters of the greatest importance; but whether I have been doing good or mischief is for time to discover. I only know that I intended well, and I hope all will end well." There had been little during his last year in France, or since returning to America, that indicated that he was contemplating anything like an immediate exit. But he suffered a bad fall about the beginning of 1788 that brought on a crippling siege of the stone, together with a wrist injury, that confined him to the house, and much of that time to his bed, until March. And in those weeks the picture of what must inevitably come to pass was perhaps etched deeper into his consciousness.

Since Mahomet could no longer go to the mountain, the mountain began coming to him. There were Philosophical and Political Society meetings in his dining room, while Benny Bache, finished with college, now had a printing plant beside the home, where he was turning out children's and adult text books. This project was far more interesting than Fitch's experiments along the Schuylkill or the Delaware, or the fact his steam ferry was making the sixteen mile trip up-stream to Burlington by the fall of that year.

Still president of the state, the Doctor commented to his French friend Le Veillard in February that "though there is a general dread of giving too much power to our *governors*, I think we are in more danger from too little obedience in the *governed*." A part of this attitude may have been stimulated by the intensity of the anti-federalist feeling in many of the states. And by mid-March he was in his seat at the daily Council meetings once again, feeling the abrasive action of politics at first hand.

In a letter of May 31 to the Rev. Mr. Lathrop he was wishing that "it had been my destiny to be born two or three centuries hence," so he might have witnessed the progress in invention, and the hoped for "improvements in philosophy, morals and politics." And on the same day he wrote former Governor James Bowdoin of Massachusetts, "Winthrop once made me the compliment that I was good at starting game for philosophers; let me try if I can start a little for you." The spring had renewed both his mental and physical vigor.

A week later he was writing Du Pont de Nemours on the subject of the new government under the Constitution. Also it is quite probable his pen was finding another purpose, for on July 17 he signed his will in the presence of three witnesses. It was a carefully drawn document, aimed at future generations as certainly as at his executors, one of whom was John Jay.

The preamble read—"I, Benjamin Franklin, of Philadelphia, printer, later Minister Plenipotentiary from the United States of America to the Court of France, now President of the State of Pennsylvania, do make and declare my last will and testament as follows." He was first, last, and always, a *printer*, which in his concept of things indicated one who could reach considerable numbers through the permanent, printed word. In retrospect, virtually all else that he had achieved rested, in one way or another, on dealing, as a printer must, with words. With the exception of the years spent in England, the smell of printer's ink had been continually fresh in his nostrils. The hand exercise of the craft may never have given him any great degree of satisfaction, but being all that the term *printer* could in those days signify had brought rich rewards, spiritual, as well as financial.

Once again he was housebound, for he was unable to take part officially in the gala parade and celebration on the Fourth of July. But he was at work again—it may have been rather casual at first—on the *Autobiography*. Also he was perhaps having just the slightest touch of second childhood, for he assured the Rev. Mr. Lathrop of Boston in a letter that he enjoyed the company and conversation of such Bostonians as "are so good as to visit me; for, besides their general good sense, which I value, the Boston manner, turn of phrase, and even tone of voice and accent in pronunciation all please and seem to refresh and revive me."

There were six Bache grandchildren—a seventh had died in infancy—ranging down the age scale from Benjamin now an employing printer just turned nineteen, to small toddlers. In fact an eighth child, another daughter, Sally, appeared on September 12. They all delighted their grandfather, and within three months he mentioned this latest addition, saying she was "a little good-natured girl whom I begin to love as well as the rest."

By October 1789 he was quite willing to relinquish the presidency of the state, for he was no longer capable of journeying to the State House, and one important meeting the previous month had had to be held at his home. But if the flesh was weak, the spirit was still willing, and a current letter to France shows that Paris continued as the scene of most of his dreams, and he would have liked nothing better than a visit there. That same day he wrote also to Dr. Guillotin, with whom he had served on the board investigating Mesmer several years before, and whose gruesome decapitating device would soon begin to work with horrifying regularity. The next day he was sympathizing with a third French friend over the latter's losses in a windstorm, and proposing hurricane and crop insurance, then unheard-of forms of protection. Seemingly there was a French ship lying in the Delaware, for the Franklin pen hastened through no less than twelve rather long letters to acquaintances in that country within three days. The first stirrings of revolution over the ocean had stopped the regular mail packet service he had helped organize.

He was writing, too, on the *Autobiography*, for the first of the above letters informed the Duc de La Rochefoucauld, who had scolded him gently for neglecting the manuscript, that the story was now advanced to his fiftieth year. But by mid-December he had not progressed beyond this point. The cold weather, and enforced confinement, had apparently provoked his ailment, yet he moved over into the last full year of his life without particular incident.

Temple, bred to diplomacy rather than farming, seems to have spent much time in Philadelphia. Although his grandfather may have felt some annoyance at the young man's unwillingness to buckle down, he also felt definite responsibility for having so trained him. What is more, he enjoyed his company, as he had that of the boy's father during the latter's earlier years. Benny Bache, nine years younger, was a better example of Franklin ambition and persistence. Among other enterprises Benny had run off four small books by an English lady, a Mrs. Barbauld, being *Lessons for Children* for ages from two to five.

His grandfather, the not-too-silent partner in this business, had sent some to Boston, thinking Jane Mecom might dispose of them to local booksellers and pick up a little extra money. However, in some manner this scheme had miscarried. But the eighty-three-year-old printer-merchant was still out to turn a dollar where he could, and wrote his sister on February 22, "As to the Books themselves, how much soever your People may despise them, they are really valuable for the purpose of teaching Children to read. The largeness and plainness of the Character [type face], and the little Sentences of common occurance which they can understand as they read, make them delight in reading them, so as to forward their Prospects exceedingly. Our little Richard not yet 5 Years old, has by their Means outstript his Brother Lewis in reading who is nearer nine." Whether this bit of sales promotion helped move the stock of juvenile readers will perhaps never be known, but Franklin enterprise was still manifest.

That summer he would be cautioning this sister with regard to addresses on his letters, "The Word *Excellency* does not belong to me, and Doctor will be sufficient to distinguish me from my grandson." Elsewhere in his correspondence it becomes evident that he was still concerned with the principal business of life as he saw it—doing good to others. The project of the moment was that of teaching young Deborah Bache, and her still smaller brother Richard, to read.

That summer, too, the Library Company was erecting its new building. In anticipation of the laying of the cornerstone, which came on August 31, the Doctor had been asked to compose a suitable inscription. With great modesty he had left his name out of its wording. But the committee in charge refused to tolerate such an omission, and promptly made reparation by writing it in. It seems improbable that the old gentleman was able to be present at the ceremonies in person, but he surely must have attended in spirit. It was then almost sixty years since he had taken the first steps which resulted in the founding of this institution which had had such considerable influence in intellectual affairs in those earlier days.

Obviously he had been unable to make the journey to New York that spring to witness Washington's inauguration as our first president. But he was most highly gratified when he read the details and heard eyewitness accounts from those who had attended from the Quaker City. He had not been well enough even to pay his respects to the president-elect on the well-nigh "royal progress" the Virginian had made from Mount Vernon to New York via Philadelphia.

As he reflected on the affair, he wrote to his companion on the

Canadian trip in 1776, Charles Carroll of Carrollton, now a senator in Congress from Maryland, saying, "I am glad to see by the papers, that our grand machine has at last begun to work. I pray God to bless and guide its operations. If any form of government is capable of making a nation happy, ours I think bids fair now for producing that effect." The missive was handed in person to the senator by Temple, still searching for a governmental post at the hands of this new government. Although he was due for disappointment, it is to be hoped that the Maryland statesman sent word back to his elderly acquaintance of his cousin's prospects. Father Carroll's name had been resubmitted to the Pope the previous year, and it now seemed certain he would soon be consecrated a bishop. Just at the moment he was busy in organizing a school, which developed into Georgetown University.

But the bladder stone had become so distressing that on September 15 Franklin had admitted in a letter, "I have been obliged to have recourse to Opium [laudanum], which indeed has afforded me some Ease from time to time, but then it has taken away my Appetite and so impeded my Digestion that I am become totally emaciated, and little remains of me but a Skeleton covered with skin. In this Situation I have not been able to continue my Memoirs, and now I suppose I shall never finish them." Actually he had been on opiates for several months.

Enforced idleness was almost as bad as pain, so when he could he kept busy with his writing. The College was being reorganized, and in June he felt that a statement of his and the other organizers' original intentions of making it primarily an English school required re-emphasis and further vindication. So he laboriously turned out a six-thousand-word document titled *Intentions of the Original Founders of the Academy in Philadelphia.* But, after his painful efforts, his proposals never were permitted to reach the trustees.

He also drew a codicil to his will that was almost as long as the original, and in which was one of the first attempts to set up a philanthropic trust. There were actually two such trusts, one in Boston, the city of his birth, the other in Philadelphia, the adopted city of his mature years. Their immediate purpose was to provide loans to young artisans desirous of becoming merchants and businessmen. Ultimately these funds, as they grew great by accumulation, were to "do good" in another manner, through the construction of public works for the felicity of mankind in general. Despite altering conditions in the following century which prevented the full benefits their donor envisioned, they were indeed a heritage in both of these cities.

Although the fall of the Bastille came on July 14, 1789, there seems to have been no word of it in Philadelphia seven weeks later, for he makes no mention of this initial act of violence in the French Revolution in a letter to M. Le Veillard on September 5. But by November he was aware of the struggle for wider liberties in progress. There is some question, however, whether he had a concept of what was ultimately in store over the ocean. There was concern for his friends in these final months of 1789, but it was lighter in touch than it might have been had he any prophetic sense of the extent to which things would go during the Reign of Terror three and a half years later.

On September 16 he admitted in a friendly, personal note to Washington that, "My Malady renders my Sitting up to write rather painful to me. . . . For my own personal Ease, I should have died two Years ago." Franklin had never been one to "enjoy" poor health, or to resort to continual allusion to it. Thus such a comment seems a clear indication of how vexing the weeks and months of continual suffering could be.

While November must have been a trying one in the Franklin-Bache home—nine-year-old Debbie had a case of smallpox from which she recovered—her eighty-four-year-old grandparent was having a most busy month. As a resolute liberal he strongly opposed a constitutional amendment that would have made the proposed upper house to be added to the state legislature representative of property interests. Also he signed his name as president of the abolition society to a document he most certainly drafted and titled *An Address to the Public*. It was an appeal for funds and for aid in combating this bondage that was so great a "debasement of human nature," and also "to instruct, to advise, to qualify those, who have been restored to freedom."

As the Christmas holidays approached he may have returned in spirit to the scenes of his childhood in Massachusetts. Out of somewhere a taste sensation popped up in his consciousness, and he got off a hurried note to sister Jane, asking that she send him a small keg of preserved codfish tongues. This she promptly did, and he enjoyed them almost to the day of his death.

On the day following Christmas, 1789, he sat down and wrote a long letter to a young thirty-one-year-old lawyer-school-teacher, whom he might have enjoyed considerably had he been privileged to know him better. His name was Noah Webster, and he had sometime before produced a pamphlet *Dissertations on the English Language,* which he had dedicated to Dr. Franklin. The old gentleman's crackling comments on the mistreatment of the language and its grammar in those days are still cogent and amusing.

As the year 1790 began to come into view, he perhaps found its advent a bit portentous. About fourteen months before, as he had closed his last term as state president, he had written Jan Ingenhousz, "I am now near eighty-three, the age of commencing decrepitude." The past year had perhaps confirmed in his own mind the truth of this statement. Yet it would never do to admit the fact with too long a face. So he approached the situation with something of a wry jest, maintaining it was no doubt fortunate that he suffered from *only three* incurable diseases—gout, the stone, and old age. The question now became simply one of how long he could withstand their combined ravages.

Nevertheless, there were perhaps others who felt greater apprehension at the lateness of the hour than he. There was a letter dated January 17 from sister Jane, in which she queried a bit ominously, "Who that know and love you can bear the thought of surviving you in this gloomy world?" Seemingly he was doddering, for he informed Benjamin Vaughan, to whom a copy of the *Autobiography* manuscript had been sent, "Not being able, however, to bear sitting to write, I now make use of the hand of one of my grandsons, dictating to him from my bed. I wish, indeed, I had tried this method sooner. . . . I have made no progress these past six months. . . . I am now grown so old and feeble in mind, as well as body, that I cannot place any confidence in my own judgment." This was a gross exaggeration as far as his mind was concerned, but his three incurable diseases were definitely taking noticeable toll of the once rugged body.

In early March he had a most welcome visitor. He was Thomas Jefferson, recently home from France, and en route from Monticello to New York to join Washington's cabinet. It might seem that the good Doctor had providentially been spared for this opportunity to have word at first-hand regarding the host of friends and admirers he himself had left behind in the land across the sea. He would wish also to know what was developing there politically. Thus the questions which welled up in the old gentleman's mind very likely were legion, and he quite probably gave his fellow philosopher a rather thorough catechizing.

At almost this same time he was composing the letter to President Stiles of Yale quoted at the beginning of this chapter. It was in truth a death-bed confession, but out of strength rather than fear, out of conviction rather than uncertainty. Tolerant rather than sectarian, there can be no doubt that he had always been deeply religious, and had more profound spiritual qualities than many unreasoning but insistent conformists. His convictions were deep and sincere, and never exhibitionist or pretentious. Perhaps no other American has been a greater humanitarian, or more zealously concerned with human welfare—material, mental, and moral. The term "do-gooder" has become customarily in recent years one of reproach. But as applied to Franklin it was a bright and splendid accolade.

The first part of this letter to Stiles had dealt with a Franklin portrait for the college library, which he had agreed to sit and pay for. But he warned that the artist "must not delay setting about it, or I may slip thro' his fingers, for I am now in my eighty-fifth year, and very infirm." But what did this mean? If he could not sit to write, how could he bear to sit for an artist for what had always seemed to him to be everlasting periods?

The truth was that from about the first of March he had felt better, been more free of pain than in months—yes, it even seemed as though one might say in years. Two weeks after the Stiles letter he sent off a biting little hoax to the *Federal Gazette*, which he called *On the Slave-Trade*, and in the true Franklin manner likened the arguments of American slave holders to those used by the hated Barbary pirates in justifying their activities.

The very next morning he wrote rather vivaciously to sister Jane. He remarked that, "I have been quite free from pain for nearly three weeks past; and therefore not being obliged to take any laudanum, my appetite has returned, and I have recovered some part of my strength. Thus I continue to live on, while all the friends of my youth have left me, and gone to join the majority." He did add as a postscript the further reassuring fact that, "It is early morning, and I write in bed. The awkward position has occasioned the crooked lines." Also he was still enjoying the pickled codfish tongues. How the good woman in Boston must have thrilled at this hopeful news! How, too, it must have pleased his Philadelphia family and friends to see him mending so unmistakably.

But this respite seems to have been short-lived. Jefferson had written him from New York, questioning with regard to the Canadian boundary and the manner of arriving at its location near Passamaquoddy Bay in the peace treaty with Great Britain. Franklin answered clearly and decisively, but with perhaps a delay of a week, protesting, "Your letter found me under a severe fit of my malady." This turned out to be his final epistle.

His cheeks may have felt flushed as he added the rather stilted complimentary close, and signed it, as he had a thousand or more others before it, *B. Franklin*. The fever was already upon him, caused by a new malady, but yet an outcome of the physical decadence overtaking him. Twice before pleurisy had felled him. Soon after the return from England, aged but twenty-one, it had all but carried him off. And now, heavily burdened with just four times that many years, the third attack was too great a distention of the odds. Nine days after his note to Jefferson this first truly civilized American had also joined the great majority.

Sparked by the flame of fever, his whole long life may have passed before him during the endless day and evening of April 17 as he charred away into terrestrial forgetfulness. And such a review would have disclosed a mighty diorama, surpassed by the experiences of few men through all time.

On the Monday following, Richard Bache, the son-in-law, wrote to Aunt Jane Mecom, preparing her for the shock, and finally closing with, "And my dear Madam *I* do most sincerely

condole with you on the loss of so excellent a friend & Brother—
I have not time at present to add more, than that he died on
Saturday last at 10 o'Clock at Night, he had not been very long
ill, & therefore we had hardly an opportunity of informing you
of it; because we had been in daily expectation of his getting
better, *but nature was at last worn out.*"

The first citizen of the world had died. None other than John
Adams had said of him: "His reputation was more universal than
that of Leibnitz or Newton, Frederick or Voltaire, and his character more beloved and esteemed than any or all of them. . . .
His name was familiar to government and people, to kings, cour-
tiers, nobility, clergy, and philosophers, as well as plebeians, to
such a degree that there was scarcely a peasant or a citizen, a
*valet de chambre*, coachman or footman, a lady's chambermaid
or a scullion in a kitchen, who was not familiar with it, and who
did not consider him as a friend to human kind."

No man better represented his age than Franklin. Yet he was
Ageless, and was so magnificently equipped that he would have
been among the leaders in any era in all of history. But, while he
realized his true value fully at all times, he was never the blatant
egoist, but rather the gentle humorist. And as he made his way
late that Saturday evening over the horizon and on into Eternity,
to become one of the large-carat jewels in the American Heritage,
one might have heard his cheery voice remark—

> " 'Tis time that I retired to Rest;
> Landlord, I thank ye!—Friends, Good Night."

Never before or since has there been an interment in Philadelphia in which *every* clergyman—parson, priest, and rabbi—in the
city led the funeral cortege. Never has there been another occasion when one-half the population of the city either took part
in, or viewed, the obsequies of an individual. Perhaps no other
major city has ever in any one man laid away so considerable a
portion of its own identity as on that twenty-first of April, 1790,
when Benjamin Franklin was laid beside Deborah Franklin in
the plot in the northwest corner of Christ Church burial ground
in that Quaker community which, by his guidance, and along
with him, had grown to greatness.

# Books About BENJAMIN FRANKLIN

Becker, Carl. "Benjamin Franklin." From the *Dictionary of American Biography*, VI (1931), p. 585–98.

Bemis, S. F. Data included in *The Diplomacy of the American Revolution*, New York, 1935.

Bruce, W. C. *Benjamin Franklin Self-Revealed*, New York, 1917.

Butler, Ruth L. *Doctor Franklin, Postmaster General*, Garden City, 1928.

Carey, L. J. *Franklin's Economic Views*, Garden City, 1928.

Cohen, I. B. *Experiments and Observations on Electricity*, Cincinnati, 1941.

Crane, V. W. *Benjamin Franklin and a Rising People*, Boston, 1954.

*Benjamin Franklin: Englishman and American*, Baltimore, 1936.

Diller, Theodore. *Franklin's Contributions to Medicine*, Brooklyn, 1912.

Eiselen, M. R. *Franklin's Political Theories*, Garden City, 1928.

Fäy, Bernard. *Franklin, the Apostle of Modern Times*, Boston, 1929.

Ford, P. L. *The Many-Sided Franklin*, New York, 1899.

Franklin Institute. *Meet Dr. Franklin*, Philadelphia, 1943.

Hale, E. E. and E. E., Jr. *Franklin in France*, Boston, 1887–8.

MacLaurin, Lois M. *Franklin's Vocabulary*, Garden City, 1928.

McMaster, J. B. *Benjamin Franklin as a Man of Letters*, Boston, 1887.

Metropolitan Museum. *Benjamin Franklin and His Circle. A Catalogue of an Exhibition at the Metropolitan Museum of Art*, New York, 1936.

Mott, F. L. and C. E. Jorgenson. (editors) *Benjamin Franklin: Representative Selections*, New York, 1936.

Nolan, J. Bennett. *Benjamin Franklin in Scotland and Ireland 1759 and 1771*, Philadelphia, 1938.

*General Benjamin Franklin*, Philadelphia, 1940.

Oswald, J. C. *Benjamin Franklin, Printer*, Garden City, 1917.

Parton, James. *Life and Times of Benjamin Franklin*, New York, 1864.

Pepper, William. *The Medical Side of Benjamin Franklin*, Philadelphia, 1911.

Sachse, J. F. *Benjamin Franklin as a Free Mason*, Philadelphia, 1906.

Smythe, J. H., Jr. (editor) *The Amazing Benjamin Franklin*, New York, 1926.

Stifler, J. M. *The Religion of Benjamin Franklin*, New York, 1925.

Stourzh, Gerald. *Benjamin Franklin and American Foreign Policy*, Chicago, 1954.

Van Doren, Carl. *Benjamin Franklin*, New York, 1938.

Woody, Thomas. *Educational Views of Benjamin Franklin*, New York, 1931.

The foregoing list is by no means exhaustive regarding complete texts, and makes no attempt to include any of the host of scholarly and popular articles from periodicals, some of which are 'of special interest, frequently giving valuable sidelights on a very remarkable character. Franklin was himself a most prolific writer, and in many instances his own best advocate, so that his writings are worthy of attention. Works of this character deserving of consideration include:

Bigelow, John. *Complete Works of Benjamin Franklin*, New York, 1887.

Cohen, I. B. *Benjamin Franklin: His Contribution to the American Tradition*, Cincinnati, 1953.

Crane, V. W. *Benjamin Franklin's Letters to the Press, 1758–77*, Chapel Hill, 1950.

Farrand, Max. *Benjamin Franklin's Memoirs*, Berkeley, 1949.

Roelker, W. G. (editor). *Benjamin Franklin and Catherine Ray Greene, Their Correspondence, 1755–1790*, Philadelphia, 1949.

Smyth, A. H. *The Writings of Benjamin Franklin*, New York, 1905–7.

Van Doren, Carl. *Benjamin Franklin's Autobiographical Writings*, New York, 1945. Mr. Van Doren also edited *Letters and Papers of Benjamin Franklin and Richard Jackson*, Philadelphia, 1947; and *The Letters of Benjamin Franklin and Jane (Franklin) Mecom*, Princeton, 1950.

# Index

peace, 71; architectural interests, 71; prayer book advertisement, 72; re-elected clerk of the Assembly, 72

As a lyricist, 73; deftness with words, 74; a confirmed "do-gooder," 75; interest in police organization, 76; first suggests a philosophical society, 76; moves his home and plant, 77; beginning of Whitefield friendship, 77; as a deist, 77, 78; brings young "Jemmy" to Philadelphia, 78; attempts magazine publishing, 78; a best seller published, 79; interest in paper trade, 79; opens plant in New York, 79; medical interests, 79, 80; botanical interests, 80; the "Franklin Stove," 80; begins organization of a scientific society, 80

Search for a partner, 83; another "Great Awakening" due, 84; American Philosophical Society proposed, 85; visits New England, 85; movement of cyclonic storms, 86, 87; Spencer's lectures, 87; Philosophical Society launched, 87; Logan contacts, 87; publishes *Pamela*, 87; his spelling and style, 88, 89; his wit, 89; his "Dutch printing office," 90; attitude toward money, 90; first editorial illustration, 90; made comptroller of postal system, 90

As a correspondent, 92; electrical experiments begun, 94; *Reflections on Courtship and Marriage*, 95; Collinson corre-

spondence on electricity begun, 96; threat of war, 96; his political aptitudes put to work, 97; establishes "Jemmy" at Newport, 97; chosen colonel of militia, 98; calls for a fast day, 98; trip to New York, 98; does guard duty, 98; buys a farm, 98, 99; Hall becomes partner of, 99; moves to new home, 99; Smith established in Antigua, 99; chosen for the Common Council, 100

Electrical experiments continue, 101, 102; talks up a school of higher learning, 103; elected Provincial Grand Master, 103, 104; acute electrical observations, 104; interest in fire insurance, 105; paper of, read before Royal Society, 105; electrical experiments written out, 106, 107; promotes a hospital, 107; suffers an electrical shock, 107; breadth of interests, 108

His financial prudence, 110; seeks post office appointment, 110, 111; continues to write for the *Gazette*, 111; works with Kinnersley, 111; hospital project advanced, 112; elected to membership in the Assembly, 112; chosen an alderman, 113; launches the *Contributionship*, 113; attempts medical application of electricity, 114; fame spreads in Europe, 114, 115; lightning rods advocated, 115, 116; the kite experiment, 115; designs a flexible catheter, 117; correspondence with "Omnis-